The Difference
Aesthetics Makes

The Difference Aesthetics Makes

On the Humanities "After Man"

Kandice Chuh

DUKE UNIVERSITY PRESS
Durham and London
2019

© 2019 Duke University Press
All rights reserved
Printed and bound by CPI Group (UK) Ltd, Croydon, CRO 4YY

Typeset in Whitman and Helvetica Neue
by Copperline Books

Library of Congress Cataloging-in-Publication Data
Names: Chuh, Kandice, [date]author.
Title: The difference aesthetics makes :
on the humanities "after man" / Kandice Chuh.
Description: Durham : Duke University Press, 2019. |
Includes bibliographical references and index.
Identifiers: LCCN 2018033901 (print)
LCCN 2018053991 (ebook)
ISBN 9781478002383 (ebook)
ISBN 9781478000709 (hardcover : alk. paper)
ISBN 9781478000921 (pbk. : alk. paper)
Subjects: LCSH: Aesthetics—Political aspects. | American
literature—Political aspects. | Art, Modern—21st century—
Political aspects—United States. | Politics and culture. |
Literature—Study and teaching (Higher) | Humanism—
Study and teaching (Higher) | Eurocentrism.
Classification: LCC BH301.P64 (ebook) |
LCC BH301.P64 C48 2019 (print) | DDC 111/.85—dc23
LC record available at https://lccn.loc.gov/2018033901

Cover art: Allan deSouza, "He gazed into the liquid
darkness in which desires drowned, from where the
body's delicious pains emerged." Photograph. Courtesy
of the artist and Talwar Gallery, New York.

For Josh, Cole, and Georgia,
With love.

The struggle of our new millennium will be between the ongoing imperative of securing the well-being of our present ethnoclass (i.e., Western bourgeois) conception of the human, Man, which overrepresents itself as if it were the human itself, and that of securing the well-being, and therefore the full cognitive and behavioral autonomy of the human species itself/ourselves.

— SYLVIA WYNTER, "Unsettling the Coloniality of Being/Power/
Truth/Freedom"

Our contemporary moment is so replete with assumptions that freedom is made universal through liberal political enfranchisement and the globalization of capitalism that it has become difficult to write or imagine alternative knowledges, to act on behalf of alternative projects or communities. Within this context, it is necessary to act within but to think beyond our received humanist tradition and, all the while, to imagine a much more complicated set of stories about the emergence of the now, in which what is foreclosed as unknowable is forever saturating the "what-can-be-known." We are left with the project of visualizing, mourning, and thinking "other humanities" within the received genealogy of "the human."

— LISA LOWE, "The Intimacies of Four Continents"

I can't help but dream about a kind of criticism that would try not to judge but to bring an oeuvre, a book, a sentence, an idea to life; it would light fires, watch the grass grow, listen to the wind, and catch the sea foam in the breeze and scatter it. It would multiply not judgments but signs of existence; it would summon them, drag them from their sleep. Perhaps it would invent them sometimes—all the better. All the better. Criticism that hands down sentences sends me to sleep; I'd like a criticism of scintillating leaps of the imagination. It would not be sovereign or dressed in red. It would bear the lightning of possible storms.

— MICHEL FOUCAULT, "The Masked Philosopher"

Contents

Preface

The Difference Aesthetics Makes offers a series of propositions intended to describe a humanism different from bourgeois liberal humanism, and to suggest how and toward what ends the humanities might be organized around
such an alternative and what work they might do. While others have responded to the manifold critiques of liberal humanism through work circu-
lating under such rubrics as post-, anti-, or critical humanism, in this book, I
try to bring to bear the subjugated or disavowed humanisms—what I provisionally and collectively refer to as *illiberal humanisms*—generated through
intellectual and creative work disidentified from bourgeois liberalism and
its cognate onto-epistemologies. I show how illiberal humanisms afford a
humanities that illuminates the role of bourgeois liberal humanism and its
accompanying humanities in the (re)production of social inequality by their
contribution to the naturalization of social hierarchies, while they also provide alternative theorizations and models for ways of being and knowing,
and the elicitation of sensibilities that accord with them. Illiberal humanisms bring forward an understanding of human beingness to be defined not
by discrete and self-possessed individuality but instead by constitutive relationality; they argue the displacement of the primacy of the visual characterizing the epistemologies of bourgeois liberal modernity by the generation
of rationalities that make sense through visceral multisensory experiences
of the world; they afford the emergence of a critical taxonomy that features
encounter without conquest and entanglement in lieu of terms and concepts inhering in knowledge paradigms that hold the political and cultural,
and economic and artistic as discretely bounded realms; and they facilitate
the articulation and elaboration of epistemes thoroughly incommensurate
with the developmental geographies and temporalities of bourgeois liberal
humanism.

It is a grounding premise of this book that the centrality of the aesthetic
to the philosophies and practical structures of liberal humanism—in this
book, exemplified by Kant's work and its impact, and by the discipline of

English and the field of American Literature—keys us into the ways that this reigning humanism sorts people into the fit and unfit, the rational and the unreasonable, Man and other, Man and woman, and Human and racialized subject. In this project, aesthetics refers to the relationships among the senses and the processes and structures of value making by which certain sensibilities become common sense and others are disavowed, subjugated, or otherwise obscured. Aesthetics in this regard may be understood as integral to the production of particular kinds of difference—for example, that of the racial and colonial order, that of sex-gender regulation—as part of the naturalized visceral experience of the world. At the same time, aesthetics are the grounds of uncommon, illiberal sensibilities. These are sensibilities incommensurate to the epistemologies and common sense of liberal humanism: they posit relationality and entanglement rather than individuality and autochthony as the grounds of human ontology; they refuse bourgeois aspirations and illuminate their parochialism; and they radically disidentify from the teleological narrative of progressive development that gives texture to liberal humanism. The aesthetics of illiberal humanisms both emerge from and afford social formations characterized by neither identity nor consensus, and instead by not only shared recognition and apprehension of the damage resulting from such potent fictions, but also a fundamental refusal to be defined or disciplined by them.

In addition to the cited and textual interlocutors animating this book, the discussions here reflect the conversations, both formal and informal, some ongoing and others only momentary, with colleagues in the richest sense of what that term means. Tita Chico, William Cohen, Roderick Ferguson, Gayatri Gopinath, J. Jack Halberstam, Laura Hyun Yi Kang, Lisa Lowe, Jodi Melamed, the late José Esteban Muñoz, Karen Shimakawa, and Siobhan Somerville have in a variety of ways been deeply a part of this project, so much so that it is often difficult for me to distinguish the thoughts that are mine from ours; I've tried to do justice to the ideas that are yours. Their generosity, brilliance, and humor are enabling in every way, in relation to this book and well beyond it.

I'm so pleased also to be able finally to acknowledge, with huge appreciation, the many others who read sometimes aimless drafts, talked with me through unkempt ideas, provided formal and informal research assistance, commiserated and encouraged, induced laughter, gave sustaining care of varying kinds, and through all of it made me try to make this book better:

Lynne Beckenstein, Lauren Berlant, Briana Brickley, Daphne Brooks, Susan Buck-Morss, Jodi Byrd, Alenda Chang, Jaime Coan, Lou Cornum, Jorge Cortiñas, Denise Cruz, Cathy Davidson, Elizabeth Lenn Decker, LeiLani Dowell, Lisa Duggan, Amanda Dykema, Christopher Eng, David Eng, Joseph Entin, Duncan Faherty, Sujatha Fernandes, Tonya Foster, Andrew Friedman, Rebecca Fullan, Nicholas Gamso, Ruth Wilson Gilmore, Jacqueline Goldsby, Marcos Gonzales, Joshua Guzmán, David Harvey, Scott Herring, Peter Hitchcock, Cindi Katz, Nicole King, Fiona Lee, Eric Lott, Martin F. Manalansan IV, Bakirathi Mani, Uday Mehta, Fred Moten, Mimi Nguyen, Zita Nunes, Tavia N'yongo, Crystal Parikh, Josephine Park, Melissa Phruksachart, Sangeeta Ray, Chandan Reddy, Robert Reid-Pharr, Joan Richardson, Danica Savonick, Cathy Schlund-Vials, Alicia Schmidt Camacho, Talia Shalev, Gustavus Stadler, Jordan Stein, Frances Tran, Alexandra T. Vazquez, Shane Vogel, and Gary Wilder—thank you.

I taught for many years at the University of Maryland, College Park, and now work at the CUNY Graduate Center. I learn an enormous amount from students at both institutions; they collectively have my thanks, as their work and engagement infuse and invigorate everything, including most certainly this project.

My thanks to Duke University Press for publishing this book. My editor, Ken Wissoker, offered astonishing support and insight—to say nothing of patience and friendship—over the many, many years it took to shape this project into a book. I am grateful as well for Elizabeth Ault's knowledgeable guidance and Christopher Catanese's and Stephanie Gomez Menzies's smart and careful work in shepherding me and this book through publication. I'm indebted to the critical eye of the readers the press secured.

Allan deSouza and Sarah Sze readily provided permission to use images of their work, for which I am enormously grateful. My thanks as well to Adam Rose and Mike Barnett of Sarah Sze Studio for facilitating these permissions. DeSouza's piece is printed here with the gracious courtesy of both the artist and the Talwar Gallery, New York. Sze's work appears courtesy of Tanya Bonakdar Gallery and Victoria Miro Gallery.

I also offer thanks to the audiences who offered generative feedback at the many places I've had opportunity to share pieces of this project: Haverford College, the University of Hong Kong, Clemson University, Yale University, Columbia University, the University of Pennsylvania, the University of Illinois at Urbana-Champaign, Indiana University, the University of Texas at Austin, New York University, Northwestern University, and Duke University. Some of these audiences heard the most undeveloped nuggets of this work way back when—my especial thanks for your patience.

Much of this book was thought and written on Peaks Island, Maine, on days enriched by people and place both. All of it was written with the care of family, both bio- and chosen. As ever, I am grateful to my parents for making everything possible, and to my sister, Patricia Chuh, for her abiding love. Of Josh, Cole, and Georgia, to whom this book is dedicated, I feel most strongly the inadequacy of words to convey gratitude and love; you have them both in abundance.

Anything worthwhile in this book results from being with this enormous, wonderful collective of people; the errant bits are completely my own.

Introduction

The Difference Aesthetics Makes

Our present arrangements of knowledge . . . were put in place in the nineteenth century as a function of the epistemic/discursive constitution of the "figure of Man." . . . Therefore, the unifying goal of minority discourse . . . will necessarily be to accelerate the conceptual "erasing" of the figure of Man. If it is to effect such a rupture, minority discourse must set out to bring closure to our present order of discourse. —SYLVIA WYNTER, "On Disenchanting Discourse"

I write in the conviction that sometimes it is best to sabotage what is inexorably to hand. — GAYATRI SPIVAK, *A Critique of Postcolonial Reason*

While it is impossible to ignore the manifold adverse effects of the corporatization and intensifying privatization of the university on the humanities, neither is it possible to stand simply in defense of the disciplinary formations clustered under the rubric of "the humanities," which have been and continue to be instrumental to the production and sustenance of social hierarchies and their subtending structures and material inequalities. This, the overarching proposition of this book, comes of acknowledging that the humanities and their corollary disciplinary structures have long been central to the organization and conduct of social life constituting Western Civilization.[1] The history of the humanities and the disciplinary structures organizing their emergence is of a piece with the history of the civilizational discourses subtending the legitimation of empire and capital, and bespeaks the onto-epistemologies that have come to secure liberal modernity's common sense. In this light, the crisis confronting the humanities calls less for their defense and instead prompts the crafting of a vision of what a defensible humanities might be and do, and how it differs from its dominant iteration.

This book pursues such a project. I try to elaborate the principles and concepts of this other humanities, derived from what I provisionally refer to as "illiberal humanisms." Radically different from liberal humanism and its cognate humanities, these other humanisms, these other humanities, have long existed and percolate institutionally largely within and through minoritized discourses. *The Difference Aesthetics Makes* records my effort to enunciate this alternative. The illiberal humanities are directed toward the protection and flourishing of people and of ways of being and knowing and of inhabiting the planet that liberal humanism, wrought through the defining structures of modernity, tries so hard to extinguish. They are part of the project of "bring[ing] to closure our present order of discourse," as Sylvia Wynter elegantly puts it, such that "the human" is and can be thought and apprehended for the fullness and radical diversity of being aggressively discounted in and by bourgeois liberal humanism and its contemporary materialization through neoliberal ideologies.[2]

This project is pointedly inspired by Wynter, from whose writings this book takes its subtitle. Throughout her capacious work, she has insisted on taking Western humanism and its manifestations in the practices of racial colonialism as objects of knowledge. Several decades ago, Wynter cautioned against the seductions of incorporation into the institution in the course of theorizing the need to go "beyond the grounding analogic of the episteme or 'fundamental arrangements of knowledge' of which our present practice of literary criticism (in effect of normal 'majority discourse') is an interconnected component."[3] This includes going "beyond the ontology of the figure of man and the empowering *normalizing* discourses with which this 'figure,' as the projected model/criterion of being of the globally dominant Western-European bourgeoisie, is still enchantedly constituted."[4] Wynter establishes, in other words, the need for us to engage the human, to think and work "after Man."

My effort to do so by drawing out illiberal humanisms and nominating them as such may be understood as an attempt to give positive weight to alternatives to liberal humanism—that is, to specify the content and contours of such alternatives so that in collective, collaborative form, they may shift the grounds of sensibility, from what we are called to stand against to what we will stand for under the penumbra of the humanities. For reasons

I discuss more fully later in this introduction, I emphasize and use aesthetic inquiry as a method necessary to bringing illiberal humanisms to the fore. Perhaps counterintuitively, because of the role of aesthetics in securing the common sense of bourgeois liberal modernity, aesthetic inquiry provides entry to the apprehension of illiberal, uncommon sensibilities. It is the procedure for calling into question the structures and processes of (e)valuation that subtend the *sensus communis* and the means by which sensibilities that differ and dissent from liberal common sense are brought to bear. This book unfolds by attending to this double-voiced quality of the aesthetic. As a method, aesthetic inquiry insists that we acknowledge a dialectical relationship between liberal and illiberal humanisms. By doing so, it illuminates the need to activate ways of knowing cognizant of the exponentially greater power and authority that has secured liberalism in the structuring of modernity, and submits that the defunctioning of that authority cannot be accomplished without the elaboration of understandings of the human and cognate rationalities afforded by subjugated knowledges. As I suggest in what follows, aesthetic inquiry emphasizes sensibility as a crucial domain of knowledge and politics; it affords recognition of both the relations and practices of power that legitimate and naturalize certain ideas over others, and the knowledge and ways of living subjugated or disavowed in the process. My effort here is to emphasize poiesis in critique—to amplify, by routing through aesthetics, the presence and potential of alternatives to liberal humanist onto-epistemologies that give rise to the narrow definition of the human around which the modern condition has been organized.[5]

I take as a point of departure for this project the by now familiar, wide-ranging critiques of liberal humanism. They have established the falsity of and damages done by its claims to universality and resoundingly decried its uses and dissemination toward the ends of imperialism and colonialism, White supremacy and capitalism, environmental devastation, patriarchy, and compulsory normativization of multiple kinds. Cathected to liberalism, this humanism has both relied on and naturalized the liberal subject as the ideal human. Accordingly, this reigning humanism advances the notion that goodness, prosperity, and freedom follow from humanity's constitution by discrete and self-conscious individuals in possession of the capacity to transcend subjective experience by sheer will tethered to the faculty of reason. Liberal humanism posits the sovereignty and autochthony of the human even as—or precisely because—it justifies the conquest and dispossession, enslavement and eradication that constitute the course of liberalism in its intimate partnership with capitalism.

While others have responded to or advanced these critiques by focusing attention away from the human—toward objects and animals, for example—I hesitate to cede the ground of humanism, a reluctance out of which this book in part grew. I think we need more rather than less attention to and accounts of human activity and behavior, accounts that, contra liberal humanism, take as axiomatic the humanity and humanism of precisely those people sacrificed to the liberal ideal. I am interested not so much in arguing who counts as human as I am in claiming humanism as a name designating efforts to proliferate ways of being and knowing radically disidentified from its liberal iteration. To be clear, I am not arguing against other approaches to thinking in difference from liberal humanism; I am, instead, arguing for the emancipation of the human from liberalism's grasp. I wish to claim rather than cede the potency of the construct, to take seriously the parochiality of liberalism's account of the human and bring forward the articulations that insist on the human as a social entity and worldly being, that acknowledge the stubborn hold of liberalism but refuse to collapse into its fold.

I write from the belief that we need to articulate a common ground through the interaction of the specificities of our uncommon bases and practices of knowledge; we—those who are committed to the twofold project of critiquing normativities and the violence of the status quo, and working toward and for alternatives—need to activate ways of going beyond the sometimes strenuous demands of disciplinarity and professionalization, ways that are not so much interdisciplinary but are instead deliberately promiscuous. The dictates of the university demand that we identify categorically—as Asian Americanists, literary critics, historians, queer theorists, and so on—as a shorthand for our intellectual and political genealogies. My elaboration in this book of an illiberal humanities derives in part from the hunch that it may act as an intellectual space for collaborating across and in spite of institutionalized knowledge formations, to challenge disciplinary divisions and the continuing stultifying consequences of liberal and neoliberal multicultural ideologies and corresponding structures. Illiberal humanities in this respect is a construct I offer to provide theoretical leverage; it acts as a counterhegemonic point of entry into illuminating the relationship of knowledge practices to structures and relationships of power. They can thus no more be contained within specific programs or units than can theory writ large. In this broad-scoping way, illiberal humanities bear the promise of gathering a critical mass constituted in and by an undisciplined relationship to the university. It is the site of the "strange affinities" of which Roderick Ferguson and Grace Hong write, a space of encounters necessary to apprehending the world in uncommonsensical ways.[6] In that spirit and against customary practice, here, I have paid little heed to remaining faithful to any intellectual tradition. I invoke Enlightenment philosophies alongside Caribbeanist epistemologies, Asian Americanist critique with theorizations of Blackness, queer theory and literary studies, and so on. My hope is that these perhaps unexpected encounters will create openings for thinking in unhabituated ways; I believe they have done so for me.

The humanisms sketched in this project are illiberal in their difference from liberalism's tenets, but are not a simple substitute for liberal humanism. Rather, illiberal humanisms bespeak an orientation that recognizes liberal humanism as but one version, one that has come to have the effect of truth through the powerful machinery of modernity. Illiberal humanisms are palpable, available to apprehension, in the thought and creative work of precisely those subjugated by and in the name of liberal humanism. In and through them, relationality and entanglement rather than individuality and authochthony as the grounds of human ontology come to the fore; bourgeois aspirations are illuminated for their fundamental meanness; and a fuller, embodied accounting of reason and rationality emerges. In this, I follow the lead of the artists, writers, and thinkers—sometimes all in one—whose work prompts sustained attention to the human after Man. Langston Hughes, Lan Samantha Chang, Leslie Marmon Silko, Toni Morrison, Ruth Ozeki, Monique Truong, Carrie Mae Weems, Sarah Sze, and Allan deSouza offer work that show and tell us of humanism in an illiberal key. I mean quite literally that I have followed their lead, in that the thinking I offer here comes of trying to make sense (out) of their work, by engaging their ideas and entering their sensibilities. Their work thus functions less as evidence for an argument than as primary interlocutors in this project. In fact, this relationship to their work and ideas is a facet of illiberal humanist pedagogy, wherein mastery is displaced by the prompt to collective thought, and subjects (critics) and objects (texts) are understood in their mutuality. Relationality, as this book suggests, is as much a principle for organizing knowledge production as it is a reference to a condition of being.

The overarching questions with which I am concerned are these: Can the humanities be oriented toward the ends of generating and proliferating imaginaries disidentified from the ideologies and logics of liberalism and derived instead from attention to the entangled histories of and ongoing connection among the impoverishment of peoples and worlds, enslaved and gendered labor, Indigenous dispossession, developmentalism, and knowledge work? What pedagogies and practices afford the generation and proliferation of imaginaries organized by the radical, irrevocable relationality of these connections? The project at hand is to identify and undo the occlusions of entangled histories by such institutions of knowledge and acculturation as universities, and thus make our knowledge practices accountable to and for them. Concurrently, it is to elicit subjects and social structures disinvested in the consignment of such knowledge to either the realm of past history or the sanitized sphere of pure knowledge, and informed and shaped instead by its ongoingness, its presence and active impact in and on the here and now.

Contexts and Genealogies

Perhaps the influence of cultural studies on this present project is already clear. Explicitly, in a theoretical register, the political edge of aesthetic inquiry rests in its function as an approach that re-sounds what Stuart Hall, in a 1980 essay, helpfully identified as one of the key governing paradigms characterizing British cultural studies of that era, namely, the "culturalist." Growing out of the work of Raymond Williams, the culturalist paradigm emphasizes the study of culture, theorized to refer to "a whole way of life" (Williams, quoted in Hall)—that is, as the analysis of "relationships between elements in a whole way of life." Hall clarifies, "'Culture' is not a practice; nor is it simply the descriptive sum of the 'mores and folkways' of societies. . . . It is threaded through *all* social practices, and is the sum of their interrelationship."[7] It is thus the task of the critic to illuminate and analyze "those patterns of organization, those characteristic forms of human energy which can be discovered as revealing themselves—in 'unexpected identities and correspondences' as well as in 'discontinuities of an unexpected kind'—within or underlying *all* social practices."[8] Oriented thus, my use of the aesthetic is with a view toward investigating how it coordinates relationships between elements in the whole way of life to which we commonly give the name modernity, including those discontinuities, those subjugated ways of life and knowing, that have persisted as integral if disavowed elements of the current conjuncture.

While Hall was writing in an era (the late 1970s–early '80s) defined by the formalization of what we have become accustomed to calling neoliberalization in economic and social policies, the project of investigating the terrain of (un)common sensibility has renewed exigency now. As the recent surge of student activism on campuses across the world attests, the intensifying inequality along the axes of race, gender, sexuality, class, and caste that describes the global condition localizes in the curricular and social experiences of students. Understood as a historical phenomenon, globalization most often refers to the contemporary establishment and multifaceted and sometimes contradictory consequences of the worldwide integration of finance, technology, economy, and culture. Thoroughly uneven in influence and effect, the widening and acceleration of interconnectedness characteristic of this era has had a pronounced effect on both the idea and practical life of the university.

The realms of the economic and the educational, intimately linked from the inception of the university, now appear increasingly to dissolve into each other such that "audit culture" all too accurately describes the global scene of education as much as that of the corporation.[9] As Ned Rossiter observes, despite the quite disparate effects of globalization across the world, there is a "distinctive homogeneity" in much of the educational policies of the globalized world.[10] The everyday lives as well as career itineraries of academics are tethered to mechanisms of accounting whereby both material resources and capital accrue to productivity measured in quantity often delinked from questions of quality or social significance, and the embrace of metrics of efficiency buttresses the increasing reliance on contingent faculty who are regularly paid unlivable wages. As the university has transformed along these lines, that it may not be viable as a site of intellectual work critical of power and policy is emerging as an increasingly compelling truth.[11] The interests of the academy, the marketplace, and the state grow increasingly to be one and the same, with resources flowing to potentially patentable research and away from work less easily commodified.

In the domain of educational policy, both within and outside of the United States, the global now serves as an aspiration (e.g., the production of a global citizenry) as well as a marketing strategy, and is deployed toward the ends of enhancing national competitiveness in the global marketplace.

Globalization has wrought distinctive divisions of labor that correlate with the shift to the particular form capitalism has taken to establish what has saliently been called the Knowledge Economy. While modes of production and labor that emerged in earlier eras continue, they have been supplemented and in some respects overwritten by the commodification of innovation.[12] The university has in this context been a distinctively important site of globalization. In a Knowledge Economy, higher education gains greater prominence as an apparatus of national competitiveness, one dedicated to the production of innovation, and the enormous expansion of state-sponsored universities across the world bespeaks this condition.[13] U.S. colleges and universities have leveraged the value of a U.S. degree in the global economic context by establishing and bolstering international branches.[14] At the same time, internationalization of the student bodies of U.S. universities and colleges has proceeded apace, with a record high of some 975,000 international students in the 2014–15 academic year. Students from India, China, and Brazil account for most of the 10 percent growth from the previous academic year, and students from China constitute a third of the entire number. The internationalization of the student body in U.S. universities is clearly a function of the sharply heavier reliance that academic institutions must have on private sources (tuition dollars and private donors and foundations) in the face of the withdrawal of public funds, but is often rhetorically justified in terms of the opportunity it provides for domestic student interaction with their international counterparts—this, in order better to be prepared for the globalized world.[15]

Within this shifting context, belief in higher education's ability to secure the social mobility promised as part of the American dream is deeply shaken. Remember that social mobility is an index of the significance of demography to life circumstances and involves complex sets of interactions between inherited and acquired capital.[16] In the United States especially, public education is meant to lessen this significance by providing opportunity to accumulate more capital regardless of circumstances of origin. The 1862 Morrill Act ("An Act donating Public lands to the several States and Territories which may provide Colleges for the Benefit of Agriculture and the Mechanic Arts") established "the endowment, support, and maintenance of at least one college [in each state] where the leading object shall be, without excluding other scientific and classical studies, and including military tactics, to teach such branches of learning as are related to agriculture and the mechanic arts . . . in order to promote the liberal and practical education of the industrial classes in the several pursuits and professions in life" (Section 4), and became the basis for the establishment of public land grant universities. Designed to address the situation of White farmers who were confronting industrialization and corollary waning of their significance to the economy, the 1862 act had an 1890 iteration, which provided for what we now refer to as the Historically Black Colleges and Universities, or HBCUS.[17] Along with the Homestead Act passed in the same year, the 1862 Morrill Act documents the seizure of Indigenous lands—some two million square miles—in the service of democracy.[18] This was not only or even primarily a process of the direct transfer of land, but rather was characterized by the financialization of land—its transformation into real estate (the land was given to states to be sold, not to be built upon directly)—and, in this regard, enacts the concept of education as an investment in (the future of the nation through) its citizenry. The democratizing function of higher education was consolidated as a governing fantasy in the mid-twentieth century, characterized in the United States as a period of relative prosperity for more of the working population. "The collective settlement," as Lauren Berlant concisely explains, "was that as long as the economy was expanding everyone would have a shot at creatively inventing their version of the good life, and not just assuming the position allotted to them by embedded class, racial, and gendered histories of devalued and unrecognized economic and social labor. The half century since the collective settlement was established embeds many generations in a binding fantasy."[19] The 1944 GI Bill (the Serviceman's Readjustment Act) underwrote a substantial increase in college enrollment, followed by the Higher Education Facilities Act of 1963 that provided for the growth of community colleges, the Higher Education Act of 1964, and the 1972 creation of Pell Grants and the Indian Education Act, which collectively extended and further concretized the principles of access and the combination of preparation for work and liberal training embedded in the Morrill acts.

It is thus in light of this history of legislative/public commitment to education as a pathway to social mobility that the current withdrawal of public monies from education plays out as a sign of both transformation of the ideal of democracy and its relationship to the economic interests of the nation. As Berlant puts it, "the revocation of educational democracy, a stand for a public investment in everyone who wanted a shot [at the good life]," translates

W. E. B. Du Bois's incisive and era-defining question, "How does it feel to be a problem?" to "How does it feel to be a bad investment?"[20] Educational policies enacted in a variety of nations that are aspirational or active participants in the global economy echo this logic and rhetoric.[21] What makes a citizen, a nation, competitive in the global marketplace? What is the value and content of education in this context?

It is unsurprising given these conditions that the defense of the humanities has largely taken the form of arguments for their instrumental relevance—for example, that businesses desire the kinds of critical thinking and writing skills that are the stuff of humanistic training, or that the encounters with diverse cultures afforded by a liberal arts curriculum are necessary preparation for the emergent global citizen. While I understand the traction such arguments have, this book takes a different tack in addressing the current situation, partly as a result of two observations. The first is the acknowledgment that insofar as such defenses are designed to forestall and reverse defunding, they have simply by and large failed. The weakness of liberalism as a defense against the voraciousness of racial capitalism and colonialism's pasts and presents is evident in every sector of society, not least in the university. Such failure presents not so much an opportunity—laden as that term is with optimistic connotation—as an exigent condition that compels reckoning with liberalism's end(s), with its participatory history in the precipitation of the current conjuncture. That is, and second, such arguments seem tacitly if not actively to affirm the rightness of the liberal vision, without regard for the destructive effects on the world and on most people of the developmental narrative advanced by the tethering of educational democracy to a liberal-capitalist vision of social mobility. In that light, I think we cannot be satisfied to remain within the dominant terms of debate. I hope with this book to bolster and contribute to a different kind of conversation, one that deliberately brackets the instrumental in order to invite attention to the foundational histories and assumptions underlying the defensive position.

I suggest that "the university" be understood as an idea and a site structured by the aspirations of a given social formation. While it is lived in the particularities of its manifestation as a specific institution, the idea of the university frames and reflects the general systems and hierarchies of value and evaluation that constitute a society's reigning ideals. Though academic discourse, however politically engaged it might be, is alone insufficient to the task of transforming the world at large, the university remains an index of broad sociopolitical, cultural, and economic conditions such that its practices and arrangements cannot not be addressed. In the United States, only a small fraction of the population will attend college; smaller still the numbers who pursue graduate education, and yet even smaller those who will join the professoriate.[22] If the twentieth century saw the deliberate expansion of access to college education under the provisions and resources of such manifestly nation-building policies as the GI Bill as well as the agendas of explicitly progressive-minded social movements, we are in this century witnessing the narrowing of educational access largely as a consequence of politico-economic policies that simultaneously increase and individualize costs.[23] That these foreclosures are occurring despite the presence and activities of politicized scholar-teachers and associated units in the university is a stark reminder that if the transformation of the university is to be meaningful in any substantial way, it cannot be by holding its perfectability as an ideal or goal to be pursued by means of striving for representational equality. Rather, we might bear in mind that the university is a specific site of the articulation of hegemonic ideologies and counterhegemonic formations; or, in other words, that the university socializes capital and the state.[24] The challenge, then, is to particularize how to take advantage of this positioning, not in defense of the university but instead to understand why and how it continues to operate as a technology of social stratification, and whether it may be made to work otherwise.

The promise of the good life at the core of the ideal of social mobility through educational investment is multiply structured as a sacrificial model.[25] Not only does it require individual sacrifice (often gendered and generational—e.g., on behalf of the children), but it also has demanded the compulsory and quite literal sacrifice of Indigenous and enslaved persons. The contemporary rhetoric of whether college is a good investment is in this regard of a piece with the principles of social mobility central to U.S. democracy; as a value, it disavows but is nevertheless contingent on the violence foundational to the nation. As Craig Steven Wilder has compellingly documented, U.S. universities are founded in the histories of conquest and dispossession, enslaved labor and global capital, that underlie the history of the United States. From the impact of the economies of slavery to the specific kinds of labor borne by people of color, and from the civilizing mission of colleges in their engagements with native peoples to the production of race through racist knowledge, "American colleges were not innocent or passive beneficiaries of conquest and colonial slavery," but instead "stood beside church and state as the third pillar of a civilization build on bondage."[26] Neither have they been institutions built upon gender and sex equality; the struggles of women to gain access to higher education unfold alongside the structurally supported social and cultural emphasis on the achievement of cis-heteronormative men of a certain class.[27] The contemporary resurgence of focus on racism and on violence against women on U.S. campuses reflects this long history and broad social context and exemplifies the inadequacy of access as a remedy for inequality organized by racial, colonial, and heteropatriarchal ideologies foundational to the U.S. nation-state. The oppositional social and political movements that transformed higher education in the late middle of the twentieth century built upon ideas and practices of dissent that were equally a part of the nation's foundation, and contested anew the ongoingness of these histories of subjugation and exclusion and of the accumulation of wealth for a few by the impoverishment of many. The contributions of higher education to such processes of social hierarchization along intersecting axes of sociopolitical identity were called to task in ways that reflect the embeddedness of education in the fabric of the social.

Contemporary forms of activism call for renewed attention to that relationship in ways that acknowledge the long history of higher education's complicity in making race, gender, sexuality, class, religion, and other categories of sociopolitical identity in all their intersectionality matter to the possibilities of life and the distribution of death, both biological and social. In part, my concern in this book is to reflect on the work of what I will refer to as minoritized discourse formations given these grounds. Practitioners of politically engaged work, including those of feminist and queer theorizing, race and ethnic studies, disability and Indigenous studies—collectively, minoritized discourses—are explicitly aware of the structural conditions within which we work, an awareness that contextualizes and informs the ways we formulate and approach our objects of inquiry. As people whose scholarly genealogies are constitutively misaligned with, even as we are contextualized by, the university's role as an apparatus of the nation-state and of capital, scholars of minoritized discourses cannot and do not easily inhabit the academy—a situation that Lisa Lowe cogently formulated two decades ago as an "inevitable paradox" resulting from the institutionalization of fields like ethnic studies.[28] Such institutionalization provides material resources and yet also submits critical inquiry "to the demands of the university and its educative function of socializing subjects into the state."[29] These institutionalized formations remain important sites for oppositional critique, and/but it is also the case that now, as Roderick Ferguson has shown, difference is contemporarily "managed" by universities in ways that attest to the effectiveness of liberal and neoliberal articulations of race, gender, and sexuality, ones that evacuate the historical materiality giving them meaning and displace the questions of power and legitimacy that drove their emergence as key terms of academic discourse.[30] Within this climate, urgency attaches to the work of creating and sustaining efforts to further the epistemological and institutional transformations of which the establishment of ethnic and women's and gender studies programs was an important part, but was not the only or end goal. By emphasizing as a key part of such an agenda the wholesale and radical rethinking of our received humanist traditions of thought, we may, I believe, better position ourselves to remember that the establishment and protection of programs is but one facet of a much bigger project oriented toward the transformation of the social field.

I offer this book also as a contribution and response to the cogent critiques of identitarian politics and paradigms that have prompted critical reflection on identity as an organizing principle for institutionalized forms of politically engaged discourse. Relatedly, my aim is to contribute to efforts to address the (neo)liberal academy, characterized by an intense compartmentalization of knowledge that registers not only in disciplinarity, but also within disciplines as well. Criticism of the politics of identity has emerged along with the institutionalization of a variety of minority discourse formations, many of which are constitutively interdisciplinary. The institutional establishment of such fields as Asian American studies, women's studies, LGBT studies, and so on has meant that existing disciplines could remain, at least at a radical level, relatively untouched by difference. Moreover, strikingly, the albeit uneven success of institutionalization correlates with increasing and multifaceted material inequality characterizing the present. What is the responsibility of politically engaged intellectual work in and to the present context?

In the present, characterized by the nonequivalent, thoroughly entangled phenomena of war, environmental disaster, new and continuing forms of settler colonialism, poverty, racism, gendered violence, and ongoing battles over the legislation of desires and intimacies by which sexuality is publicly materialized, it is imperative to think hard about how the academy can proliferate alternatives to and critiques of the ideologies that would have us accept the inevitability of the status quo—which is to say, how it can proliferate pedagogies and practices of alterity through criticism and research and practices of imagination that originate from other(ed) grounds. Along these lines, I hope this book will encourage and invigorate the kind of work that is determined to collaborate across institutional boundaries, to challenge the stultifying consequences of (neo)liberal multiculturalism both within and outside of the academy, from standpoints that attempt in a variety of ways, all important and all delimited, to speak the condition of injustice and induce more livable worlds into being. This is not to posit the academy, academic work, or certainly this book as a remedy to neoliberal culture and politics, but instead to ask whether and how these conditions enjoin critical attention to our role in the reproduction of hegemonic social formations.

Accordingly, we might ask anew, how do and might the knowledge and teaching principles and practices we elaborate, occupy, and employ be recruited toward the broadly ethicopolitical aims of something like greater justice? Of lessening the determinative effects of the circumstances of the accidents of birth? Of illuminating the ways that the nonequivalent accidents of geography, class structure, racialization, gender relations, sexuality, indigeneity, and so on organize the material conditions of existence in aggressively hierarchical ways? These "accidents" are of course anything but random or neutral. Instead, they are structurally and culturally conditioned, coordinated by political and social relations unfolding in multiple scales. Naturalized narratives of the willful and rationally intentional liberal and neoliberal subject responsible for securing her or his own good life (the liberal-ethical subject), or the continuing stronghold of a developmental notion of civilization (dependent on the liberal-political subject), that asserts and assumes the privileged destiny of humanity, disavow that overdetermination. In concert with the abundance of meticulous studies that endeavor to suss out the purposeful grounds of these accidents, my hope is that this book will suggest ways that aesthetic inquiry has something distinctive to contribute to this work. This book unfolds by attending to particularities, to incommensurabilities, to incomparability, each as made available by aesthetics, in hopes of—with the hope of—suggesting the difference aesthetics makes.

The chapters that follow elaborate the characteristics introduced here. In the remainder of this introduction, I focus on explaining the importance of aesthetics to the project of bringing to bear illiberal humanisms. As I discuss in what follows, the history of the aesthetic gives it distinctive purchase in the critique of bourgeois liberalism and its corollary structures of knowledge, and makes aesthetics signally important to the project of thinking, working, and living after Man. Aesthetic inquiry as mobilized in this book orients critical focus on the conditions of possibility that subtend the dominant order, to the production and sustenance of the sensus communis—of common sense—and insists upon the double valence of sensibility as a reference to both what is held to be reasonable and what is viscerally experienced. Derived from subjugated and/or otherwise minoritized art and writings, aesthetic inquiry indexes the difference aesthetics has made and continues to make in the service of the Order of Man, and simultaneously gives texture and specificity to illiberal humanism.

On Aesthetic Inquiry

In the register of academic discourse, this book recalibrates the ways in which aesthetic inquiry and cultural studies appear to be oriented toward quite different and even fundamentally oppositional ends. Such an understanding is evident in the familiar story of the culture wars of the later twentieth century. In the context of literary studies in the United States, this story tells of the shift to cultural studies approaches underwritten by Marxist, post-structural, and postmodern theories: "works" become "texts," and the definition of literary value and the politics of canonicity come to the fore as flashpoints of critical debate. Catalyzed by activists and critics (sometimes one and the same) of the post–civil rights era, that shift resulted from their illumination of the interrelation of education, acculturation, and social stratification.[31] A variety of scholars taking ethnic studies and feminist approaches denounced divisions between "high" and "low" culture and undermined the idea of a bias-free subject as the arbiter of universal value. Aesthetics, strongly associated with such conservative formalist movements as New Criticism and aestheticism—movements working in the service of deeply entrenched hierarchized notions of culture—receded from prominence, and textual and curricular diversification increased quite substantially. In brief, where established modes of literary study aimed to advance a putatively disinterested practice of evaluating greatness based on objectively neutral formal properties, feminist critics and scholars of ethnic literatures, among others, argued the nonneutrality and ideological underpinnings of objectivity and disinterestedness.

One consequence of the culture wars was the yoking of studies of ethnic and women's literatures to the institution of U.S. literary studies as a corrective to the erasure of minoritized subjects from the naturalized scene of the curriculum. In effect, the scholars/activists of that era were recognizing and responding to the racialization, class ordering, and gendering of literary studies by means of aestheticization, or in other words the production and hierarchization of difference according to a process of (e)valuation that disavowed its own historicity. The interrelated politics of canonicity and representation that organized the culture wars in the U.S. academy converged in such a way as to inaugurate cultural studies as an approach critically aware of such materialities and politics. For those working with canonical texts and writers, this shift to a cultural studies approach entailed acknowledging the ideological work and material specificity of cultural expression and practices of classification, including aesthetic inquiry. Curricular diversification and the ongoing and unevenly successful efforts to establish institutional formations (programs, institutes, departments) that take as their primary objects of study minoritized cultures, histories, and so on, describe this chapter of the culture wars.

Another and parallel story accompanies this one and takes as its protagonists those working with minoritized literatures, for whom the consequences of this shift from "literature" to "culture" and "work" to "text" were quite different. For one, that academic practices are ideological was a founding premise of minoritized discourses, meaning that its critics had a different point of departure for negotiating the role of aesthetics in critical practice. Even as minoritized literatures were being institutionalized by challenges to the idea of universality, the paradigm shift to cultural studies also complicated minoritized discourses' relationship to aesthetic inquiry by bringing with it what in hindsight has been understood as an overemphasis on minoritized writings as political or anthropological documents rather than artistic creations. Coupled with the institutional validation of minoritized literary studies as a sign of a commitment to diversity, such literatures have in the main been framed and studied in terms of authenticity, racism, and resistance rather than literariness per se. In other words, "greatness" and "difference," aesthetics and politics, were made to diverge, with the former tacitly if not explicitly associated with politically conservative scholarship, and the latter connoting various forms of minoritized discourse. Ethnic and women's literatures have in this respect been conceptualized as important to study *because* of politics.[32] Critically discussed and institutionally valued through standards of authenticity and bureaucratic investments in diversity, the distinctively aesthetic qualities of such work and the metacritical questions of whether or to what ends it is important to study those distinctive qualities has been underaddressed.[33] My point is not to argue the greatness of minoritized literatures per se; rather, it is to observe that in the segregation of aesthetics and politics, the aesthetics of minoritized literatures—the sensibilities and the genre of the human and cognate rationalities brought forward by them—have remained covered over.

I am among a number of critics who have taken up some version of these matters in the field of literary-cultural studies. This contemporary turn toward aesthetics finds broad traction in part because of the fatigue in such fields as Asian American studies with the kind of political critique that is somewhat predictable in its rendering of resistance, agency, and subjectivity. Some have emphasized formalist modes of criticism while others have centered affect as a critical approach alternative to rationalist political critique, and this latter work has enabled us to ask about our affiliative attachments to our objects of inquiry, as well as highlighting the limitations of rationalist critique in accounting for the complexities of lives and histories, subjectivities and politics.[34] The aesthetic turn and the affective turn are closely aligned moves in this sense—that is, in the ways that both are bracketing politics (as in, "the politics *of*") to allow for other kinds of knowledge and other modes of apprehension to emerge. The historicity of the aesthetic and its relationship to the humanities—to aesthetic education in particular—underwrite its thematization in this book.

The aesthetic is perhaps most familiar as a term used to describe a set of characteristics (as in "the aesthetics *of*") and judgments thereof, or precisely in contradistinction to politics (or, in other words, as without immediate material consequences and distant from the poles of power). Associated strongly in common critical discourse with the critical faculty of judgment and bearing conflicting legacies of deployment, the aesthetic can seem simultaneously so overdetermined and expansive a term as to be analytically meaningless. These uses belie its importance. Embraced or disavowed, its persistent presence in the intellectual traditions that ground the epistemologies organizing our received knowledge practices is indicative of the ways in which the aesthetic is deeply embedded in the history and structures of modern thought.[35] Its persistence is thus suggestive of the promise that aesthetic inquiry holds as a method of illuminating the historicities and particular shape that dominant humanism and its corollary institutions take.

More specifically, the aesthetic's history as an axis along which the kinds of persons idealized as the modern liberal subject have been distinguished from those incapable of achieving such subjectivity speaks to the long-lived ways that it has operated as a limit test in the articulation of liberal humanism and underwrites its analytic and poetic power.[36] The turn away from theological explanations of human ontology and toward scientific rationalism that crystallizes in the eighteenth century posed as a central philosophical task the need for Reason to prove itself the secure ground out of which Truth would emerge.[37] How can we come to know ourselves? How do we achieve self-consciousness in ways alternative to deistic, theological understandings of the human's relation to the natural world? If all selves are sovereign—individual and unique—upon what basis are they (should they be) connected? Upon what basis does humanity cohere? The aesthetic experience—understood in this Enlightenment context as the pleasure experienced in the encounter with the beautiful and the sublime in especially the natural world—highlighted the limits of scientific rationalism to account fully for the aspirational humanity posited through the debates out of which Enlightenment emerged.[38]

We can in light of this history understand critical recognition of the nonneutrality of standards of evaluation as registering a first-order distribution that occurs at the *proto*-political level to define and classify humanity according to the capacity for aesthetic judgment. The ability to make proper aesthetic judgments—to be capable of achieving proper awareness of the truthful beauty of something—is a fundamental characteristic of the idealized modern subject, that enlightened representative of human potentiality central to Western modernity.[39] This mythic subject, Man, stabilized through the nineteenth-century Western European consolidation and expansion of nation and empire and the concomitant subordination of a host of dissenting ideas and philosophies.[40] This history—and this is broadly Jacques Rancière's point—registers the ways that politics are constitutively aesthetic. In other words, this radical, constitutive comparison that sorts humans into different kinds based on their abilities to reason through aesthetic experience may be understood as itself aesthetic.[41] In short, aestheticization produces racial difference as sensible in both valences—as reasonable (common sense) and as affectively available to apprehension.

What I am rehearsing in this summary form is how the problem of human ontology—What is the nature of human beingness in the absence of a deistic explanation?—is answered in the aftermath of Enlightenment by suppressing the contradiction between positing sovereign, distinct individuality and establishing the general properties of humanity. Kant's anthropological writings especially register the taxonomic production of racial difference as organized by geography and especially biology.[42] Such "biocentricity," Wynter has shown, narrowly casts the definition of the human as primarily biological rather than social, with the effect of consolidating the ascription of fundamental differences among capacities to the seemingly irreducible register of the natural.[43] Considerable uncertainty as to the grounds and boundaries of human subjectivity characterized the Western European eighteenth century, and the scientific racism of the era reflects a drive to order captured in the taxonomic imperative.[44] In broad strokes, we may observe that post-Enlightenment, such uncertainty is managed by an appeal to universal humanity in the form of identity, buttressed by the coextensive emergence of the nation-state as the dominant geopolitical form of modernity. The philosophical subordination of difference to identity that ensues inaugurates representational and identity politics.[45] Backed by the policing authority of the nation-state, the liberal citizen-subject acts as the formal category of such a politics, which effaces and abstracts the very material conditions of its emergence, namely, those of empire and capitalism.[46] Corporealized into sub- or unhuman bodies by the materializing processes of capital, empire, and the imposition of the nation-state as the naturalized and dominant geopolitical formation, the incapacity for proper aesthetic judgment signaled the difference between those who would and would not realize human potential by achieving full self-consciousness.[47]

Given this history, it is no wonder that aesthetics has been met with wariness if not complete dismissal. This history also raises the question, however, as to what might come of bringing into the foreground the possibilities that are suppressed or occluded by the effacement of the potentiality of aesthetic encounter. In other words, if modernity is understood to be characterized by a compulsory aesthetic othering, mining the radical unpredictability of art and being—before its designation as "art" and "human"—bears promise for reconceiving otherness itself.[48]

Historicize in this long view the contemporary—the age of Derridean deconstruction and the radical challenges to the naturalness and inevitability of such a definition of humanity—and consider in these terms the postmodern assertion of the manufacturedness and violence of the modern narrative of a coherent, universal humanity. Moreover, put the ontological and epistemological uncertainty elaborated by postmodern critique in conversation with the dominant discourses on contemporary globalization that herald the abrogation of national sovereignty concomitant with the rise of transnational capitalism, and the urgency of attending to the antinomy of the universal and the particular emerges with renewed force. For, what we are living in now is a condition in which the economic, hyperrational, and deeply individualist subject has displaced the sociopolitical (civic) subject as the avatar of the universal.[49] Accumulation serves as the pathway to, if not self-consciousness, then self-fulfillment, and purchase power is the defining feature of civic life. The economic, of course, no more exhaustively captures the textures and complexities of life than does the political fully account for the operations of power. The arguments that insist on the paranational movements of capital that characterize contemporary history push us to consider the consequences and possibilities inaugurated by recognizing this time as a time of massive historical and onto-epistemological change akin to and animated by the intensity and scope of transformation associated retrospectively with the age of Enlightenment. This is to observe that we live and operate with the dense, unified temporality of "crumpled time" wherein the presentness of the past is acutely apprehensible.[50] This means reckoning with the conquest and colonialism, racism and cis-heteropatriarchy, upon which bourgeois liberalism is not only founded but also continues to operate; it means, following Jodi Byrd, displacing the lamentability of the production and dispossession of Indians with the grievability of Indigenous peoples continuing to claim sovereignty within the concretized structures of settler colonialism.[51] It means, following Lisa Lowe, understanding the "intimacies of four continents" as the deep foundations upon which the contemporary world has been built.[52] It means, following Christina Sharpe, sinking into the wake of slavery and the ways that its dehumanization pervades the very material substrate out of which the contemporary takes shape.[53] It means, following José Muñoz, sussing out the desires, the erotics, queer to and queerly persistent despite the powerful ideologies and institutions that would eradicate them.[54] These are the orientations of illiberal humanisms.

The distinctive contribution of minoritized discourses to matters like these rests in their general and persistent reminder that modernity and its cognates largely fail to produce peace or proliferate freedom or stability for the majority of the world.[55] The translation of Sovereign power (the power of the Sovereign) to sovereignty (the power of the citizenry to self-regulate) that modernity narrates has been coextensive with a variety of historical and ongoing violence, executed regularly in the name of the national sovereignty. Ongoing Indigenous struggles and ex-colonial nationalisms speak to the power of sovereignty—literally, understood as bearing power over life and death, and conceptually, as a compelling aspiration that registers the sovereign nation's fantastic (or perhaps phantasmatic) ability to distribute hope.[56] Self-knowledge and intentionality go hand in hand to enliven a mimetic relationship between political and individual sovereignty—or so the story goes according to liberalism. That state of identification is not only grossly unevenly distributed (this is what minoritized discourses have shown over and over again), but is also dependent on a willfulness difficult if not impossible to sustain. Contrary to the pedagogies of (neo)liberalism, individuals cannot overcome the accidents of birth simply by dint of sheer will. Challenging those pedagogies is especially vital in the U.S. context, characterized as it is by its exceptionalist and meritocratic ideologies.[57]

In this light, what Bruno Latour provocatively declares of the classification of knowledge practices resonates strongly: we have never been modern.[58] That is, history belies the inevitability of progressive Enlightenment as a mode of securing the future and full realization of humanity. It is, then, for all these reasons that we might turn to aesthetics. For, like modernity's others, the aesthetic inhabits the suppressed contradictions of modernity. The subjective experience of art, of difference, as a realm that has been subordinated to general Reason names modernity's alterity. The aesthetic is, categorically, the particular that is subsumed by the universal.

Jacques Rancière helps to clarify the political stakes of aesthetic inquiry. Aesthetics for Rancière refers in a broad sense to what he calls the "distribution of the sensible"—the modes by which activities and objects are associated with certain perceptions and ideas, resulting in the identification of art as such. In his view, aesthetics "refers to a specific regime of identifying and reflecting on the arts: [it is] a mode of articulation between ways of doing and making, [and of] thinking about their relationships."[59] This distribution manifests historically as distinct but overlapping regimes, which are various orders that serve as the grounds of a common social experience and to organize that experience by delimiting the roles that individuals may play in civic life. Analogous to the ways that for Kant, a priori concepts translate experience into understanding,[60] aesthetics for Rancière condition "what presents itself to sense experience"—they are structures that proffer and frame what can be heard and seen.[61] Understood in this way, aesthetics may be recognized as simultaneously political (that is, conditioned by relations of power and their material manifestations) and the grounds upon which the political is constituted and perceived. The material conditions of history may not only be indexed by aesthetics (the regulation and distribution of sensibility and artistic capacity), but are also themselves fundamentally aesthetic in that they are brought forward to be sensed by (historiographic, archival, methodological) practices that (re)shape the sensibilities held in common. This returns us to asking again after the terms by which the ideal (neo)liberal subject is naturalized by and enters the domain of common sense. By keying us into the sensus communis, aesthetic inquiry affords critical recognition of the terms and aspirations of the dominant social order of which common sense is both a product and a facet. It allows us to specify how corporeality and cognition interact within the bounds of and through the parameters of a specific regime of sensibility.

In classical, Aristotelian terms, sensus communis actively referred to corporeality—to that which enables the specific senses (sight, hearing, touch, taste, and smell) to coordinate syncretically what each distinctively perceives.[62] This corporeal common sense leaves the specificity of each sense intact, and understands each as equally but incommensurably contributing to the ability of the body to apprehend the world it traverses. In contrast to the primacy of sight, of the privileged economy of the visual in the apparatuses of modernity, which subtends the privileging and double meaning of representation as referring to both political standing and reflective image, this nonmodern understanding gives rise to a human subjectivity formed in fuller, embodied relation to the world. As used in this book, aesthetic inquiry reactivates this fuller meaning, suppressed by the long-dominant Kantian tradition in the prioritization of a narrow understanding of cognition. Kant uses "sensus communis" to refer to the a priori accounting for the possible judgment of others that is a part of the act of the judgment of taste; it is a necessary condition for specifically aesthetic judgment: "it is only under the presupposition that there is a common sense . . . I say, that the judgment of taste can be laid down."[63] This sense-in-common is a requirement to judge something beautiful, for we must presuppose the possible agreement of others, the possible correspondence by and communicability of our experience of the beautiful to others, in order for aesthetic judgment to be understood as partially objective, that is, as in relation to the characteristics of a specific object. The judgment of taste is thus for Kant a "subjective universal," a construct that intersects the subjectivity of aesthetic experience with the objectivity of cognition.[64] In short, the sensus communis refers to common sense as an invocation of what is presumed to be reasonable. A series of questions follow, ones with which this book is concerned: How is the sensus communis that is the condition and measure of reasonability formed? What are its governing structures, its sources of authority? How is that knowledge made to stand as a product of reason? By what legitimating authorities? By what right and what understanding of reason?

Within these questions lies the overtly political edge of aesthetic inquiry. As Rancière explains, community is a condition of politics, and community is itself cohered by sensibilities held in common, that is, the sensus communis. These sensibilities are understood to be partitioned in that they organize intelligibility: it is an "order of bodies that defines the allocation of ways of doing, ways of being, and ways of saying, and sees that those bodies are assigned by name to a particular place and task; it is an order of the visible and the sayable that sees that a particular activity is visible and another is not, that this speech is understood as discourse and another as noise."[65] This partitioning of the sensible, which is the common sense, determines the boundaries of the community (who belongs) and who may speak in and for it (who is authorized). Political engagement thus requires aesthetics, which means the apprehension of the ordering of sensibility by the sensus communis.[66] Corporeal, cognitive, and political, the sensus communis links the phenomena of sensation to the operations of reason and the subtending orders and ideologies of a time and place. It is in this regard a way of understanding the aesthetic as emergent from and affording critical attention to the forms in and by which body, mind, and sociality are related and take shape within a whole way of life.

Propositions

The chapters that follow sink into ideas introduced here. Chapters 1 and 2 together explain why and how it is that liberalism organizes the humanities in ways that continue to racialize and hierarchize people, contrary to its abstract values but very much in accordance with its historical formation and uses. These chapters work in tandem to promote deliberate disidentification from the practices, horizons, and the human and humanism of the liberal order. Lan Samantha Chang, Allan deSouza, Carrie Mae Weems, Langston Hughes, and Toni Morrison precipitate heightened sensitivity to the promise of foregoing attachment to the received humanities. They help us apprehend and overtly politicize the sense and sensibility of disidentification, toward the ends of disarticulating humanism and the humanities from liberalism.

The latter half of the book, then, turns to considering how, from this disarticulated, disidentified state, alternative humanisms and humanities are unconcealed. Illiberal in their incommensurability with liberalism's dictates and parameters, and amplified in writings by Leslie Marmon Silko, Ruth Ozeki, and Monique Truong, these alternatives generate models of organizing a humanities grounded in aesthetic rationality. These latter chapters, in other words, sketch a praxis of an illiberal humanities.

Through their discussions, these chapters forward a series of propositions that it is my intent to offer. In summary form, they are as follows:

1. Given the function of the contemporary/liberal humanities as an apparatus of modern U.S. nationalism, and given the long history of the contribution of the liberal humanism that subtends the humanities to the decimation of peoples, cultures, and lands, it is necessary to disidentify deliberately and organizationally from them.

2. By remembering that the visual is cathected to liberal representational politics within the dominant regime and, especially, to secure the racist common sense of the human of liberalism through the production and disciplinary regulation of the beautiful, the urgency of the project of bringing this current order (of Man) to closure through aesthetic inquiry unconfident in the primacy of the visual is brought to bear.

3. The disarticulation of humanism and the humanities from liberalism involves the delegitimation of the rationalism that secures the

authority of liberal ideology. This process elucidates an illiberal understanding of the human and corollary rationality based in the historically grounded, embodied knowledge subordinated within the liberal regime, which may provisionally be referred to as an *aesthetic rationality*.

4. Among the effects of disidentification and disarticulation in these contexts is the reclamation not only of the grounds of what constitutes reasonability but also of the constitution and meaning of the universal. The realization of a university that correlates with this reclaimed universal emerges as a project for the illiberal humanities.

With these propositions, with this book, I mean to issue invitations, to elicit interest and engagement with the ideas that come of the work and worlds that the dominant order works so hard to suppress, eradicate, and dismiss. They bring to bear sensibilities—feeling, thinking, knowing, and being— that are of the thickness of history and life, that orient us toward neither hope nor despair, but simply to work that is under way and that needs doing in order to proliferate the humanities after Man.

Chapter 1

Knowledge under Cover

Disidentification is about recycling and rethinking encoded meaning. The process of disidentification scrambles and reconstructs the encoded message of a cultural text in a fashion that both exposes the encoded message's universalizing and exclusionary machinations and recircuits its workings to account for, include, and empower minority identities and identifications. Thus, disidentification is a step further than cracking open the code of the majority; it proceeds to use this code as raw material for representing a disempowered politics or positionality that has been rendered unthinkable by the dominant culture. — JOSÉ ESTEBAN MUÑOZ, *Disidentifications*

I have begun to suggest the distinctive importance of aesthetic inquiry to the project of disarticulating the humanities from liberalism. That importance may be understood in short form in this twofold way: One, aesthetic inquiry emphasizes the link between what is held to be reasonable and what is viscerally experienced. In that way, it brings forward the doubled meaning of sensibility (what is held to be reasonable and what is available to the senses) and the sensus communis as a key domain of political struggle. Two, aesthetic inquiry, turned on the aesthetic itself, elucidates the historic and ongoing uses of art—of its meanings, its constitution and definition—in the service of dominant regimes of power (i.e., liberal modernity) as well as by those subjugated by and within them. The suppression of experience and onto-epistemologies incommensurate with the logics of the dominant is of a piece with the dehumanization through colonialism, settler colonialism, and racism justified by the developmental telos of liberalism. The aesthetic and the subordinated—"the minor"—accordingly are aligned, a shared positioning that gives aesthetic inquiry special purchase in the project of bringing alternative humanities to bear.

In this chapter, I invite us to consider the impact of aesthetic inquiry, understood in this way, on our understanding of the power and operations of the privileged paradigms of the liberal humanities, exemplified by those organizing knowledge production and prioritization in the discipline of English and the field of American Literature. I follow the lead of writer Lan Samantha Chang, and draw from visual art by Allan deSouza and Carrie Mae Weems, as I make the case for deliberate disidentification from the liberal humanities.[1] Chang's novella, *Hunger*, helps us apprehend such humanities in contemporary form as an apparatus of the U.S. nation-state, and unfolds the meanness and inadequacy of the aesthetic education it offers. Bound to the ideologies of the modern nation-state as exemplified by the United States, they require both a disavowal of its foundational and ongoing violences, which is effected through the production of ignorance under the guise of knowledge, and a prioritization of abstract ideals over empirical realities. DeSouza and Weems, together with Chang, invite us to think here specifically about the implications of these insights on the horizons and practices of minoritized discourses in the academy, as well as those of fields like American Literature, which have become multicultural in ways that attest to the pervasiveness and power of liberal common sense. What emerges is a reminder of the continuing force of U.S. nationalism and its ability, through its promulgation of liberalism, to conserve power and resources for a few at the expense of a great many. Aesthetic education through the received humanities buttresses these exclusionary ideologies and practices. The governing proposition of this chapter is this: While their defunctioning cannot alone forestall the injurious activities of the U.S. nation-state, we can at the least stop submitting to its demands as we claim the humanities as a ground for bringing forth sensibilities that grapple with rather than cover over its constitutive violence.

In this regard, my address here is directed to those of us who, in light of the strategy of "represent and destroy" that is liberalism's response to racism and settler colonialism, seek ways of working in and through the university against and beyond the liberal order.[2] There is much unavailable to our immediate control in remediating the structures and effects of racism and colonialisms, but the creation of curricular and other structural pedagogies that refuse inducement to identify with liberalism and with the U.S. nation is well within our reach. Under the aegis of the humanities, I believe we can amplify the work of antiracist critique, Indigenous and settler colonial studies, ethnic studies, gender and sexuality studies—of, in short, the work issuing from and within the dispersed administrative/classification units of the institution, and emergent from the people and communities subjugated or otherwise minoritized in the service of upholding the rightness of the liberal order. I envision our work as putting into place, as others who came before us did, ideas and practices that will allow us to look back on this time and identify what we were collectively able to do despite as well as because of institutionalization, and despite as well as because of the political economic conditions and policies that subordinate the importance of aesthetics to the production of common sense. What will the humanities have stood for, what will they have been and done, in this long era of normalized war making in the name of humanity, impoverishment in the name of progress, surveillance and multifaceted suppression of dissent in the name of civic society, and mass incarceration of especially Black and Brown people for the sake of the public good? How do we put into place concepts and structures to realize a humanities that elicits subjectivities and social formations that demand and secure the conditions necessary to the flourishing of people rather than nations, of lives rather than ideas?

Both the exigency for and the difficulty of contesting the received iteration of the humanities come of the assaultive pressures on higher education that characterize the current conjuncture. Neoliberalization, the process whereby personal responsibility delinked from history and the deployment of free-market ideology in every facet of life are compulsorily mandated, is plainly legible in the defunding of public higher education that has continued apace since the 1970s. The minimal funding that is now available— down to about 34 percent on average, from a high of about 60 percent in 1975 (in national average terms)—is contingent on market-driven performance standards that simultaneously assert the inadequacy of government and the efficiency of corporate structures to administer all aspects of society, and education most decidedly. These policies have led to sharp increases in tuition—as much as 247 percent since the 1970s at flagship state universities, and by about 164 percent at community colleges. By as soon as 2050, if current trends continue, most states will entirely cease to support public higher education. In what regard such education will continue to be public is unclear, except insofar as this redistribution of tax dollars evacuates its meaning as related to providing access to higher education to the general populace.[3] Now, with concerted emphasis on STEM (science, technology, engineering, and mathematics) fields deemed necessary to success and national competitiveness in the global workforce, outcomes toward and relevance to those goals serve as primary measures of institutional performance. It is thus that it seems necessary to defend the humanities as a means of resisting the rationality that authorizes and resources certain kinds of knowledge at the expense of others.

At the same time, it is also increasingly clear that long-standing arguments for the humanities, including those that insist on their utilitarian and political value—the teaching of critical thinking and support of ethical development toward the ends of sustaining democracy—have limited persuasiveness in this state-supported, political economy–induced climate of self-interested competitiveness. In a crudely pragmatic sense, such arguments simply have been ineffective in forestalling or reversing defunding policies; liberalism's weakness as a remedy for neoliberalization is resoundingly evident in educational policy.

That weakness is, I believe, indicative of the ways that neoliberalization exposes rather than initiates the collaboration among capitalism, colonialism, and liberalism that characterizes and animates U.S. national identity formation as the exemplary modern nation-state. In other words, the rationalization of the humanities along these lines affirms the values and concepts of bourgeois liberalism and settler colonialism as they obscure how neoliberalization is precipitated by rather than a sharp departure from them. To be sure, the humanities are not solely or perhaps even primarily responsible for neoliberalization, but in their affirmation of liberal ideology, they have facilitated its establishment as policy and common sense. I would suggest that the much-rebuked "one percent" may be understood not as aberrant to the bourgeois liberal project but rather as its logical conclusion: that subject arguably embodies the Adamsonian ideal of a life of comfortable leisure; it is the enlightened, achieved subject of modernity. Aesthetic education, the purview of the humanities, has long trained the privileged classes who had access to *studia humanitatis* to embrace the private, property-owning individual of liberalism as the apotheosis of humanity.

In their received form, they are a legacy of the nationalist and robustly patriotic ideologies of the U.S. nation-state characterizing the post–World War II and Cold War eras—ideologies that give specific shape to the long life of liberalism. That the humanities have been complicit in the further-ance of U.S. nation and empire building in these ways is apparent not only in the histories underlying the establishment of higher education—the civ-ilizing mission executed through education that accompanied militarized efforts to exterminate and dispossess Indigenous peoples and the accumu-lation of wealth through the stolen land of those peoples and stolen labor of enslaved peoples—but also in their explicit recruitment toward patriotic ends in the twentieth century.[4] While the study of human expression and behavior has existed since antiquity, the humanities crystallized as a mean-ingful rubric in the interwar years and became overtly nationalist in the overlapping post–World War II, Cold War, and civil rights movement eras.[5] An affirmation of the distinction between *Bildung* (self-knowledge) and *Wis-senschaft* (knowledge of the natural world) crystallized in the Enlighten-ment and post-Enlightenment European contexts, the establishment of the humanities in the U.S. university seemingly settled debates regarding the relative importance of science over ethical development.[6] The formally com-partmentalized organization of university life was to allow humanists and scientists to coexist in pluralist harmony, familiar to us now in the hardened institutional structures of higher education. In the middle-late twentieth century, with heightened awareness of the military and economic domi-nance of the United States in the global world order, the threat of nuclear war, and the demands of insurgent power and rights movements, the hu-manities were rationalized in the United States on patriotic grounds.

We can see this nationalist mobilization of the humanities in the found-ing of the National Endowment for the Humanities in 1965 as an indepen-dent federal agency. This is a signal event in the consolidation of the belief that the arts and the study of the best of human achievement, as the hu-manities were described at the time, were vitally important to realizing the dream of American greatness. The 1964 *Report of the Commission on the Hu-manities*, coauthored by the American Council of Learned Societies, Coun-cil of Graduate Schools in the United States, and the United Chapters of Phi Beta Kappa, recommended the establishment of the NEH in order that the "highest achievements" of humanity might serve to guide Americans and the United States in "kindling aspirations" and acting with concern for "man's ultimate destiny" on the global stage.[7] The authors argued that the humanities were crucial to the conveyance of such "enduring values" as "justice, freedom, virtue, beauty, and truth," as well as to the acquisition of cross-cultural knowledge and to modeling "excellence of . . . conduct . . . [to] entitle [the United States] to ask others to follow its lead."[8] Without such training, what is diagnosed as "a novel and serious challenge" posed by "the remarkable increase in their leisure time" resulting from technological advancement could lead to "trivial and narcotic amusements," which are posited as clearly against the national interest.[9] The values and vision of the humanities articulated in this report expressly pull forward the ideology of the founding fathers to argue their importance to the telos of the United States, destined to be a superior civilization produced by generational advancement from war to the arts, from the utilitarian to the reflective.[10]

If driven by somewhat less overt patriotism, current rhetoric declaring the crisis of the humanities echoes the ideology of this earlier context. Consider, for example, a 2013 article in the *New Republic* by Gordon Hutner and Feisal Mohamed titled "The Real Humanities Crisis Is Happening in Public Universities," which opens with the declaration, "You've probably heard several times already that the humanities are in 'crisis.' The crisis is real." Their call for a "new deal for the Humanities" argues for redress of the withdrawal of support for the liberal arts on the basis of the contribution that the humanities—the "noble tradition" of the liberal arts—make to "enriching society." Representative of a dominant strain of arguments for the defense of the humanities, such rhetoric bespeaks the continuing force of liberal ideology and finds traction in the face of the produced and imposed austerity that public higher education is currently confronting.

My concern, in brief, is that though we may well be at (or amid) a turning point regarding the humanities and higher education, a danger of this moment is that present conditions provide the opportunity for the reentrenchment of liberal values integral to the U.S. nationalist project. If we allow that to happen, we are effectively obscuring and indeed affirming the histories and ongoing practices of dispossession and denigration justified by liberalism. In other words, what I am getting at is that given that bourgeois liberalism has been instrumental in the justification of U.S. imperial and colonial maneuvers, the affirmative recruitment of its concepts warrants pause even in the face of neoliberalization. The militarism and political economic expansionism of the United States historically and currently advances under cover of liberal values in ways that are anything but abstract.[11] What Lisa

Lowe has astutely termed the "ruse of freedom" conjured by bourgeois liberalism's close partnership with racial capitalism has facilitated everything from slavery and indentured servitude to colonial occupation, both historic and ongoing, to contemporary forms of war making for the sake of rescuing victimized women, always imagined to be elsewhere.[12] Neither have liberal solutions been effective remedies for eradicating the forms of violence organized along the intersecting axes of sociopolitical identity. They have instead proliferated into and as the legitimation of the security state—the sanctification of belief in personal and national sovereignty that authorizes the innovation and enactment of regulatory and disciplinary mechanisms designed to protect the public from the criminal, the citizen from the terrorist, the legal from the illegal migrant.[13] In short, and as the discussions that follow elaborate more fully, if we take seriously the long-lived ways in which the humanities have served U.S. nation building from its founding to the contemporary, we cannot but also take seriously the need to disidentify with rather than defend them.[14] These histories, that is, explain how the humanities are organized in such a way as to promote identification with and attachment to the liberal order despite both its participatory history in producing, and corollary overweening inadequacy as a response to, the necropolitical state activities and effects characterizing the current conjuncture.

Lan Samantha Chang's aestheticization of the hollowness yet powerful appeal of the promises of happiness and prosperity tethered to U.S. national identity makes sense of this history of the humanities. Chang's attention to the (im)potency of aesthetic education helps us apprehend and understand how the liberal humanities—the purview of aesthetic education and an engine of modernity—produces ignorance in the guise of knowledge.[15] It is an ignorance empowered by the apparatuses of the U.S. nation-state in ways that induce commonsense attachment to bourgeois liberalism's promises despite its manifold failures to secure freedom, happiness, and prosperity as empirical realities; it is an ignorance resulting in material consequences captured by an immutable hunger arising from deprivation and dissatisfaction that cannot be resolved by individual will. Beyond acting as a prompt for critical investigation, Chang's work bespeaks the specifically aesthetic nature of knowledge practices and the authorized institutions that advance them. Her novella identifies how ideas come to be experienced as truth or falsehood through institutional and state mechanisms far beyond the control of any individual, and identifies those mechanisms as reiterating the material diminution of lives along the intersecting axes of race, gender, sexuality, and class. What it registers and bespeaks, in other words, is the structuring of inequality as an integral part of bourgeois liberalism's cherished institutions of aesthetic education and the heteronormative nuclear family.

Is This All There Is?

Hunger opens in New York City in 1967. "I often dream about the restaurant where I met Tian," Min, Chang's narrator tells us, and continues, "I see myself walking toward those [double doors of the Vermilion Palace, the restaurant in which she worked]—a slight, brown girl with hair like an inkbrush, tilted eyes, and a wary mouth."[16] Min recalls that a "chill went beneath [her] skin" and made it impossible for her to stay warm in the first months of her life in New York City; it is music that brings her to her senses, that grounds her in America:

> I could not taste my food or feel the softness of my narrow bed. I had been in the city for two months before I even noticed the music school. And then one evening I heard a student practicing. Walking past a basement window, I caught the thread of a violin melody, high and sweet as a woman's voice. The sound rose up through a crack in the window and between the safety bars; it shimmered through me, a wave of color, blooming past the gray tenements and toward the narrow sky. I drew one cold, sweet breath of air and truly understood that I had arrived in America.
>
> A few days later, I saw Tian. He might have been to the restaurant a dozen times before, but I do not remember seeing him until after the music.[17]

"For the first time," Min remembers upon serving Tian, whom she would later marry, "I felt warm."[18]

We come to learn that Min's narration is posthumous as well as retrospective, a fact revealed only late in the story.[19] By the time Min dies of cancer, Tian has long passed on, and her daughter Ruth has fled the home while the other, Anna, resignedly remains. "My body was being left behind," Min explains of her death. "The world's winds took hold of me. The earth began to rush below, and I who had once dreamed of leaving Brooklyn—I decided I would not let go. I held on like a metal filing, bracing myself against the force of the earth. I held on. I will not leave. I have held on, to this day."[20] As

Hunger closes, we see Min waiting: for Anna to return and her "daughters to meet again"; for that time "when no one on earth will remember our lives."[21]

Published as the eponymous piece of Chang's 1998 short story collection, *Hunger* unfolds in the U.S. post–civil rights era as it melancholically insists upon dissatisfaction and inadequacy rather than freedom and prosperity as qualities inhering in the promises of the U.S. nation. A story of people fleeing the Cultural Revolution, through Taiwan and then to the United States, the world *Hunger* paints is decidedly aesthetic: Chang offers in *Hunger* a meditation on the production and effects of common sense by and within authorized institutions of the modern nation-state, namely, the nuclear heteronormative family and formal aesthetic education.[22] Couched as a familiar immigrant family drama, this apparent privatization of the immigrant narrative emphasizes the aesthetics of politics at the level of everyday life.[23] As its opening passages suggest, *Hunger* posits the enlivening effects of aesthetic encounter—of the ways in which embodied and grounded being emerges through sensory encounter with music—an insight that is thickened and complicated by the story's attention to the institutional forces that sharply delimit the transformative potential of such encounter. Chang marks a distinct contrast between the invigorating force of the music floating out from the basement, fugitively escaping the figural undercommons of the music school, and the stultifying effects of formal aesthetic education. The experience and practice of music, the feminized sound issuing from the violin, contrasts sharply against the patriarchal vision of the masterful teacher and racially discriminatory institution of education put forward by the story.

There are of course any number of immigrant narratives that attest to the emptiness of the American Dream. This is certainly true of literatures that thematize the experiences of migrants from Asian countries, and Chang's novella shares this genre's interest in the barriers to assimilation and prosperity that contradict the American Dream. *Hunger*, moreover, employs the conceit of intergenerational family conflict widely familiar in the narration of transformation from immigrant to citizen. Striking in Chang's iteration, however, is her attention to aesthetic education in the rendering of this arc. Through that attention, *Hunger* offers itself as a meditation on the faith in aesthetic education's ability to cultivate a good liberal subject that is a hallmark feature of bourgeois liberalism. Even more specifically, it speaks to and of the insularity rather than transcendence that describes a life dedicated to liberal aesthetic education.

Tian, for example, who fled China by swimming half a mile to a refugee ship, his cherished violin held above the water, and who works diligently once in the United States to secure a permanent position on the faculty of the music college only to be passed over in favor of a White candidate, is at greatest freedom in the tiny sound-proofed practice room of their home. Obsessively believing in music as the pathway to a fulfilling life, Tian gives fierce instruction to his daughters, especially Ruth, the musically gifted of the two. Music, which compels him to seek freedom, and which enlivened Min, transforms in the institutional contexts of education and patriarchal family into a force of violent prohibition.

Ruth's refusal to pursue a career in music follows from the torrent of verbal abuse from her father for her imperfect mastery of technical skill. Anna, meanwhile, is technically proficient and yet receives only indifference from Tian, lacking as she does musical genius. The all too persistent stereotype of the overbearing Asian patriarch is cast here as the exemplary figure of the Pedagogue, he who privileges mastery and demands obsessive fealty to the transcendent power of the aesthetic over and above actual lives. Neither does *Hunger* find satisfaction in the dispassionate stance of scholarly distance: that Anna becomes an academic specialist in East Asian antiquities, a life that provides tidy order, bespeaks in the loneliness that accompanies it the banality of the institutional solution. Music, which brought life to Tian and Min, is found as the story closes to be trapped in the walls of their home, like Min herself, made into a haunting presence of unfilled promises and potential.

Hunger functions in this story as a dense metaphor that collates immigration, aesthetic education, and the heteronuclear family as institutions inadequate to the flourishing of life. Each of these promulgates belief in individual advancement and happiness, a sensibility that is shown by Chang to be cruelly optimistic.[24] The bourgeois ideals to which Anna attaches, the dream of individual freedom pursued by Tian, and Ruth's refusal of and escape from the household (she regularly exits and enters the home surreptitiously through a bedroom window), together delineate the felt/thought dissatisfaction precipitated by these normative liberal institutions. Chang sketches a resulting hunger so powerful as to overcome even death: in Min, we are called to acknowledge this foundational hunger as the force that constrains her even after death. The story leaves us asking, simply, is this all there is?

Where Are We in This Story?

"Is this all there is?" is a question that initiates the crafting of different horizons, ones defined neither by the nation nor by its defining ideologies and institutions. It is an invitation to critique not the failure of the individual to succeed, but instead the paucity of available options for life. And it is, I think, a question particularly salient to apprehending what the humanities might come to be when defense is displaced in favor of more radical engagement. In these ways, Chang's emphasis on the inadequacies of liberalism's promises resonates with Sylvia Wynter's cautionary insistence that we "cast a critical eye on . . . the price at the level of emancipatory knowledge that would have to be paid for our newly licensed functioning within the present organization of rational knowledge," and with Roderick Ferguson's likewise cautionary enjoinder to recognize the "will to institutionality" that can orient the interdisciplines to the effect of muting their radical politics.[25] Anna's careful curation of Asian antiquities figures such domestications of difference. In the novella, the individual, whether extraordinary by virtue of artistic prowess or tethered to institutional regimes of order, cannot produce the conditions whereby emancipated life is empirically evident. Assimilation to the present order, attachment to the promises of institutionalization, gives rise to foreclosure—to a narrowing of life—rather than to its flourishing. In this regard, *Hunger* allegorizes the institutionalization of ethnic and gender studies in the U.S. academy specifically with regard to the liberal multiculturalization of humanities curricula. The numerous social scientific accounts of the marginalization, "presumed incompetence," "microaggressions," and discrimination against women of color in the academy are echoed by Chang such that these phenomena, experienced by individuals and groups subjectively, may be understood as precipitated by these normative institutions.[26] Not individual decision making or personality, but instead the conditions of possibility and common sense that would have us believe that these phenomena are purely subjective, come to the fore as the objects of critique.

Think in these terms of curricular design, and specifically of the principles of field coverage and disciplinarity and acknowledge their effectiveness in inducing the willful ignorance required to sustain the posited universalism and rightness of bourgeois liberalism. Fundamentally a liberal model of representation, coverage, or the administrative equalizing of subject areas that describes the basic architecture of higher education, quite effectively covers over the developmentalism and attendant racialization, class ordering, and gendering that subtend and sustain it. As David Lloyd has noted, the concept of representation emerging from Enlightenment philosophies takes narrative form, positing a developmental telos of humanity that moves from those who are primarily sensual beings (the savages and primitives as well as women of the liberal philosophical discourse of the time) to the penultimate figure of disinterested reason exemplified by the propertied Western Man.[27] Proximity to that figure of disinterested reason indexes the capacity for representativeness of human capacity, correlating to the capacity to govern. By extension, we can recognize that representation as a remedy for inequality effectively reproduces the teleology of modernity, which consigns certain bodies of knowledge, to borrow Dipesh Chakrabarty's formulation, to the waiting room of history.[28] In other words, the point of arrival—the structure into which assimilation concludes—remains the center of gravity, the standard against which "later" arrivals are measured.[29]

The immigrant narrative registers this procedural affirmation of extant standards, and serves in this sense not as a faithful record of experience so much as a genre of modern nationalist and settler colonialist ideology. Liberal representational politics—multiculturalism—cannot but fail in its attempts to redress exclusion by diversification, because it is of a piece with these ideologies of the modern nation-state. Or, rather, precisely because it attempts to solve the problem of exclusion by means of representational diversity, it affirms and idealizes assimilation as it disavows the significance of history and empirical reality. The legally performative language of naturalization reminds us that immigrants are to become, as if by nature, citizen-subjects of the U.S. nation; this is a demand for an exhaustive assimilation, one that requires both the willful denouncement of history and occlusion of the ongoingness of settler colonialism. The choices offered by the modern nation-state are stark: metaphorically speaking, we can, like Chang's Anna, assimilate insofar as accepting the limited roles assigned to us—to represent the minoritized subject, the oriental(ist)—or, like Ruth, absent ourselves entirely.

The nationalization of the humanities and their recruitment toward patriotic ends provides a framework for understanding the traction that curricular multiculturalism—this structured insistence on formal equality by organization around the principle of field coverage—has had in the U.S.

academy. Such formality effectively displaces substantive debate in favor of a purposeful civility that is nothing if not a performance of bourgeois manners. Claims of autonomy and assertions of mutual respect for mastery of specific bases of knowledge justify and animate such civility, reproducing an ideal of the scholar as an exemplary figure of the disinterested, neutral subject. Administratively tidy, this model efficiently cooperates with what Melamed has argued is the "official anti-racism" that is liberal multiculturalism, which simultaneously dematerializes race and promotes diversity and inclusion as solutions to racism.[30]

The procedures and effects of this ideology are distinctly palpable in the field of American Literature, which continues to be paradigmatically organized by the overrepresentation of Melville, Hawthorne, Emerson, and Thoreau, its "original elements." The assimilationist trajectory enabled by the field coverage model reiterates a segregationist sensibility reflected in and constructive of the continuing functionality of a hierarchical division between American Literature and its subordinated others, which plays out as a distinction between aesthetics and politics that conserves the authority of the field's original elements, including the priority assigned to the White masculine subject. The 2004 special issue of the journal *American Literature*, coedited by Christopher Castiglia and Russ Castronovo, helps us recognize this condition, though perhaps in ways unintended by its editors. Titled "Aesthetics and the End(s) of Cultural Studies," this issue was designed to show, the editors explain in their introduction, how attention to "the materialities of aesthetic production" and to "the unpredictable nature of . . . social conditions and settings" characterizing cultural studies methodology renews engagement with aesthetics as a politically salient aspect of American literary studies.[31] Their introduction proceeds from laying out these conceptual grounds to turn, in the next breath, to "take, for instance, Herman Melville's novella, *Benito Cereno*."[32]

The ease with which Melville is invoked to instantiate the political possibilities of thinking aesthetics in a cultural studies tenor is striking. The casualness of exemplification tells us more about the field's embrace of liberal multiculturalism and the mobilization of aesthetics toward its ends than, I would suggest, it provides insight into the political potential of aesthetic inquiry per se. Castiglia and Castronovo note, "aesthetics . . . need not be a turning away from differences."[33] In such a statement resides the occlusion of the history of aesthetics in the production of differences, a history in light of which the prospect of "turning away" is rendered moot. This temporally inflected, positional distinction registers further in the significance attached to *Benito Cereno* as the exemplary text that illuminates the relationship between aesthetics and cultural studies. According to Castiglia and Castronovo, the novella renders Captain Delano as the contemplative aesthetic subject, in contrast to Babo, the leader of the slave revolt, who emerges as the "revolutionary aesthetic" subject. Delano in this account is defined by an investment in self-transformation while Babo is defined by a capacity to "shape the heads—perspectives, ideologies, sympathies—of others."[34] The privileged White masculine self-interested subject and the disenfranchised Black masculine political subject are recognizably figures of a liberal multicultural imaginary. The reputed unpredictability of aesthetic encounter turns out to be rather predictable in associating Black masculinity with the revolutionary political sphere and White masculinity with contemplative self-interest. Through this reading, the editors advance their argument that aesthetics, far from being a mode of disengagement, "invite the possibility of constituting and producing subjects at the site of dialogue and power."[35]

This reach for Melville reflects a version of American Literature rooted in the dominance of the era of Great Books methodologies, which are themselves rooted in the fervent nationalisms of the early twentieth century that organized our inherited arrangements of knowledge. Polemically stated, my point is that despite its claims to post-Americanist and postnationalist hermeneutics, American Literature remains bound to its original elements. Castiglia and Castronovo's essay is but one example of a more general phenomenon that registers the embrace of Melville as, as Donald Pease has explicitly put it, providing the dominating "frame narrative" of the field.[36] There is something obviously tautological occurring here: Melville has indeed been central to American Literary history, because he has been upheld as such by Americanist critics; and because he is central to American Literary history, he can be made to speak transcendentally to sketch the future of the field. The instance of Melville becomes generalized in this way and reinscribes his hypercanonical status.[37] We seem to arrive, unchanged, at our point of departure, a hallmark characteristic of liberal multiculturalism.

That is, this reach for Melville iterates liberalism's erasure of history such that all differences appear identical in kind. Within this schema, because all texts are equally valid, Melville is identically different from all others.

Such a move deftly sublimates the hierarchizing effect of taking yet again Melville's writings to be the textual equivalent of the everyman. The reinscription of the White male writer as the authoritative speaker on racialized subjectivity, aesthetics, cultural studies—in fact, on any matter—cannot but cause critical pause. In that pause rests the opportunity, perhaps even the enjoinder, to recognize that this move also attests to the problem of sympathetic identification with the subjugated. Here, I recall Avery Gordon's incisive argument that casts such identification as a "treacherous mistake," one precipitated by a desire for distance from the "onerous inheritance" that is slavery.[38] In her discussion of Toni Morrison's Beloved and the ways it has been taken up into the sociological imagination, Gordon astutely observes that "few teachers . . . would identify with the schoolteacher, the educated master."[39] Rather, sympathetic identification flows to the enslaved, thus effectively bypassing "the sedimented power relations in which we lived then and live now."[40] Morrison's novel, Gordon submits, "suggests that it is our responsibility to recognize just where we are in this story, even if we do not want to be there."[41]

This responsibility, I have tried to suggest, cannot be met by faithful appeal to liberal values, nor without critique of the mean inadequacy of the knowledge and ways of living authorized by the liberal humanities. Consider, for example, the organization of Asian American cultural studies around the subjugated Asian—the internee, the immigrant prohibited from assimilation, the would-be migrant excluded from the nation's borders. The proper subjects of Asian Americanist inquiry have long been a structuring topic of debate in the field.[42] Laura Kang has challenged Asian Americanist literary critics to reflect anew on this matter, by astutely observing the "Asianization" of capital in the 1990s and a corollary "Americanization" of debt (especially to China), coeval with the affirmative (rather than resistant) role that Asian American subjects have played within global capitalism.[43] Kang presses us to ask, "What does it mean for Asian Americans to be well-compensated agents of 'late (global) capital'?"[44] While critically acknowledging the continuing persistence of an "unabashed American Orientalism," Kang argues the necessity of accounting for—of taking up as the figures of Asian Americanist critique—those who "express [an] uncritical and even proud identification with Wall Street and finance capital."[45] Instead of dismissing such subjects as self-hating, anomalous subjects interpellated to a false consciousness, what would it mean for Asian Americanists to take seriously these identifications with the very systems that Asian American studies intends to resist?

Homologously, we may ask what it would mean for American Literature to become accountable for Delano as much as Babo—to produce, in the course of studying the wages of slavery and racial capitalism, identification with the regime that precipitates the well-compensated agent rather than, or in addition to, the subjugated other. The ethics of objectification come to the fore as the scene of academic work, and impolitic questions arise: What explains the attachment to the scene of subjection that characterizes (Asian) American Literature? What is at stake, and for whom, in the organization of the field around identification of and with injury—rather than, in contrast, epistemological and institutional complicity with racial capitalism and colonial modernity? Self-subalternization not only benefits from the suffering of others, but also, in its most well-intended forms, reiterates the importance of sympathy to liberalism. The individualization of affect that is systematically, structurally produced is a favored trick of liberalism. Made into matters seemingly personal, sympathy and guilt go hand in hand to convince us that individualized care for the other as well as the self rather than structural change is the cornerstone of social transformation.

We are, in other words, plotted—willingly and not—into a system that, if we are to avoid self-affirming liberal/sympathetic identification as a facet of politically engaged research and teaching, requires a thoroughgoing assessment of the subject position of the producer of knowledge. These positions are perforce differentiated, and quite sharply so, along the intersectional axes of race and gender, indigeneity and national origins, class and sexuality, and so on, which map the differential distribution of relations to institutional authority and resources that characterize the academy. At the same time, no matter where and how we are located, it is necessary to question the conditions that prompt and the effects of subjective identification, which cannot be made into an excuse for neglecting difference, racial or otherwise. The point, decidedly, is not to induce guilt or blame—modalities that, like sympathy, merely confirm the subjective ego. Rather, the task at hand is to address differential relations and conditions of legitimacy and authority as a consistent part of critical praxis.

Disidentification and the Incommensurate Subject

I believe one way we may go about doing so is to take seriously the methods by which the potent fictionality of liberal ideology can be ameliorated by attending to the aesthetic. I suggested in the introduction that the aesthetic and the Other of modernity may be understood to have in common subordination in the modern order. Cast as "minor" in the world shaped by bourgeois liberalism, the aesthetic/the Other is that order's condition of possibility. To be minor in the modern project is not merely to be marginalized, but is instead to be proto-political or, in other words, the condition that precedes and subtends modern onto-epistemology. Fundamentally, there is an incommensurability between the "major" and the "minor" of modernity that is erased in the process of naturalizing modern subjectivity.[46]

As Natalie Melas points out in her reflection on the field of Comparative Literature, commensurability is a condition that refers to a precedent judgment—to the determination of a required qualitative equivalence which is a necessary condition for an evaluation of relative merit to advance.[47] (Commensurability gives rise, for example, to the enjoinder to compare apples to apples, or to not compare apples to oranges.) In the absence of such similarity in kind, "better" or "worse" are meaningless terms of comparison. Determined at this radical level to be qualitatively different, those whose humanity is consequently cast as uncertain have no entry to a discourse on personhood; they are constitutively in nonidentity to modern subjectivity. Constituted in difference from—as *in kind* different from—the individual who can aspire to be the abstract citizen-subject standing for human potentiality, this Other is produced by the logic of commensurability that rationalizes modernity's constitutive violence.

The minor of modernity may thus be understood to be incommensurate—to mark a position wrought by qualitatively different modalities of being. In contrast, conceived of as a conventionally liberal political subject, the minority is part of the distributive logic of modernity; its legibility as a political subject depends on the distributive/representational logic of the nation-state. Given the power of the nation-state to regulate the distribution of sensibility through the regulation of material conditions of life, the urgency of vigorous support for the minority as a political subject is clear. And/but, it is also clear that such political subjectivity cannot but be limited, because it is a category of normative distribution. We cannot afford to ignore the trenchancy of identity given the bio- and necro-political power of representational politics, but it also must be recognized that such politics are themselves grounded in a disavowal of radical alterity. We must try, as Lowe enjoins us, to imagine the "what could have been"—to craft and work within "the space of a different kind of thinking, a space of productive atten- tion . . . [to what has been sublated or lost], a thinking with twofold attention that seeks to encompass at once the positive objects and methods of history and social science and the matters absent, entangled, and unavailable by its methods."[48] The incapacity to reflect properly on aesthetic experience upon which radical otherness is predicated returns here to focus critical light on the scene of the aesthetic encounter. It is the scene in which the individual's incapacity can be attested, evidence of which supports the appropriateness of the distribution of sensibility enacted by modernity. The incommensu- rate subject bears no obligation to hew to the dictates of modern rationalism and, in fact, categorically cannot. It stands, then, as a figure of unmanaged radical difference.

In this way, the critical privileging of incommensurability gives rise to a hermeneutics of disidentification that enjoins focused attention to the aes- thetic state. I mean aesthetic state to function in a doubled sense—on the one hand as a designation of the ways in which the nation-state functions as a formal part of the dominant "regime of visibility"—vis-à-vis Rancière—to regulate what (and who) can be seen and heard.[49] On the other hand—and at the same time—the aesthetic state refers here to the potentiality embed- ded in an encounter with an object that appeals in extraordinary ways to the senses. The aesthetic state in this latter sense is a state of suspension between the subject and object wherein predictability and intentionality are arrested: neither the subject nor object is perfectly delineated or coherent in this encounter. Sense perception (a specific form of experience) and cogni- tion (the faculty of reason) open to each other in encountering an aesthetic object; the aesthetic state names the indeterminacy that results. It is in ef- fect the state of subjectlessness.

The image of Allan deSouza's "He gazed into the liquid darkness in which desires drowned, from where the body's delicious pains emerged" (figure 1.1) manifests this condition. Part of a series he produced at the turn of the twenty-first century, in both its crafting and the resultant image, this work renders the extraordinariness of the aesthetic object and augurs the potentiality of difference that resides in the aesthetic state. The image is on

1.1 Allan deSouza, "He gazed into the liquid darkness in which desires drowned, from where the body's delicious pains emerged." Photograph. Courtesy of the artist and Talwar Gallery, New York.

one level a painterly addition to the long tradition of U.S. landscape painting and photography that aestheticized the land as a welcoming, conveniently uninhabited frontier. The rough surface of what appears to be eerily barren earth backlit by a horizon line of yellowing light, together with its sensually and psychically evocative title, gesture beyond the frame of land and photo to the fluid unknowns beyond. Without knowledge of deSouza's methods, it is perhaps impossible to see the body in the image. In fact, the detritus of the human body sculptures the surface: hair, fingernail clippings, and earwax are reorganized and reclassified into a seemingly nonhuman landscape. This photograph instantiates a(n illiberal) worldview in which truth claims attached to bodies, and those that affiliate certain bodies to specific spaces, are held to be radically suspect.[50] Its evocative emptiness makes present the histories and aesthetics of violent dispossession subtending the production of the American landscape as beautifully empty—*terra nullius*, as a space in waiting.[51] Although it is part of a series of works that invoke racialization and the relationships of land to identity and personhood articulated and naturalized through the establishment of the modern nation-state as the dominant geopolitical organizing mode of the past several centuries, deSouza's piece refuses apprehension through the commonplace vocabularies of race or nation. And though its title associates a masculine gender identity to the image, the gaze, in its objectlessness, leaves such identification open-ended such that it removes us to the proto-political realm. This image in these ways marks the link between subjectlessness and the aesthetic.

More specifically, deSouza's photograph works by connecting the sensory (experience) to the conceptual on multiple levels. The prioritization of a surface that reads simultaneously as landscape and skin in the image raises, as William Cohen has asked in a different context, "a fundamental question about embodiment: what does skin cover?"[52] DeSouza's photograph likewise focuses on skin's function and metaphoricity through its visual cathection of bodies and land. Expressed through the absent presence of the body and compounded by a psychic life involving desire, pleasure, and pain invoked in the title, the photograph literally brings into the foreground of critical inquiry the grounds of embodiment. Here, detritus metonymically refers to (a) body, yet that body cannot serve as a social signifier. Nor does it posit interiority as the proper location of human essence. Instead, it signals a vestibular position of disidentification: outside of proper integration, without organization; or, in other words, in nonidentity to the body.[53] It is perhaps from and into this vestibular space that "he gazes," a gaze that is objectless and focused instead on a yet unknown, unbounded horizon. The "liquid darkness" of deSouza's photograph functions in this way as a figuration of the aesthetic state. The aesthetic marks the boundary between experience (desire, pain) and judgment (deliciousness, taste). Working against the teleological quality of narrative, however, the aesthetic state, because it is formally external, does not dissolve or become incorporated into stable judgment: it remains vestibular, irresolvably precedent to judgment. Thus experience remains polychronically present in the act of judgment, always threatening to erode the status of knowledge.

This Kantian version of an aesthetic idea, as Andrew Bowie explains, refers to "that representation of the imagination which gives much to think about, but without determinate thought, i.e., *concept* being adequate to it, which consequently no language can completely attain and make comprehensible."[54] In the aesthetic relationship to an object, "the freedom of the imagination not to be bound by existing concepts enlivens the powers of cognition, enabling them to develop further."[55] In other words, the encounter with art arrests subjectivization (the coming to consciousness of the self in its relation to the world) and precludes its definitive closure into the universal subject of modernity. The Other posited by the dominant philosophy of modern subjectivity as precisely the individual fundamentally incapable of beauty—incapable, that is, of making proper sense of the experience of beauty—occludes the open-endedness of aesthetic encounter. Recall that central to critiques of aesthetics has been analysis of its insistence on the universality of experience as an albeit paradoxical cognate of sovereign subjectivity. The emphasis in the Kantian tradition on the relation of uniquely individual experience to the subject's sense of equivalence with others puts the particular (the subjectively unique) in the service of the universal (the categorical equivalence of reason, the basis of sovereign subjectivity) in such a way as to subordinate particularity. But aesthetic judgment operates distinctively, and it is that distinctiveness that is helpful to the present project. Even in Kant's systematic ordering, the judgment of taste holds a special place because of its relationship to freedom. In his terms, to identify something as beautiful requires that it be judged as "the object of an *entirely disinterested* satisfaction or dissatisfaction."[56] That is, aesthetic judgment—the cognition of pleasure derived from the aesthetic object—is a result of an indifferent encounter, of an encounter with an object to which we have no prior attachment or knowledge; of a surprise, an opening or opportunity because, unknown to us in advance, it/we cannot but be free of expectation. It is a "*free* satisfaction," without constraints (such as moral ends) or usefulness (interestedness) underlying its determination as such.[57] In this way, "the beautiful is that which apart from concepts is represented as the object of a universal satisfaction."[58] Our subjective judgment of beauty, because it is disinterested, presupposes agreement but "does not *postulate* the agreement of everyone."[59] The judgment of taste, or the naming of something as beautiful, is a representational act that bespeaks an individual's relationship to the idea of the universal, which describes a shared conceptual ground— the holding in common of concepts that make possible communication among individuals, that is, the sensus communis. Or, to put it otherwise, radical particularity finds its connection to the universal in the judgment of beauty.

Especially salient to the present discussion is the way in which the aesthetic subject is constituted as such by the condition of incommensurability. In contrast to the teleology posited by Kant's rendering of the relationship of the aesthetic and the powers of cognition, the vestibularity of the incommensurate subject reminds us that although development into the enlightened citizen-subject is the trajectory imposed by modernity, such subjectivization is neither inevitable nor an apposite account of humanity. The incommensurate subjectivity emergent from disidentification is, in other words, nonteleological.

The increasing preoccupation of aesthetic philosophy with beauty subsequent to the Western European eighteenth century and the naturalization of attendant forms of subjectivity and governance bespeak an attempt to regulate the direction of aesthetic subjectivization. Despite the etymological roots of "aesthetic" in sensory experience more broadly, aesthetic philosophy has focused on the adjudication of beauty and the relationship of that judgment to the prospects of humanity. Against such an emphasis on aptitude, deSouza's image demarcates the horizon as simultaneously the vanishing point and the point of departure for desire. For deSouza, the potentiality of humanity is not at issue; rather, he asks after how that potentiality is imagined and produced.

It is significant that in deSouza's image, the correspondence between desire and corporeality appears as a question. As Judith Butler's theorization of performativity, Hortense Spillers's theory of "flesh" and its disarticulation from "body," and Gayle Salamon's investigation of embodiment have provided, there is a fundamental correlation between the ways in which we conceive of bodies as discrete and coherent and how subjectivity is, within the regime of capitalist modernity, understood to be distinctively sovereign.[60] The body has been a focal point of critical interest across many fields, perhaps implicitly because this correlation leads to a variety of corporeal assumptions, each with attendant consequences.[61] In pointing us to the space between flesh and embodiment, deSouza refuses resolution into singular, sovereign entities. Whatever body/subject might be read into or out of this image, we cannot but take to be incommensurate with the disorganization that flesh connotes. Aesthetic experience is here rewritten, from the grounds upon which a sense of self is fashioned to the grounds upon which consciousness of otherness—*of being other than the apparently inevitable self*—is evoked.

From another vantage, Carrie Mae Weems interrupts the modern epistemic correlation of sight, truth, subjectivity, and knowledge with pointed commentary on racialized, gendered, and heteronormative representational politics. In *Mirror, Mirror* (1987), Weems showcases the withholding of the authorized place of privilege from Black women in ways that highlight the disidentified state of the incommensurate subject.[62] The image features a Black woman holding a rectangular wall mirror in front of her, but her gaze is askew, toward the mirror's frame. In the mirror is pictured a female figure shrouded in white translucent fabric looking directly at the woman and holding a glittery ten-armed star against the mirror. Beneath the image, in bold, all-capital letters is the caption, "LOOKING INTO THE MIRROR, THE BLACK WOMAN ASKED, 'MIRROR, MIRROR ON THE WALL, WHO'S THE FINEST OF THEM ALL?' THE MIRROR SAYS, 'SNOW WHITE, YOU BLACK BITCH, AND DON'T YOU FORGET IT!!!'" Weems illustrates the cutting potency of beauty as an instrument of racism in its irrevocably intersectional form. Here, a pointed comment is made on the literary-aesthetic as a site of the production of such gendered racism, and the pedagogies that begin in childhood to shape and naturalize the social order. But there is also the refusal to accept that nomination, the impossibility of behaving appropriately that is invoked. Like the classic Disney-fied evil stepmother to whom the mirror is beholden, the woman holding the mirror is an outlier to the bio-heteronuclear family: she poses a threat to the reproduction of the social order. Powerful and dangerous, it is against her authority that Whiteness must struggle. The idiom of beauty, of the aesthetic, is unmistakable in both the fairy tale and Weems's rescripting of it to invoke the histories of subjugation through which Black womanhood categorically emerges. In her gaze, directed toward the hand that holds the mirror rather than at the reflection, is the possibility, the suggestion, of the fragility of the epistemology and order that holds Snow White to be the pinnacle of beauty. What would it take to let go of the mirror, to shatter the authority of representation? How to make use of the power that is not given but is instead, has always been, already hers? Articulated through the linguistic and visual rhetoric of beauty, Weems's work evokes a radical disidentification from the economies of value advanced by dominant aestheticization.

That is, Weems's image registers the fundamental inadequacy of racist onto-epistemology to speak the truth of being. Not only does she mark its derogation of Blackness through a violent pedagogy of interpellation, but she also puts into relief the unreliability of the visual to produce truth. Sight itself is implicated in the sustenance of the racist onto-epistemology enunciated by the mirror and captured by the image. Seeing askew from the racist episteme, Weems implies, may mean foregoing the privileged place of representation itself. The resonance with Fanon's theorization of racist-colonial interpellation through the visual—captured neatly in the seminal phrase "Look, a Negro!"—unfolds through Weems's work as a reminder of the specific history of the foundational role that the regulation of Black women's embodiment plays in the course of producing and sustaining the dominant regime. Here, the double voice of the aesthetic and its resultant ability to acknowledge at once both aestheticization as a racial project and the aesthetic as a site of disidentification are markedly clear. The Black woman exemplifies the incommensurate subject insofar as the figure, as Weems presents it, marks a position of critical alterity cognizant of but irreducible to the dominant regime.[63]

The incommensurate subject, enacting disidentification, in other words, inhabits the conjuncture between the proto-political and the political and instantiates "being singular plural," in Jean Luc Nancy's formulation. Each iteration of identity and subjectivity, whether those unmarked identities of the dominant or the specified categories by which minoritized peoples are made legible, is seen from this standpoint as an invocation of a particularization of the identity/difference dialect.[64] Methodologically, the centering of incommensurate subjectivity illuminates the proximity of the particular iteration (the Black woman) to the radical difference that is its condition of possibility (being itself). Identity is a consequence of a doubled disavowal of difference, and the spectrality of difference points to difference in both content (as produced through the dialectic of identity/difference) and form (that formlessness gives way to the dialectic of identity/difference as its form).

Identity understood as an articulation of form and content—what we might think of as its metaphoricity—speaks to its meaningfulness as a literary and representational construct. Such an understanding registers in, for example, the long-established mutually productive relationship between nation and the bildungsroman, and more generally through Benedict Anderson's influential emphasis on the coincident significance of imagination, print culture, and the establishment of the modern nation-state.[65] In the act of becoming, or being made into, "the people," modernity's nation depends simultaneously on suppressing the contradiction between individuality and uniformity (difference and identity) and insisting on the status of the nation as the natural, inevitable, and distinctive form of representing the people. The nation-state, like the sovereign subject, forms through the paradox of insisting on particularity (the distinctiveness of a particular people) and uniformity (that in form, all modern nations, like all modern subjects, are equivalent). In this equation, particularity must be subsumed in favor of uniformity, whether by direct suppression or exclusion, or by legislating the sameness of all difference. This is the grounds of the liberal politics of representation, where representation is understood to be the achievement of identity with the nation-state.

It is toward this insight that Chang, deSouza, and Weems guide us as they press upon us the need to disidentify with the liberal humanities. In their respective ways, they remind us that aesthetic education in a liberal key is deeply implicated in the production of deprivation and dissatisfaction rather than the freedom and happiness it promises, and identifies inducement to faith in the political economic form of U.S. liberal democracy as a facet of such education. In this, they echo the abundant evidence of the large-scale decimation of lives and worlds necessary to securing and maintaining the liberal order that is modernity. Critical acknowledgment of these material consequences warrants deliberate disidentification from the liberal humanities, an analytic procedure that at once arises from the experience of its inadequacy and is necessary to puncturing the ignorance/truth effects of the liberal order. Lest we become like Min, attached beyond life itself to a fantasy of resolution and comfort promised by the institution, we are called to pause, to challenge the systems that at once give and take authority, that confuse and so distract from the need to bring closure to the present order.

The orthography of liberal humanism as it structures the knowledge arrangements of the humanities fosters a viscerally held belief in the rightfulness of the liberal order, a belief that, because it cannot be sustained in the face of empirical reality, conditions an insatiable longing and nostalgia for a mythic, halcyon past tethered to a notion of an ideal future to come. It is, in Chang's idiom, a hunger that provides entry to the deprivations that are the material effects of bourgeois liberalism—the multifaceted starvation and diminution of humans that occurs in the name and through the structured support of liberal humanism. We are enjoined to create and proliferate pedagogies and practices that delegitimate and displace the sensibilities induced by the ignorance/knowledge produced by liberal humanism and elicit the generation of radically disidentified forms of knowing.

Chapter 2

Pedagogies of Liberal Humanism

Don't just enter the music, but descend into its depths. —FRED MOTEN, *In the Break*

I have been proposing that disidentification from the liberal humanities comes of a combination of intellectual activity and embodied knowledge, from sense making through critique and sensory encounter. It is a result of critical and affective apprehension of the need for deliberate, willful, and organized refusal to affirm the ability of the liberal humanities to represent or advance humanity, grounded as they are upon the narrowest and meanest of definitions of Man, and supportive as they are of the political economies and corollary structures that require impoverishment and denigration. The sedimentation and embrace of the pluralist representational model of field coverage that is the architecture of the received humanities reiterates liberalism's reliance on hierarchization along these lines, an ordering that explains its usefulness to racial capitalism and the settler colonial nation-state. Liberal humanism justifies domination by providing for the differentiated capacity for exemplary humanity on the basis of geography and gender difference made to appear natural, commonsensical. The sensus communis in this regard functions as the ground of struggle over authority and meaning and structured economies of truth and value. Aesthetic education in its received form attempts to align perception with conception in the production of this common sense; disciplinarity is a name for this procedure, and definitionally reminds us of the punitive consequences of misalignment, willful or not. Indeed, bourgeois liberalism precludes assimilation to common sense for those cast as ontologically lacking competence. Sensible as a matter of felt experience, and elaborated through the knowledges subjugated by the liberal order, disidentification can be deliberately mobilized as a critical modality to refuse the frameworks of liberalism. I am accordingly encouraging us to mobilize the disidentified aesthetic of precisely those incompetent (according) to liberalism as the center of gravity of a humanities disarticulated from liberalism.

Taking as axiomatic the humanity of those who have been cast as subhuman abrogates the common sense that identifies liberal representation as the horizon of equality. Or, perhaps more satisfyingly, recognition of bourgeois liberal humanism as but *a* humanism, one in which Man is made to be synonymous with human, as Sylvia Wynter argues, initiates the elaboration of the humanities after Man. Historicizing this liberal humanism as emergent in the course of the increasing secularization of Western Europe, Wynter notes that this "de-godded" human, no longer guaranteed supernaturally (divinely), autopoetically describes-creates himself as of Nature. Thus producing Man-as-Nature (ontologically biological rather than social), this humanism rescripts its constative act with the seemingly neutral act of description.[1] Our task is thus twofold: one, to illuminate its particularity and nonneutrality and the effects of its forcible universalization through modern-colonial projects; and two, to bring forward other humanisms, other humanities, resistant to the systems and ideologies that require the vulnerability and disposability of people and worlds in the name and for the sake of humanity.

That aesthetic education has contributed to the occlusion of the parochialism and pernicious effects of liberal humanism is evident in the history and politics of literature. We will remember that literature crystallized in Western Europe as reference to a distinct mode of writing coeval with the rise of bourgeois individualism and corollary putative autonomy of the aesthetic sphere. The emergence of literature in this late eighteenth–early nineteenth-century era buttressed the sanctification of private property and the idea of sovereign subjecthood defined by the principle of a private (interior) world distinguishable from the public (external) sphere, a distinction that is a fundamental precept of bourgeois liberalism. The failures of the French Revolution to produce radical democracy and the class struggles that ensued gave shape to literature as a mechanism of revolutionary thinking, but one specifically indifferent to the processes and conditions of material distribution. Literature, in short, is a phenomenon and artifact of the bourgeois liberal revolutions of the Enlightenment and post-Enlightenment eras. Literary criticism in this view participates in the "arrangements of knowledge . . . [that] were put in place in the nineteenth century as a function of the epistemic/discursive constitution of the 'figure of Man,'" as Wynter puts it.[2]

Contestations over the meaning of literature may thus be understood as contestations over the meaning of the human and its cognate world. The question of who can represent—who can stand for and as—the human percolates beneath the inquiry into literature's constitution and boundaries. The proliferation of administrative categories that mark the institutionalization of minoritized knowledges—Literature by Women, Asian American Literature—compounds the problem of representativeness by externalizing through nomination difference from the humanity that literature tacitly and historically designates. Within the economy of field coverage, which is to say the liberal representational field, such categories preserve the original, disavowing the particularity of the exemplary human of literature's history while simultaneously positing the particularity rather than exemplarity of the human in work by minoritized writers often emerging from subjugated communities.

My point is not to argue for any version of color blindness in the definition of literature, nor is it to diminish the struggles that created space within the academy for subjugated knowledges to find footing.[3] Rather, I want to emphasize that at stake in the enduring question, What is literature?, is the definition of the human. Understanding of these stakes is everywhere present in subjugated knowledges, pronouncedly so in work by writers who thematize anti-Black racism and the ascription of Blackness to being. The literary-intellectual traditions of these writers robustly establish that the onto-epistemologies and aesthetics of liberal humanism valorize the necropolitics of the U.S. nation-state. From dehumanization through the literal commodification of people to the overweening use of criminalization and incarceration, a variety of methods enact state-sanctioned and/or extralegal production of group differentiated vulnerability, to invoke Ruth Wilson Gilmore's trenchant definition of racism, to produce Black as a racial identity.[4] The longevity and depth of anti-Black racism in the formation of the U.S. nation, of course and however, fail(ed) to extinguish the actual humanity of people racialized in this way; instead, the fundamental cruelty of bourgeois liberal humanism emerges with sharp clarity.[5]

In this chapter, I follow this line of thought that links the critique of liberal humanism with the poiesis of Black literature, specifically by moving with and through Toni Morrison's 1983 short story "Recitatif" and Langston Hughes's 1934 short story collection, *Ways of White Folks*. The humanism Hughes aesthetically affords powerfully illuminates the terrible and terrifying beauty of anti-Black racism within the liberal humanist regime. He insists upon the material impact of aesthetics—of matters of beauty as matters of power and politics—as a necessary part of an antiracist project and as an organizing principle of a humanism and humanities disarticulated from liberalism. Together with Morrison, who demonstrates the potency of racial common sense in the production of knowledge and ignorance, Hughes emphasizes the interruptive power of aesthetics. Like Wynter, they call for retrieving the human from the grasp of liberalism, which both disallows Man to stand as exemplary and suggests the stakes in elaborating an illiberal humanism. In the process, they help us understand how liberal humanist pedagogies enacted through the administrative rubrics that manage difference may be short-circuited. For, what they show is how literature (a category through which understanding of the human is produced and consolidated) may be modified by the designation of difference. That is, they invite us to embrace the adjectival function of "Black" and similar designations, in their association with literature.

Where "modification" in common usage connotes incremental rather than radical change, we might in this present context consider the project of fashioning the humanities after Man as a form of genetic modification that takes us, in Wynterian fashion, from the liberal abstract and parochial iteration to the constitutive sociality of the human.[6] A humanities organized around the figuration and constitutive (ontological) grounds of the human locates the prospects for and prohibitions to human potentiality in a whole way of life. That is, it critically centers the cultural (ethnoclass, in Wynter's terms) specificity of, and takes as its object of knowledge, humanism itself.

Modifying Literature

Langston Hughes's short story "Home" closes with this:

> The little Negro whose name was Roy Williams began to choke on the blood in his mouth. And the roar of their voices and the scuff of their feet were split by the moonlight into a thousand notes like a Beethoven sonata. And when the white folks left his brown body, stark naked, strung from a tree at the edge of town, it hung there all night, like a violin for the wind to play.

Roy Williams, the "very well-dressed, but awfully thin" virtuoso violinist who returns to Hopkinsville, Missouri, after years of training and performing in Europe thus dies at the hands of a White mob. Published in 1934 as part of his short story collection *Ways of White Folks*, and like the volume as a whole, "Home" links Blackness and artistry, and the violence of Jim Crow racism and its thoroughgoing relationship to aesthetic sensibility, in ways that key into the problematics with which this chapter and this book are concerned. In Hughes's story, the all-too-familiar historically drawn trope of the hanged Black man takes on an expressly aesthetic cast. The lyricism of Hughes's rendering deepens the brutality leading to Roy's death; so, too, the poetics of Hughes's staging interrupts the familiarity of the trope, calling attention to itself not as about the relation between aesthetics and minoritization, but as rendering that relationship itself. The story does not represent so much as instantiate the intimate link between the definition of art as such and the processes and politics of racialized subject formation. Or, in other words, at stake for Hughes is at once the necropolitics of racism and its inextricability from the aesthetic realm.[7] This story's closing scene vividly enjoins us to ask, how is it that the hanging brown body comes to function as here an objet d'art? What structures and epistemologies make possible, normalize, and perhaps even require, this aestheticization, this transmogrification of human into object? What sense is to be made of the attachment of aesthetic value to the brutalized Black body, of Hughes's mordantly ironic commentary on racism and art?[8]

The insight Hughes offers as to anti-Black racism—not only that Blackness should be produced by categorical violence but also that that violence might be found beautiful—is profound. There can be no satisfying interpretation of Roy's story, and yet, that it makes sense—that it is the logical conclusion of anti-Black racism—is unavoidable. The dark irony of Hughes's vision rests in the interplay between his own ability to craft language so powerfully and the inadequacy of artistic prowess (figured as Roy's virtuosity) alone to negate or transform this material, epistemological terrain.

This "scene of subjection," as Saidiya Hartman evocatively renders the problematic of Black subjectivity, reproduces the violence and onto-epistemology of chattel slavery.[9] It stages the ongoingness of violence as a condition of freedom by cathecting violence to aestheticization.[10] Or, in other words, Hughes poses as an aesthetic matter the nature and possibility of freedom as a defining characteristic of humanity in and through representation. Representation for Hughes, and in ways that echo Hartman, delimits freedom by requiring and operating through an epistemological frame in which the Black subject cannot (be allowed to) stand as the exemplary figure of freedom, namely, the artist. As Fred Moten puts it, caught between the poles of "objectification and humanization," the Black subject is produced by a representational dialectic that already determines the onto-epistemological horizons of Blackness.[11]

This story and the collection in which it appears critique the reigning model of representational politics established in the aftermath of the Enlightenment, with its inauguration and idealization of the bourgeois liberal subject. Conceptualized as the subject properly capable of participating in political life, this subject is rendered over and against those who are not (yet) fit for governance. This capacity for political participation is derived from aesthetic training or, in other words, through the production of identification with the liberal bourgeois version and vision of humanity.[12] Modern aesthetic education is thus fundamentally teleological insofar as it functions as the mechanism by which individuals develop into proper subjects. Canonicity forms around and reflects this developmentalism in that the works selected for the canon are those that offer proper training, that is, that figure the truthfulness of this liberal bourgeois humanism, which projects an essentially teleological view of humanity.[13] The problem of representational politics is in this regard the liberal humanist ontology that subtends the subject of representation.

In this light, the scene of subjection understood to illuminate the problematic of Black subjectivity may be recognized as exemplifying the general process of subject formation in the terms of liberal bourgeois humanism. Neither marginal nor anomalous to the dominant philosophies and practices of modernity, minority difference is a prerequisite of representational politics: this humanism clarifies its developmentalism by means of employing a contrast between those fit for full participation in the modern/ human project (the liberal bourgeois subject) and those who are developmentally delayed (the primitive, the savage). As Moten puts it, the challenge before us is to ask, "Is there a way to subject this unavoidable model of subjection to a radical breakdown?"[14] Or, stated differently, in what ways might the relation of politics and aesthetics be refunctioned such that the developmental telos of liberal humanism that requires subjugation is short-circuited? Hughes's interest in precisely this relationship is instructive.

Fourteen stories that collectively and sometimes individually describe a social field characterized by intimacies and alienations constitute *The Ways of White Folks*. The first two stories introduce themes that repeat throughout the collection, namely, the im/possibility of love under conditions of inequality, and the experience of aestheticization from the perspective of the aesthetic object. Hughes in these ways identifies the state of racialized existence in the Jim Crow era not as a break from but a continuity of what Hartman has described as a "slave humanity."[15]

"Cora Unashamed," the collection's opening piece, meditates through the figure of Cora Jenkins on the peculiar behavior of (some) "white folks" as expressed by their fixation on appearances to the exclusion of living fully. A lifelong resident of Melton, "one of those miserable in-between little places, not large enough to be a town, nor small enough to be a village," utterly charmless and "150 miles from any city at all—even Sioux City," Cora is given to us through a second-person conversational narration, the intimate nature of which will be carried through the collection as a whole.[16] "Cora was like a tree—once rooted, she stood, in spite of storms and strife, wind, and rocks, in the earth," the narrator offers early on (4). "Treated . . . like a dog" by the Studevants, for whom she is the "maid of all work," Cora has no choice but to withstand the circumstances of her job: "The Studevants thought they owned her, and they were perfectly right: they did. There was something about the teeth in the trap of economic circumstance that kept her in their power practically all her life" (4). Having thus introduced the story's main figure, Hughes turns to eliciting the reader as a participant in the story world: "You want to know how that could be? How a trap could close so tightly?" the narrator asks, making the reader responsible to the story unfolding (4). We learn that Cora was one of eight children, the oldest child of the "only Negroes in Melton, thank God!" (4); that her siblings have left, leaving her the primary caretaker for her sick mother and drunkard father; that after caring for the seven younger children, she left school in the eighth grade to begin working for the Studevants.

The focalizing drama of the story surrounds illegitimate children and death, first, of Cora's pregnancy by a transient White boy, Joe, who always smelled of horses and was "some kind of foreigner," with "an accent, and yellow hair, big hands, and grey eyes" (6), and the short life and death of Josephine, the child who will die of whooping cough at an early age. Cora, we are told, "was humble and shameless before the fact of the child" (7), but "not humble before the fact of death": "As she turned away from the [grave], tears came—but at the same time a stream of curses so violent that they made the grave-tenders look up in startled terror" (8). The other child she loves, Jessie, the Studevants' somewhat dimwitted and socially awkward daughter, is impregnated by a White boy of social status unacceptable to her parents and surreptitiously is taken away to terminate the pregnancy despite her fervent protest. Jessie's death soon follows, catalyzed by the combination of bodily violation and heartbreak. Again neither humble nor shameful in the face of death, Cora finally breaks with and from the Studevant household when the wake and funeral, cleansed of any reference to the conditions that led to Jessie's death, cannot be tolerated. She screams the truth of the events in a way "that has remained the talk of Melton to this day" (16). In the aftermath of the drama, the narrator closes calmly, "Anyhow, on the edge of Melton, the Jenkins niggers, Pa and Ma and Cora, somehow manage to get along" (18).

While the Studevants are figures of plantation mentality, representing the kind of Whiteness so utterly self-involved in the preservation of its status that there is no sacrifice or violence too great for its purposes, the Carraways, whom we meet in "Slave on the Block," the second story of the collection, typify the "people who went in for Negroes," whose self-definition is firmly embedded "in helping a race that was already too charming and naïve and lovely for words" (19). The typologies of the Studevants and the Carraways are repeated in *The Ways of White Folks* and become a way of identifying which "ways" of which "white folks" are the object of study and curiosity for Hughes. The Studevants are collectors of the "Art of Negroes," and Hughes makes little effort to contain his disdain for the mentality behind that collecting: "In their collection they owned some Covarrubias originals. Of course Covarrubias wasn't a Negro, but how he caught the darky spirit!" (19). The catalog of their collection echoes the familiar recitation of figures of African American Culture: Paul Robeson, Bessie Smith, Countee Cullen. One would imagine that Langston Hughes would be collected alongside these others, a slyly delivered implication that takes great pleasure in the biggest joke of all, namely, the paucity of White folks' imagination. "As much as they loved Negroes, Negroes didn't seem to love Michael and Anne," the narrator explains, dropping the reasons for such lack of affection mediated by "maybe," to soften the sting of the devastating critique that the Carraways are simply beneath the Negroes: too gushy, trying too hard, in the wrong neighborhood—by all counts, simply inadequate.

This point is elaborated by the plot of the story, which follows Anne Carraway's efforts to make "the most marvelous ebony boy . . . , a boy as black as all the Negroes they'd ever known put together" (20), into the subject of a painting she titles Boy on the Block. Putatively hired to help with housework, Luther does less and less actual labor in the house, becomes more and more familiar and less servile, and comes into the habit of walking around the house shirtless in anticipation of serving as the model for Anne's painting. He is so utterly indifferent to the Carraways that he does not bother to stay awake for his modeling sessions, requiring Anne to change the composition of the first painting she attempts rather than trying to awaken him. Michael and Anne are rhapsodic—the term Hughes uses—about Luther as himself beautiful, repeatedly marveling (again, Hughes's language) at his gorgeousness. "And he was an adorable Negro," the narrator admits, "not tall, but with a splendid body. And a slow and lively smile that lighted up his black, black face, for his teeth were very white, and his eyes, too" (24). Luther exists as adjective for the Carraways, as the exemplary figure of Blackness ("'He is the jungle,' said Anne when she saw him. . . . This ebony boy. The essence in the flesh," 21). When it turns out that he behaves not as an adjective but as a willful ("impudent") subject asserting himself to Michael's mother, he cannot remain in the household. The narrator conveys in the most concise manner that the problem, from the Carraway perspective, is simply that "Luther talked." Punctuated thus, the brevity of the line concisely captures the central tension between objectification and humanization playing out in the story. "'Oh,' Anne moaned distressfully, 'my "Boy on the Block"!'" she declares upon Luther's exit (31).

With these opening stories, Hughes articulates racialization as firmly bound to the economics of bourgeois aspirations, which are contingent on authorized or censored speech. It is Cora's unauthorized publication of the Studevants' secrets and Luther's impudent speech that lay bare the partitioning of sensibility necessary to the unequal distribution of material resources underwriting the kinds of Black subjectivities sketched by Hughes. "With noise is born disorder," Jacques Attali declares; the racial capital order rendered in Hughes's stories cannot accommodate the sonic resonance of the commodity that speaks.[17] Pervasive in *The Ways of White Folks* is the sense that the visual is firmly tethered to this order: from these opening stories to the epistolary story titled "Passing" that formally and thematically connects visual perceptibility to maintenance of public order, to the embodied resemblance between (a White) father and (a Black-White) son in "Red-Headed Baby" and the final story of the collection, "Father and Son," that requires violent disavowal to protect the racialized economic order. Color, whether the deep blackness of Luther or the muted whiteness of the sons in these latter stories, regulates material distribution.

Hughes recognizes, too, that this is a distributive ordering that is inescapably gendered. If the disavowal of fatherhood by White men has the effect of securing the passage of property to other White men, mothering by women, as it does in "Cora Unashamed," is overdetermined by racial and socioeconomic position such that both White and Black motherhood comes to figure the deliberate process by which social reproduction of the status quo is executed. By "deliberate," I do not mean necessarily willful—though it is that, too, as in "Cora Unashamed"—but rather, that it requires a structured effort often in the form of the excision of the disruptive figure and reinstatement of ordered domesticity. However well-meaning the mothering White women in this collection—Mrs. Pemberton's dutiful adoption of the orphaned son, Arnie, of their deceased former servants in "Poor Little Black Fellow" and Mrs. Ellsworth's condescending patronage of the talented pianist Oceola Jones in "The Blues I'm Playing," for example—they participate in reproducing firm boundaries between Black and White worlds, coded as the difference between the impoverished and the wealthy. Neither do the characters outside of familial bonds remain ungendered. The unnamed first-person narrator of "A Good Job Gone" finds himself required to enact rituals of male bonding with his employer at the expense of the narrator's pursuit of education; and Miss Reese of "Home" is notable as a spinster, the status that might well contribute to her inadvertent disruption of the social order.

If the mechanisms and possibilities of speech, of making noise, are differentially distributed by gendering, *The Ways of White Folks* nonetheless insists that sound can interrupt the social order more immediately, perhaps more effectively, than can visual representation.[18] Though Attali perhaps overstates it when he writes that "more than color and forms, it is sounds and their arrangements that fashion societies," he makes a suggestive case that the history of the transformation of noise into music, and the emergence of different kinds of music, is the history of changes to and in the socioeconomic field.[19] This understanding of aesthetics echoes Rancière's theorization of politics as naming a fundamentally aesthetic field whereby the distribution of sensibility and the designation of social roles tells the story of the boundaries of participation and their subtending conditions. What Hughes does, however, is emphasize the effects of the partitioning and differential prioritization of the senses. Against the primacy of the visual as the sensory truth-producing apparatus, Hughes reminds us of the ways that multiple and nonequivalent senses serve as the knowledge-producing mechanisms of the human body. That is, by linking disruption of the racial order to sound, that most ephemeral of phenomena, Hughes invites us "into the break," to borrow Moten's formulation, of a radical aesthetics that undermines the privileged position of representation and its attendant processes of subjectification/subjection.

The five senses we designate—touch, taste, sight, hearing, and smell—functionally determine the normative human body. We identify a disordered, diagnosable body when sight produces taste (synesthesia) or pain cannot be felt (analgesia). Cognitive studies suggest that these normative pathways are installed in the course of development; infants experience greater fluidity, often processing sensory data in what are sometimes referred to as the prelinguistic centers of the brain.[20] The senses provide entry into the world; they are the mechanisms for interaction between the limits of our selves and that which is held to be external to them. That the visual has been the privileged sense of Western modernity correlates with the centrality of representation to the modern project.[21] Simultaneous was the deprioritization of music in philosophy in favor of the image and the written text.[22] This is in some ways despite the pervasive interest in and strong claims regarding music's potency that are present across the swath of some of the most influential philosophers and theorists normatively constituting the Western tradition. These structuring conditions favored the naturalization of the association of literature with the visual; thus understood, literature is, as Rancière submits, "a historical mode of visibility of writing, a specific link between a system of meaning of words and a system of visibility of things."[23]

So it is with this sense of literature as a partitioning of sensibility in place that the disruptive aurality of *The Ways of White Folks* may be apprehended. Noisy speech but also music—the blues, jazz, classical music, opera, spirituals—organize Hughes's story worlds throughout the collection. Hughes both presages Rancière's claim that who may be recognized as an artist in a given historical context indexes the broader distribution of sensibility, or in other words, the dominant aesthetico-political regime, and restages the centrality of sound—of orality, aurality, and musicality—in philosophy across the ages.[24] While it is commonplace to associate the Harlem Renaissance, with which Hughes is so closely identified, with jazz and, more broadly, Black racialization in the United States with music ranging from spirituals to the blues to jazz to rap, I am less interested in describing the aesthetics of Blackness and more in thinking about what the copresencing of sound and the visual tells us about the aesthetic per se. In other words, I want to suggest that what on one hand appears as a way of theorizing Blackness is also and at the same time a way of theorizing the aesthetic, and specifically, its role in helping us identify as well as in producing the sensus communis.

Of the stories, "Home" stands out for the sound sense it emphasizes—that is, for the ways in which it makes available for apprehension the consequences of the partitioning of corporeal sensibility. Roy's development as a musician is thematically linked to his mobility: he leaves Hopkinsville as part of a minstrel show and follows a jazz band to Berlin where "hard work and hard practice" in the company of master teachers culminate in his ability to play "music, real music!"[25] Called to perform upon his return, Roy crafts a program featuring Brahms, Beethoven, Bach, and César Franck and, despite burning with fever from the unnamed illness he bears, when he played, "the notes went bursting out of the windows and the colored folks and white folks in the street heard them. The classic Mr. Brahms coming out of a nigger's house in the southern end of Missouri. Oh, my God!" (39). A tongue-in-cheek declaration of alarm, there is something substantive to the suggestion that the improper place of Brahms is precisely what is at stake—that is, the freedom to travel across space and time, which is inextricably connected to shifting the distribution of sensibility.

The story takes us immediately into another performance, this time at the Shiloh Church, with an audience of Black and White, and "Methodist and Baptist both came, forgetting churchly rivalry" (39). Thus at first, Hughes seems to suggest that music fulfills the romantic ideal of making social differences insignificant, of catalyzing community by acting as a kind of universal language. The story quickly disabuses us of this idealism.

When Roy performs for this crowd, the story shifts from third- to a first-person stream-of-consciousness commentary that demarcates the duration of the performance. This technique at once marks his estrangement from the communities, Black and White, of his putative home, and designates the curious phenomenon of being at once the aesthetic subject and object: "They're all looking at me. The white folks in the front rows and the Negroes in the back. Like one pair of eyes looking at me" (40). The speaking object cannot be heard until the music plays. Instead of the object of the gaze, he is the object that speaks, an impossible figure realized.

This section of the story (section V) is transitional, serving as Roy's reentry to his former home. It mirrors in function Jules Massenet's "Méditation" from his late nineteenth-century opera Thaïs, which figures centrally in this section. Notably, "Méditation" is an intermezzo piece (the entr'acte), which comes between scenes in Act II of the opera. Like Massenet, Hughes emphasizes desire and longing in a way that produces an erotics of subjectivity. This section is explicitly elliptical and is the place in the story where we encounter Roy as a desiring subject instead of primarily the object of desire.

> This, my friends . . . I should say, *Ladies and Gentlemen.* (There are white folks in the audience who are not my friends.) . . . This is the *Meditation from Thaïs* by Massenet. . . . This is the broken heart of a dream come true not true. This is music, and me, sitting on the door-step of the world needing you. . . . O, body of life and love with black hands and brown limbs and white breasts and a golden face with lips like a violin bowed for singing. . . . Steady, Roy! It's hot in this crowded church, and you're sick as hell. . . . This, the dream and the dreamer, wandering in the desert from Hopkinsville to Vienna in love with a streetwalker named Music. . . . Listen, you bitch, I want you to be beautiful as the moon in the night on the edge of the Missouri hills. I'll make you beautiful. . . . The *Meditation from Thaïs.* . . . (40–41, ellipses original)

Massenet's opera, first performed in Paris in 1894, tells a story of religious conversion to Christianity by the eponymous character. Set in Egypt in the Byzantine era, the story is one of thwarted desire and human passions: Athanaël, an ascetic, Cenobite monk, attempts to convert the beautiful, pleasure-seeking Thaïs to Christianity putatively for the most selfless of reasons, only to realize that he is driven by his fleshly desires for her rather than by the purity of love of spirit. Meanwhile, Thaïs, though initially recalcitrant in the face of Athanaël's explanations of the road to eternal life, upon contemplation decides her life based on earthly pleasures is meaningless and commits herself to conversion. The "Méditation" is her meditation; the music transitions this figure to Christianity and a life in a convent. The opera ends with Athanaël, having realized his erotic desire for Thaïs, repudiating a life committed to the eternal while the dying Thaïs describes the opening of the heavens and the welcome of the angels.

By his invocation of the "Méditation," Hughes figures music as simultaneously corporeal and immaterial, as transforming the significance of life itself and the desires that give it purchase. His emphasis on dreams throughout this section—on the dreams of "Mr. Brahms" to "sing[] across the world"; Roy's own dream of playing Carnegie Hall; and the references to Athanaël (41)—correlates the noninevitability of designated subjectivity (as Black) to the aesthetic state. Roy notes, "Jesus, I dreamed like that once before I got sick and had to come home" (40). Home forecloses dreaming, imposing an identity, a life, that inhibits the flourishing of desires. This is Hughes speaking of a "dream deferred" long before that famous poem ("Harlem") is published (in 1951), of the formation of Black subjectivity that adequates racialized subjectivity dangerously to the waiting room of history. What is clear in "Home" is that the dream that is deferred is not one of representational equality but of unfettered possibility and desire, an aesthetic wherein Blackness—which is to say, being—is. In contrast to the traditions that posit music's ability to transcend difference, music is difference itself; or rather, following Hughes, it is the medium that makes present the noninevitability of ways of being and knowing naturalized by the primacy of the visual that is an organizing principle of Enlightenment modernity.

The common (in literary criticism) understanding of ekphrasis following from W. J. T. Mitchell as referring to the use of one mode of expression (the visual) in another (the written) might in this regard be reconceived as a questioning of the privileging of one sense over another. To be clear, textualized music (musical notation, compositions on paper) is a kind of written language and thus is not music (sound) itself. So this is not an argument for learning to read music (though it is not opposed to reading music either). Rather, it is an invitation to consider the centrality and limitations of reading (by sight) as in the processes of racialization. Let me return again to Hughes to explain.

Section V of "Home," the intermezzo, closes with Roy's introduction to Miss Reese, the "old maid musicianer at the white high school," as his mother will refer to her.

> . . . O, dream on the door-step of the world! Thaïs! Thaïs! . . . You sure don't look like Thaïs, you scrawny white woman in a cheap coat and red hat staring up at me from the first row. You don't look a bit like Thaïs. What is it you want the music to give you? What do you want from me? . . . This is Hopkinsville, Missouri. . . . Look at all those brown girls back there in the crowd of Negroes, leaning toward me and the music. First time most of them ever saw a man in evening clothes, black or white. First time most of them ever heard the *Meditation from Thaïs*. First time they ever had one of their own race come home from abroad playing a violin. See them looking proud at me and music over the heads of the white folks in the first rows, over the head of the white woman in the cheap coat and red hat who knows what music's all about. . . . Who are you, lady? (41–42, ellipses original)

Miss Reese approaches him at the concert's conclusion, shakes his hand, and makes Roy "glad she knew what it was all about. He was glad she liked music" (43). This initial contact is mirrored in the event that catalyzes Roy's demise. Meeting her on the street late one evening, Roy, "forgetting he wasn't in Europe, . . . took off his hat and his gloves and held out his hand to this lady who understood music. They smiled at each other, the sick young colored man and the aging music teacher in the light of the main street" (47).

> Roy opened his mouth to reply [to a question Miss Reese asks about a Heifetz recording of a piece by Sarasate] when he saw the woman's face suddenly grow pale with horror. Before he could turn around to learn what her eyes had seen, he felt a fist like a ton of bricks strike his jaw. There was a flash of lightning in his brain as his head hit the edge of the

plate glass window of the drug store. Miss Reese screamed. The side-walk filled with white young ruffians with red-necks, open sweaters, and fists doubled up to strike. The movies had just let out and the crowd, passing by and seeing, objected to a Negro talking to a white woman—insulting a White Woman—attacking a WHITE woman—RAPING A WHITE WOMAN. They saw Roy remove his gloves and bow. When Miss Reese screamed after Roy had been struck, they were sure he had been making love to her. (47–48)

The pre-personal grounds of their initial contact at the close of the concert transform here to the impersonal-categorical reading of this scene of encounter. The (mis)reading Hughes stages overtly identifies the primacy of the visual in the materialization of sexualized racial difference. Where sound and touch (the handshake) harbor in this story the possibility (not always realizable) of dreaming a different world at the level of the individual, sight is deeply implicated in maintaining the structuring socialities of Whiteness. Hughes amplifies, raising the volume by capitalization and syntactical pacing, using diacritics to inscribe sound into writing.[26] Hughes demarcates the impossibility of fully presencing sound in writing, calling simultaneous attention to the potency as well as the limitations of writing as visual record.

Wrapped, then, within an indictment of racialized violence is an emphasis on making words do something other than make narrow sense (as Logos) as a mode of going beyond indictment to poiesis. *The Ways of White Folks* is not content with the horizons of representation; rather, it offers through sound, as sound, an aesthetics that cannot be captured by the (visual) concept of horizons itself. This is the collection's literariness, which emerges as a quality that has less to do with the distinctiveness of Hughes's use of language than with the entry it provides to alterity.

I have been suggesting that Langston Hughes in his distinctive way makes the case that, and of course, the human-as-object (the figure of enslaved humanity) does not await hegemonic ontological determination in order to be in the world, but rather, that the human-or-object is figured as such by an epistemological privileging of representational visuality within the distribution of sensibility we call modernity. As Moten establishes so powerfully in the idiom of materialist theory, commodities speak, make noise, demand to be heard, and, indeed, can be heard in and for the fullness of a being that is fugitive from the imposed ontology that questions their essence.[27] In order to hear, to re-member hearing as part of the corporeal *sensus communis*, we remember that "writing's description of sound (the literary representation of aurality) is also a de-scription of sound, a writing *out* of sound, that corresponds . . . with a denial, both conscious and unconscious, of the very idea of the whole."[28] This is a strategy of bringing to bear the corporeal substrate, the visceral body that is vanished by the abstractions of modernity, not in order to claim a primacy of sound over sight, but instead to assert the compresence of these nonequivalent senses, the compresence of incommensurate senses and sensibilities that is only minimally captured by the concept of reading. There is something radically democratic about this re-membering that heralds an equality of noise-making beings, eschewing the temporal hierarchization of bourgeois liberalism's representational politics.

Literature, understood in Rancière's framing as a "historical mode of visibility of writing, a specific link between a system of meaning of words and a system of visibility of things," indexes the distribution of sensibility that secures for words "the power of framing a common world."[29] The establishment as well as the regularity of categories like Asian American Literature and Literature by Women attest to literature's aesthico-political quality; these are rubrics that are evidence of the contestations over the visible and the sayable that readily correlate with debates over canonicity and curriculum. So, too, does literature's historicity, its crystallization in Western Europe as a distinct mode of writing that keeps supportive company with the rise of bourgeois individualism and corollary putative autonomy of the aesthetic sphere. Coupled with the establishment of literary criticism as a professional field, a process contextualized by the increasingly nationalist flavor of universities, literature's historicity bears witness to its political function. That we designate a certain kind or set of writing as literature is in itself political, not (only) because of its exclusionary function, but (also and) fundamentally, because it identifies a specialized domain of the sayable and visible that could/would not exist as such outside of a particular aesthetic regime.

Rancière usefully proposes that the aesthetic regime of the arts be understood as "the true name for what is designated by the incoherent label 'modernity'" because of the ways that it establishes a relationship between humanity and time.[30] Because it exists in a tension between its enclosed status as art and the absence of modes of classification or evaluation as such, the aesthetic regime—like modernity—restages our relationship to the past; it installs a temporality that rereads the historicity of the past as a way of understanding the present and the future. As Rancière explains, "it devotes itself to the invention of new forms of life on the basis of an idea of what art *was*, an idea of what art *would have been*."[31] In other words, modernity rereads the past in terms of the operations of regimes of visibility. It does not negate the past so much as posit an aesthetic relationship to it whereby we are able to assign modes of visibility governing the identification of art. By doing so, modernity (or, more properly, modernism) creates the possibility for different forms of visibility—for Rancière, for more egalitarian forms of art and life.

By interrupting the primacy of the visual, Hughes's work orients reading toward the act of attending to the unwritten. Accordingly, we are turned in literary criticism to listening for that which remains unrepresented and that which makes representation possible. The literary thus presents—thus makes present—that which is normally construed as bygone. From this position, the compulsory fiction and narrowness of bourgeois subjectivity as the achievement of human potentiality is laid bare. And in this regard, Hughes's writings may be understood to be part of the project of "setting upon our literary and cultural heritages and their orders of discourse," rather than one of "continuing to adapt to their generating premises and non-conscious systems of inference."[32] From Literature as a technology for inculcation into the order of the primacy of Man-as-Human to literature as a vehicle for activating a different order of discourse describes the impact of modifying literature.

Un/Learning Modern Epistemology

What might literary criticism be and do in such a different order? Understood to be a means of bringing forward aesthetics disidentified from common sense, literary criticism of this kind iterates the problem of representation to be not of verisimilitude or of equality through diversity, but instead as located in the confluence of racism and valorization of the visual's ability to produce truthful knowledge that characterize modern epistemology. Such criticism would accordingly undertake the work of disallowing the correlation between visual markers of bodily difference (the corporeal schema) and knowledge of person, character, or being, without foregoing or disavowing the ways that that correlation has secured deep inequities in the material lives of the racially subjugated.

Toni Morrison provides a model for such an approach in her short story "Recitatif." First published in 1983, this work sharply critiques U.S. liberal representational and identity politics for their inadequacy as modes of addressing racism. "Recitatif" illuminates the potency of common sense in the production of knowledge and ignorance, understood in their inseparability, in the course of the heightened attention it pays to class politics. Morrison tells the story of Twyla and Roberta, characters who meet at a shelter (St. Bonny's) for children because Twyla's "mother danced all night and Roberta's was sick."[33] Twyla is the story's narrator, and the one whose recounting captures the vicissitudes of memory in the recollection of details. The two spend four months together at St. Bonny's—"nothing in time," Twyla later observes (249); their subsequent chance encounters structure the story. While racial politics are everywhere present in "Recitatif," Twyla's and Roberta's racial identities are never assigned. Metatextually, Morrison in this way thematizes the will to knowledge, both the desire to fix and the inadequacy of fixing racial identity as a means of knowing self and other.

Diegetically as well, "Recitatif" takes up the problem of interpretive means and authority, as the scenes of encounter are anchored by a different iteration of an event involving Maggie, introduced as "the kitchen woman with legs like parentheses," from their time at St. Bonny's (245). Initially described as "old and sandy-colored" and rumored to have been mute, Maggie, in Twyla's memory, fell one day in the orchard. Later, though, Roberta will insist that she had been pushed and assaulted by a group of mean older girls, and by Twyla; she will assert that Maggie was a "poor old black lady," only later to recant the certainty of her recollection and her claim of Twyla's participation. The story closes in a final chance encounter in a diner on Christmas eve, with the now-wealthy Roberta dressed in a "silvery evening gown and dark fur coat," and Twyla, now with a son in college and in financial conditions that make the purchase of a Christmas tree a notable decision, revisiting again the question, "What the hell happened to Maggie?" (261). Roberta is given these last words, which are uttered as she dissolves into tearful anguish. Closing thus, Morrison emphasizes both accountability and the impossibility of representational justice.

We are refused the story of what really happened, our will to knowledge as frustrated as Twyla's and Roberta's. That this serves as more than a story of individual lives is evidenced by the care Morrison takes in staging each encounter within the shifting climate of racial politics. At St. Bonny's, Twyla's first experience of Roberta is one of nausea from being "stuck in a strange place"—sharing a room—"with a girl from a whole other race" (243). Twyla declares, "'My mother won't like you putting me in here,'" recalling that "every now and then [my mother, Mary] would stop dancing long enough to tell me something important and one of the things she said was that they never washed their hair and they smelled funny" (243). But in the diverse setting of the institution—"all kinds of kids were in there, black ones, white ones, even two Koreans" along with the "New York City Puerto Ricans and the upstate Indians who ignored us" (244)—the girls form a bond out of common alienation.

Eight years old and both with failing school grades, neither literate nor "real orphans with beautiful dead parents in the sky" (244), Twyla and Roberta attach to each other because Roberta does not ask too many questions about Twyla's mother. "I liked the way she understood things so fast," Twyla explains, "so for the moment it didn't matter that we looked like salt and pepper standing there" (244). Reticence rather than inquisitiveness, opacity rather than exposure, provides for a necessary connection. There is relief in impersonality that overcomes, in Twyla's memory, her inherited bigotry. There is compassion in accepting unknowing in Morrison's world, surely a comment on the demands for self-exposure and self-knowledge of the liberal order.

Morrison, in other words, provides a textual model of what José Quiroga eloquently identifies as the tactic of "open masking" in queer politics, as a means of questioning representational critique's however unintended affirmation of racist epistemology. Quiroga explains that the

> mask entailed a liberatory act in its own right. It destroyed the dialectical opposition between the visible and the invisible, between the *visibility* of homosexuals and their *invisibility* in the population at large. . . . By allowing the invisible to incarnate, as a presence, the social polity in itself construed its own public rite. It produced a zone of contact that mediated rupture: it operated from the point of view of structural play, instead of from the blinders given by systems and taxonomies.[34]

Such a practice "does not entail hiding or 'closeting' something," he explains; rather, "it is a form of speech that is transparent in different terms for different members of the reading audience, who have been initiated into one of its many circuits of meaning."[35] Rather than attempt to assume an omniscient position as the critic, the acceptance of open masking as a strategy that is always in play emphasizes the saliency of the circuits of meaning and economies—the governing rationalities—and the processes of initiation into them. "We demand the right to opacity," Glissant insisted, and Morrison's work shows how that demand and right may be put into practice.[36]

When in a later encounter at Howard Johnson's, where Twyla is a waitress, Roberta mocks Twyla's ignorance of Jimi Hendrix and barely acknowledges their previous relationship, their earlier mutuality is punctured. This break, it becomes clear as the story unfolds, figures a growing difference in class positions, marked here by the difference between Roberta's appearance (with "hair so big and wild," wearing a "powder-blue halter . . . and earrings the size of bracelets") and Twyla's (in waitress uniform, with "the blue and white triangle on my head, my hair shapeless in a net, my ankles thick in white oxfords").[37] Roberta "laughed a private laugh that included the guys [she was with] but only the guys, and they laughed with her too" at the news that Twyla lives in Newburgh, the town in which "half the population . . . is on welfare" (250). Roberta will come to oppose school desegregation by bussing while Twyla will be in favor; Roberta, who comes to live in Annadale, the "neighborhood full of doctors and IBM executives," will have a chauffeur, while Twyla's foray into a Food Emporium filled with inessential goods will make her feel "foolish" (252). Increasingly, their differences are marked as class differences, and Twyla muses, "Everything is so easy for them. They think they own the world" (251). Morrison in other words enacts intersectionality, attending to the materialities of sociopolitical differences without giving race authority of meaning. What and who is Black or White is subordinated to the environment, the material conditions, that allow for certain relations and modes of being and not others, that, in short, precipitate the personal. There is no catharsis or epiphany in Morrison's world, no resolution to the question of what happened to Maggie that serves as narrative closure. Omniscience is denied to both characters and readers. In lieu of mastery of knowledge, we are left with the work of apprehending the conditions that induce both care and violence, and the refusal of paradigms that deter our attention to them. That violence was done to Maggie is clear; ignorance of its details does not release us from accountability.

This event, the occlusion of which both troubles and enables Twyla's and Roberta's lives, is elliptical in form. These pauses, these enactments of recitative that are the connective tissue linking their lives, are given priority in Morrison's story. These pauses do not indicate the absence of meaning but point instead to its foundations. Maggie, denuded of sensibility by and in Twyla's and Roberta's accounts, and by those who abuse her (including, possibly, Twyla and Roberta), invokes the occlusion and disavowal of the histories and ongoing conditions of violence, racialized labor, and dispossession upon which the U.S. nation is founded. Morrison's work is cautionary in its insistence on acknowledgment of the costs of institutionalization. The remedy here is not so simple as giving voice to Maggie, but rather requires taking up as object of inquiry the pedagogies that require both her abjection and suppression of knowledge thereof. This is a comment on the exclusionary nationalism of the U.S. nation, according to which, tautologically, only those subjects who demonstrate social mobility are afforded the opportunity for advancement. Twyla and Roberta are not success stories emplotted into bootstrap narratives, but rather, characters caught up in worlds that require the subjugation of some for the advancement of others.

Literariness, Undisciplined

If aesthetic education has been central to the divisive effects of Enlightenment philosophy's postulation of a putatively abstract citizen-subject representative of the best of human potential, a literary critical pedagogy informed by such an understanding bears the promise of engaging in the broad proto-political questions that subtend the meaningfulness of the category of literature itself.[38] This is to argue for approaches to ethnic literary studies wherein neither "ethnic" nor "literature" is the presumed object of knowledge; instead, the critical and pedagogical work undertaken might be precisely that of elucidating the human(ism) that emerges from work so categorized.

The stakes in such a move reside both within and far beyond the academy. Everywhere today, the urgency of defunctioning anti-Black racism announces itself. The "cultural logic" of lynching, as Jacqueline Goldsby argues, is of a piece with the consolidation of U.S. modernity in the nineteenth and early twentieth centuries. "Lynching," Goldsby submits, "can be understood as an articulation of the social world's organization at any given point in time."[39] The contemporary salience of her claim, together with the resonance of Hughes's story of the criminalization and killing of Black people rendered threatening on sight, attests to the continuing murderous impact of the epidermal schema. Empirical reality belies the dominant common sense that holds that racism was effectively mitigated by legal apparatuses—the Reconstruction amendments, the civil rights acts, the end of de jure segregation. Whether through mass incarceration or other forms of state-sanctioned killing, violence continues to be a normalized means of Black racialization and gendering. These contemporary manifestations of the cultural logic of lynching are as spectacular as those on which Goldsby focused, though now it is largely through viral social mediation that they circulate.[40]

While transformations to literary study will not directly forestall anti-Black violence, I believe they might help us discontinue or at least interrupt the historic and ongoing intimate link between Literature and racism. Hughes's and Morrison's prompts to remember and interrogate common-sense reliance on the visual gain contemporary traction in this context. They ask us to train our critical senses on the dominant social field and its normative pedagogies of racism and racialization, to modify rather than discipline literary studies, and invite us to organize the humanities accordingly.

Chapter 3

Making Sense Otherwise

He cried the relief he felt at finally seeing the pattern, the way all the stories fit together—the old stories, the war stories, their stories—to become the story that was still being told. He was not crazy; he had never been crazy. He had only seen and heard the world as it always was: no boundaries, only transitions through all distances and time. —LESLIE MARMON SILKO, *Ceremony*

For a long time we have divined both order and disorder in the world and projected these as measure and excess. But every poetics led us to believe something that, of course, is not wrong: that excessiveness of order and a measured disorder exist as well. The only discernible stabilities in Relation have to do with the interdependence of the cycles operative there, how their corresponding patterns of movement are in tune. In Relation analytic thought is led to construct unities whose interdependent variances jointly piece together the interactive totality. These unities are not models but revealing *echos-monde*. Thought makes music. —ÉDOUARD GLISSANT, *Poetics of Relation*

I have tried in the foregoing chapters to bring forward the aesthetics of work that collectively and distinctively orient our sensibilities toward disidentification from liberal humanism and its corollary pedagogies and arrangements of knowledge. They do so in a variety of ways: by invoking the noncorrespondence between the liberal genre of the human and the being(s) compelled to live in a world dominated by its forcible imposition; by asking us to think in ways contrary to the dictates of the liberal order, to think/

work aesthetically, which is to say, of and through perception and persistently attuned to the conditions that prioritize and legitimate certain modes of knowing by the subjugation of others; and by acknowledging how questions of artistry and artistic value are also always questions of politics and history.

In calling into question the order in which racism, dispossession, and impoverishment make sense—in which sensibilities that find these conditions acceptable and even valuable, and which affirm and thereby buttress them—aesthetics incommensurate to common sense challenge the rationalization of the liberal/modern world. They encourage us to focus on the consequences and structures of enforcement of determining what and who are presumed or judged reasonable and not. In this, they echo the manifold and diversely grounded calls to bring forth "alternative rationalisms," to trace "another reason," to *ab*-use Enlightenment.[1] We are enjoined both to delegitimize the rationalism that secures settler colonial, racial capitalist modernity, and to construct structures and elicit subjects fundamentally intolerant of its logics.

In this chapter, in the company of Leslie Marmon Silko's *Ceremony* and Ruth Ozeki's *A Tale for the Time Being*, I focus on the importance of claiming the grounds of rationality as part of the work of delegitimizing liberal onto-epistemologies and their supporting structures, and proliferating in their stead those organized by and around a governing principle of uncontingent care. What is cast as irrational, unhinged, and/or incompetent in and to the liberal order emerges through Silko's and Ozeki's works as invitations to question the political and symbolic economies that precipitate such designations. Rather than debate their truth or falsity, we are turned by them toward the interrogation of their precipitating conditions and their sources of authority and legitimacy. This orientation describes what we may think of as the *aesthetic rationality* these writers bring to bear—aesthetic in its grounding in visceral-empirical history and experience, and in its disidentification from and incommensurability to rationalism in a liberal or neoliberal key. Such defining characteristics of liberalism as individual and national sovereignty and insistence on progressive enlightenment through the accumulation of putatively disinterested knowledge and individuated self-consciousness are rendered by illiberal aesthetic rationality to be patently if potently nonsensical.

I am especially interested in the thematization of rationality given the intense insistence on and celebration of individual choice and decision making that are hallmark features of the current conjuncture—features that update liberalism's long-rooted cherished concepts of discrete individuality and self-consciousness.[2] The affirmation of meritocracy as a neutral metric and corollary disavowal of the sociality and historicity of the individual is part of the ideological support accompanying and subtending the upward distribution of capital and resources in the neoliberal era. Accordingly, dominant rationalism serves as the explanation for, rather than being understood as a condition of, the success of a few and the failure of most: failure is rationalized by asserting freedom of individual choice and behavior, evidence of which is found in the success of those few who heroically surmount history to achieve individual success.[3]

These qualities pervade the instrumentalization of education and knowledge characterizing the contemporary era. Educational policy explicitly features the binding of innovative thinking to boosting the national economy and its global profile, and induces entrepreneurship designed to further those aims as the ultimate objective of public education.[4] These policies direct education to uphold the liberal mandate to *think* oneself free, combined with freedom conceptualized as choice plus purchase power under neoliberalization—the freedom to buy and own (things, education, experience, even happiness)—in short, to affirm the long-lived collaboration between liberalism and capitalism.[5]

These conditions highlight the role of rationalization—the production and legitimation of what counts as reasonable—through policy and structure in the consolidation of common sense. Dominant rationality secures itself as the purveyor of truth, by authoritatively (with institutional force) discounting as irrational knowledge and ways of knowing arising from other(ed) grounds. Individualization and personalization are enormously effective procedures by which such dismissal can be effected: how much tidier it is to locate success and blame in an individual rather than take up the weightier work of sussing out and grappling with the complex conditions of (im)possibility that subtend choice and behavior.[6] The contemporary overweening emphasis on mentoring as the U.S. academy's favored method of addressing structural inequality, and the seeming necessity of self-promotion as a means of navigating institutional terrains, appear in this light as practices aligned with (neo)liberal rationalism. It takes no special insight to notice how they reiterate the long-lived tradition of self-help bolstered by U.S. nationalist ideology: bootstraps and meritocracy have since the nation's founding been integral to its privileged imaginary.

To these perhaps familiar criticisms of (neo)liberalism, Silko and Ozeki lend intensity and focus. They deflate the authority of the (neo)liberal not so much by mounting arguments against it, but instead by showing that violence and devastation of and against the well-being of both people and planet are its logical conclusions. Their critiques are neither bound by nor beholden to the narratives of humanity that are a seminal part of liberalism's orthography. Instead, the aesthetic rationality they throw into and as the world, find both untenable and dangerous the abstract ideals of freedom and happiness that modernity holds as humanity's horizon. It is by attesting and attending to worlds *disordered* by normative/liberal geographies and temporalities that Silko and Ozeki elicit understanding of the chaos produced by (neo)liberal rationalism.

Indeed, the certainties of time and place—the common sense that temporality and geography are referential rather than ideological contrivances—do not withstand Silko's and Ozeki's respective elucidation of this disordering. Time in their hands serves not as a commodity of which there can be too much or too little, nor as a unilateral force according to which pasts are discretely held apart from presents and futures. Instead, time names a condition of radical connectedness, a condition that requires neither revelation nor discovery to apprehend, but instead to which it is (im)possible to (not) be attuned. This is a condition of simultaneity; it is every time at once, and the presence of every place in every other. And it is, I will suggest, this sense of time and its cognate onto-epistemologies that allows us to reckon with the foundational and ongoing violence rationalized by liberalism.

It is, finally, that Silko and Ozeki help us key into what such reckoning entails—what practices and concepts, what imaginaries and supportive institutional arrangements—that makes their attention to rationality so vital. For, one of the challenges confronting minoritized discourses now is precisely the need to generate ways of making sense beyond the paradigms of identity and representation, an effect of which has been to hold discrete what are in fact deeply imbricated histories, formations, and conditions. As the foregoing chapters have discussed, the field coverage model organizing the academy reifies the identity and representational politics of liberalism such that administrative rubrics (e.g., Asian American Literature, African American Studies, and so on) are mistaken as references to discrete and stable objects and traditions that need only be fully represented to achieve equality. That such politics and arrangements cannot accommodate the interarticulation of settler colonialism, modern nationalism, gender and sexuality, indigenization and racialization, has become markedly clear.[7] Jodi Byrd gives compelling shape to this situation in the identification of the lamentability of conquest and Indigenous dispossession within liberal/ settler colonial imaginaries, in contrast to apprehension and understanding of the grievability of the ongoingness of settler colonialism's necropolitical effects.[8] Part of the challenge Byrd identifies in elucidating how the temporal protocols of the liberal order, wherein conquest and dispossession are cast as the lamentable past, exclude the presentness, the ongoingness of settler colonialism, is precisely that of asking how we may reckon with the entanglements of race and indigeneity, and of racism and settler colonialism, in ways that account for this cacophonous condition.

What does it mean to reckon with rather than rationalize foundational and ongoing violence? What conceptions of truth and reason, and what politics accord with reckoning as a mode of knowing? The contemporary is indebted to the violence justified by liberalism, which articulates in these distinguishable but inseparable ways; the problem before us is, how will we account for and address that indebtedness?

As what follows suggests, I propose that the address of such questions involves the elucidation of a subjugated genre of the human, one wherein it is possible to apprehend the human as a being not in but *of* time. Silko and Ozeki help give shape to a conception of human beingness incommensurate to the liberal version, one that reminds us of the intimate and inseparable link between being and knowing, ontology and epistemology. What I think of as, and what I'm endeavoring to elaborate under, the sign of illiberal knowing (its procedures and truth effects) and of illiberal being (the plural singularity that José Muñoz, drawing on Jean-Luc Nancy, theorized as brownness, about which I say more later) afford apprehension of the interconnectedness of people and histories wrongly but purposefully given to us as discrete by the favored concepts and paradigms of modern ontoepistemologies. The distancing in time and place that U.S. nationalism requires, for example, which necessitates the separation of a migrant past from a national future, which relegates conquest and dispossession as past history, and which regularly relies on the production of foreign enemies to rationalize war making and concomitant environmental devastation, collapses in the face of the reality of that state of entanglement. This is not an erasure of difference or distinction, nor the positing of a reality characterized by a pluralist harmony. Rather, it is an embrace of the world as it is, in its thickly imbricated, cacophonous complexity.

Being, Before and Beyond

It is not surprising that work emergent from Native America should advance the delegitimation of the liberal order and its corollary logics, given that Indigenous dispossession refers not only to the expropriation of land but also to the rationalism that justified the transformation of land into property that could be owned and stolen under the aegis of the U.S. nation's self-proclaimed manifest destiny.[9] Ongoing struggles for sovereignty—for self-determination and self-governance—register this twofold impact, cognizant as they are of the dark irony of having to argue in the terms forcibly imposed through settler colonialism.

This theoretical and political aporia precipitates what Silko's novel makes sensible as a condition of bearing the unbearable wrought by the U.S. nationalist project. In *Ceremony*, U.S. nationalism, expressed as its conduct of war and its consequent decimating impact on people and planet, particularizes the conditions produced by and in the name of the liberal order. First published in 1977, the novel situates World War II and the Cold War within the long arc of colonialism's and imperialism's constitutive roles in U.S. nation building.[10] Identifying as nuclear the forms that they take in the twentieth century, Silko attends to the specificity of the damage they wrought in this era as she collates settler colonialism with U.S. empire building in Asia.[11] Explicit in connecting nuclear warfare against Japan in World War II with the toxicity produced on Indigenous lands and in Native peoples by uranium mining and nuclear arms testing, by connecting colonial occupation of Indigenous lands with that of the Philippines, *Ceremony* produces a geography that recognizes and overwrites the spatial and temporal protocols of U.S. nationalism. Silko excoriates the rationalization of territorial occupation under the sign of manifest destiny and its justificatory principle of *terra nullius* as it plays out in the occlusion and deaths of people living in precisely the areas central to the production of the technologies of nuclear warfare, that is, the southwestern United States, by means of showing that this logic is the present—or rather, that it is present. The novel suggests by doing so that while it is impossible to undo the death and toxicity by which the U.S. nation secures its sovereignty and global standing, the refusal of its logics is not only possible but necessary for survival.[12]

The novel is organized around Tayo, the "half-breed" who returns to the Laguna Pueblo as a battle-weary veteran of World War II. Still immersed in the experience of war, including his witness of the death of his beloved cousin Rocky, Tayo's efforts to constitute a coherent sense of self describe the novel's plot. As *Ceremony* opens, Tayo is just emerging from a state of utter dissolution of body and mind, which we come to understand results from the rationalization of killing and dying for the sake of the U.S. nation. Silko's figuration of Tayo bears witness to the ravages of U.S. nationalism in the forms of imperialism and (settler) colonialism; he is a character who bears in his body and being those effects. The child of a Laguna woman and an anonymous White man—one of a number with whom his mother consorts to the approbation of her family—Tayo grows up sharing a bedroom with Rocky, who encourages Tayo to make his life in the "white man's world" rather than with the "people back home." It is Rocky who precipitates, without malicious intent, Tayo's joining the military by introducing him to the army recruiter as his brother: Tayo cannot resist this gesture of familial belonging and becomes a soldier out of gratitude for fraternal solidarity. Reminded repeatedly by his Auntie (his mother's sister and Rocky's mother) of what she believes to be his shameful illegitimate beginnings, Tayo longs for kinship. Silko renders in this way the intimacy of the link between the geopolitical—the disruption of Indigenous kinship relations by the U.S. nationalist project—and the personal and familial.

In Rocky's death and in Tayo's inability to inhabit fully the overtly patriotic position of the individual willing not only to die but also to kill for the nation, Silko marks how the U.S. nation continues to take life to secure its own sovereignty and global standing, and the nonchoice that assimilation to such patriotism in fact is for those disidentified from the liberal order. Ordered to kill, Tayo viscerally intuits that to do so for the U.S. nation is to be a part of the same machinery of conquest that made Indians of the peoples living on the continent. The novel provokes questions—Just who is the enemy? For what reason is killing and dying justified?—that sharply illuminate the deeply suspect logic that requires giving oneself over to the U.S. nation, even if it were possible to do so.

Silko couples this insight to an understanding of the radical interconnectedness that subtends this disidentified state. Surrounded by death, Tayo consubstantially identifies with the corpses, with the "skin . . . not much different from his own":

> The skin. He saw the skin of the corpses again and again . . . skin that was stretched shiny and dark over bloated hands; even white men were darker after death. There was no difference when they were swollen and covered with flies. That had become the worst thing for Tayo: they looked too familiar even when they were alive. When the sergeant told them to kill all the Japanese soldiers lined up in front of the cave with their hands on their heads, Tayo could not pull the trigger. The fever made him shiver, and the sweat was stinging his eyes and he couldn't see clearly; in that instant he saw Josiah standing there; the face was dark from the sun, and the eyes were squinting as though he were about to smile at Tayo.[13]

This memory, this experience of dissolving realities and visceral identifications, constitutes Tayo's sickness well beyond the incident itself: "Tayo stood there, stiff with nausea, while they fired at the soldiers, and he watched his uncle fall, and he *knew* it was Josiah; and even after Rocky started shaking him by the shoulders and telling him to stop crying, it was *still* Josiah lying there."[14] Tayo cannot be made to believe that his Uncle Josiah was not in fact present in the Philippine jungles. This is not a willful refusal but rather an unwilled incapacity to inhabit the logic of the nation. Provoked both by recognition of the humanity of, and by glimpsing the presence of Uncle Josiah in those designated as enemies, Tayo's decomposition marks as unbearable the liberal/modern onto-epistemologies that give authority to war making. Feeling deeply responsible both for his inability to save Rocky from dying and for his part in the war, Tayo's exhaustive disorientation is at once irrational and wholly understandable; it is the logical if disavowed conclusion of the necropolitics of settler colonialism and U.S. nation building.

Normative time and the geographies resulting from the world crafted through the attempts of modern nations to secure their own power on the world stage cannot contain this other rationality, in which Tayo's dissolution makes sense/is reasonable. The metaphor of decomposition Silko employs is multivalent: it refers at once to the disassembly of human bodies and of the Indigenous body politic, and to the perdurance of nuclear toxicity and corollary pernicious effects on land and its inhabitants, as it connotes the psychic and emotional defrayal, the loss of composure and extraordinary effort to maintain or regain it in the face of chaos-producing forces.

To address and live in the compresence of incommensurate rationalities, according to Silko, is afforded neither by securing identity with Laguna Pueblo cultures conceptualized as ahistorically fixed, nor through performative identification with dominant onto-epistemologies. Rather, as indicated in Josiah's—and, as I discuss later, Betonie's—figurations, it is necessary to craft traditions anew, to found ceremonies capable of acknowledging and thus addressing the ongoingness of the modern/colonial condition. The conveyor of Laguna traditions to Tayo, Josiah embodies generosity to the nonidentical through his embrace of his nephew. In contrast to Auntie, whose strictly regulated domesticity Tayo experiences as exclusion, Josiah creates community through the hospitable welcome of difference. Josiah's openness to those with whom he shares no blood ties enables rather than dilutes his ability to sustain the Laguna Pueblo. It is this openness and embrace Tayo cannot ignore in the Philippines; it is this sense and logic of mutuality Silko brings to bear.[15]

Silko emphasizes the nonidentical and refuses blood genealogy as a means of determining belonging or community—through Tayo's "half-breed" status, through Josiah's openness, through a definition of family wrought through performative rather than legal lines, and through the idea of ceremony itself, as presented in the character Betonie.[16] A multiracial Navajo medicine man who acknowledges the historical antagonisms between Laguna and Navajo peoples, Betonie guides Tayo through his healing ceremonies in ways that affirm the world of connectedness Tayo intuits and experiences. The ceremonies, Betonie explains, "have always been changing," even as they have remained consistent:

> The people nowadays have an idea about the ceremonies. They think the ceremonies must be performed exactly as they have always been done, maybe because one slip-up or mistake and the whole ceremony must be stopped and the sand painting destroyed. That much is true. They think that if a singer tampers with any part of the ritual, great harm can be done, great power unleashed. . . . That much can be true also. But long ago when the people were given these ceremonies, the changing began, if only in the aging of the yellow gourd rattle or the shrinking of the skin

around the eagle's claw, if only in the different voices from generation to generation, singing the chants. You see, in many ways, the ceremonies have always been changing.[17]

The limitations to willful agency are sketched in Betonie's explanation: the aging gourd, shrinking skin, and shifting voices that transform to allow, seemingly contradictorily, for ceremonial continuity, acknowledge but do not give primacy to human activity. In the course of the novel, ceremonies function as signposts, as points of arrival and departure, as moments and sites of pause and remove, as promises of healing and reminders of long-lived genealogies of people, traditions, lands. Silko proffers the sacred and the ritualized as questions as much as themes. What is held sacred, by whom? From what authority or grounds does reverence stem? How does the sacred become customary? What do we ask of the ritualized, the ceremonial? The ceremonial serves in this way as a category through which Silko invites us to apprehend the material lives of ideas, and to consider how ideas become belief, presumptively external to rationality and yet its grounds of truth. Through Betonie's account, we can see the long history of the ceremonial in the explanation of the human of liberal modernity, from a being divinely guaranteed, as Sylvia Wynter explains, to one who "defined itself no longer as Spirit but as Natural Reason carefully cultivated."[18] The ceremonies that yoked the human to the divine had to be rewritten in the age of Enlightenment such that Man could emerge supreme.[19] The seeming paradox Betonie articulates—that ceremonial continuity is characterized by change—marks a rationality in which time is capacious, one in which change and continuity are neither oppositional nor mutually exclusive. Rather, their compresence characterizes being beyond and before (the order of) Man.

Silko invokes this other, ancient order in Betonie's explanation to Tayo of the reasonability of Josiah's presence in the Philippines and the familiarity of the putative enemy. Betonie explains, "'The Japanese,' . . . it isn't surprising you saw him with them. You saw who they were. Thirty thousand years ago they were not strangers. You saw what evil had done: you saw the witchery ranging as wide as this world."[20] This witchery, Tayo comes to understand, revels in destruction and traffics in dissemblance:

> The liars had fooled everyone, white people and Indians alike; as long as people believed the lies, they would never be able to see what had been

done to them or what they were doing to each other. . . . If the white people never looked beyond the lie, to see that theirs was a nation built on stolen land, then they would never be able to understand how they had been used by the witchery; they would never know that they were still being manipulated by those who knew how to stir the ingredients together: white thievery and injustice boiling up the anger and hatred that would finally destroy the world: the starving against the fat, the colored against the white. The destroyers had only to set it into motion, and sit back to count the casualties. (191)

Silko's insistence on the power of belief to cover over truth makes unmistakable the (ir)rational needs of the modern/settler nation to occlude the very elements that would preserve rather than destroy the world. This is neither an aphoristic insight nor a parable that she offers in Betonie's words, but instead an attestation that makes sense of history as ongoing. The timescale of this operation is vast: this temporal thickness is part of what the destroyers have covered over. Tayo's is the experience of all-time erupting through the given/dominant plane of reason: which is truly (un)reasonable, the decision (not) to kill on behalf of an idea, a nation, founded in intentional death, or the embrace of the connectivity of people in and over time? What appears to be a hallucinatory imagining of Josiah out of proper time and place is scripted by Silko as an eruption of this other rationality into the field of common sense.

We may think here of how the ceremonial subtends common sense, often through quotidian practices: in the pledge of allegiance schoolchildren are taught to recite well before the meaning of the words and rite can be apprehended; in the secular blessing that is the obligatory performance of the national anthem to open sporting events; and in the unremarkability of "God bless America" as the sign-off for every politician's speech. Repetition and reiteration renew the sacrality of the U.S. nation and transform lies into common sense.

Deliberate participation in ceremonies incommensurate to those of the settler nation precipitate Tayo's relief and regaining of composure, a process by which Silko identifies the power of Indigenous knowledges to illuminate the world in all its complexity. Having participated in several healing ceremonies, Tayo finds relief while hiding in an old uranium mine, once operated by the U.S. government but abandoned after it repeatedly flooded and other sources were located. There, Tayo flashes into the truth Betonie describes:

> He had been so close to it, caught up in it for so long that its simplicity struck him deep inside his chest: Trinity Site, where they exploded the first atomic bomb, was only three hundred miles to the southeast, at White Sands. And the top-secret laboratories where the bomb had been created were deep in the Jemez Mountains, on land the Government took from Cochiti Pueblo: Los Alamos, only a hundred miles northeast of him now. . . . There was no end to it; it knew no boundaries; and he had arrived at the point of convergence where the fate of all living things, and even the earth, had been laid. From the jungles of his dreaming he recognized why the Japanese voices had merged with Laguna voices, with Josiah's voice and Rocky's voice; the lines of cultures and worlds were drawn in flat dark lines on fine light sand, converging in the middle of witchery's final ceremonial sand painting. From that time on, human beings were one clan again, united by the fate the destroyers planned for all of them, for all living things; united by a circle of death that devoured people in cities twelve thousand miles away, victims who had never known these mesas, who had never seen the delicate colors of the rocks which boiled up their slaughter. (246)

Ceremony amplifies ways of being and knowing that apprehend, altogether, the "world as it always was: no boundaries, only transitions through all distances and time" (246). Tayo's journey is the descent into chaos and finding there both devastation and enduring life. It is the "circle of death" that overlays the Japanese and Laguna peoples; it is the circulation of toxic matter— the uranium, the matter of the exclusionary nationalism of modernity—that connects the anonymous intimately together.[21] The repossession *Ceremony* narrates exceeds without forgetting or erasing the violence of colonial modernity. This is a history that cannot be undone, the unintended effect of which is to sharpen through destructive means the unity of people and planet that witchery had interrupted. The unbearable truth that must be borne is unconcealed: nuclear annihilation makes visible the unity that settler colonialism/nationalism covers over.[22]

The clarity of illiberal enlightenment emerges from the grounds of devastation, the muddiness of flux and chaos of debris, as much as it does from the overtly ceremonial. Indeed, Silko's novel suggests an irrevocable intimacy between these that is the condition wrought by U.S. settler colonialism and empire building. The geographies and temporalities of liberal modernity cannot withstand the truth of Silko's world. That which renders Tayo into madness and debility, which makes war and creates unlivable conditions, is thrown into relief as the rationalism that must be refused and refuted.[23] In its stead, care for unknown others, care uncontingent on the personal, the familial, the identical, the national, is resoundingly unconcealed.[24]

According to the logics within which connectedness and unity make sense, are reasonable in both thought and felt experience, truth of being resides not in the idea of transcendence of individuality but instead in the irrevocable relationality of being. The dehumanization wrought by enslavement and dispossession did not extinguish this beingness, but covered over it so thickly through the sacralized rituals of nationalism—of war and conquest—that they are made submarine, of the undercommons.[25] As Tayo sees not Japanese nor enemies but people recognizably worthy of life and infinitely grievable, the discord between the virtue of patriotism and its actual consequences fractures the manufactured truthfulness of given, dominant reality. Within the cacophony of reckoning with the unavoidable difficulty of the grounds of entanglement that enable living, that require suffering and the erosion of life, resides the rationality that comes of disenchantment with the potent magic that gives patriotism and modern nationalism their sacrality.

What appear to be entities of and in discrete places and time are shown to be indefinite, in-finite. Tayo precedes and surpasses himself, a figuration that inverts the idea of self-possession from its liberal iteration as ownership of a sovereign, discrete selfhood, to the self as a being in and of time, of all that has passed and all that will shape the contours of what will come. To stand with Tayo is to reckon with the world dis-organized by liberal colonial rationality, and to find neither happiness nor hope in that understanding, but instead clarity of a different order of reality. Attunement to this other order does not erase the consequences of modernity's establishment as the world historical dominant; it is not in itself a remedy for them. Instead, as Silko figures in Tayo, such attunement to relationality is at once comforting and utterly discomfiting. This enlightenment—so decidedly different from Enlightenment—produces the subject aware of humanity's historicity as much as the unity of being, of being as time. Whether such attunement/enlightenment can foster the development of ideas and structures able to sustain and protect without reiterating the exclusionary violences of the still-dominant regime remains to be seen. Yet it is clear that such changes cannot be made without it. For the remaking of common sense is a necessary facet of the inducement of subjects not only aware of this condition of relationality, but who experience it viscerally as truth, as the grounds of determining what is reasonable and not, and who may thus collectively demand and produce structures organized by this aesthetic rationality.

Irrevocable Relationality

The task here, in other words, that Silko's and, as I elaborate below, Ozeki's works elicit is to craft and illuminate the sensibility and rationality that accords with the self of relationality rather than possessive individuality. This means not only making it available to the senses, but to make sense of and with it—that is, to craft the parameters of reasonability with and around it. The relationality that belies the seeming autonomy and discreteness of the I does not correlate with the Cartesian assignment of human beingness to cognition. Rather, the relational I posits the historic, material conditions of its emergence, operating as a figuration of the plural singularities that is time itself. Each moment, each I, carries in it every moment of being; what is reasonable accordingly is tested against whether thought or action emerges from and addresses itself to relationality, understood not to be a chosen condition (one does not enter into relationality but is/becomes attuned to it) but rather the condition of possibility of being itself.

Ozeki gives further specific texture to these ideas, and in two ways that are of especial concern here. First, resonant with Wynter's identification of Man as but one genre of the human, *A Tale for the Time Being* emphasizes how the relational I calls forward and operates in a genre incommensurate to that of liberal modernity, namely, those of the bildungsroman and the private propertied self it throws into the world. Beyond and before the genre of Man, and aligned with Silko's, Ozeki's work suggests there are forms of living and being that can never fully be captured, and indeed, the elusiveness of which is one of its defining characteristics. As with Silko, Ozeki's work's defiance of category (it is at once a novel and not) is arguably illiberal: it not only finds fault with but also supplants the liberal order by rendering a logic incommensurate to liberal rationality. In form, relationality overwrites categorization and brings forward in its stead the sensibility of the in-finite.

Second, Ozeki's work does so thematically, through the idioms of Zen Buddhism and quantum physics, and by a critique of exclusionary nationalism that finds common cause with Silko's work. The coincidence of Silko's and Ozeki's concerns with the inducement of subjects willing to kill and die for the nation prompts us to acknowledge the possibilities for collective action that arise from the grounds of disidentification-in-common. No longer are we in the logics that give rise to "special interests" or to possessive identity; rather, we are called to identify such common grounds as arise from uncommon sense.

Formally, *A Tale for the Time Being* is a novel only in the loosest sense. The book offers explanatory footnotes that gloss the Japanese and idiomatic terms that appear in Nao's diary, and appendixes (five of them) that provide information on quantum physics, Zen Buddhism, a quantum theory thought experiment known as Schrödinger's cat, and a physicist named Hugh Everett, all of which shape its thematics. The book features two primary narrators whose stories unfold in alternating chapters. One narrator is Nao, and it is her diary we are reading; the other is Ruth, and her story feels like a memoir, but is told in third person. Ruth, a writer living on a remote island in British Columbia, discovers Nao's diary and some other documents tucked away inside of a Hello Kitty lunchbox, which is itself sealed inside a barnacle-covered plastic bag. Writer's block that has stalled work on the memoir she is writing inspires the walk along the island's shores on which she discovers this bag. She lives on this island with her husband, Oliver, an artist who is preoccupied with the Eocene era and in the course of the narrative endeavors to populate the island with ginkgo trees and other species that hail from premodern times.

The voice of sixteen-year-old Nao, which is short for Naoko, is the first we hear. She opens the first chapter of the book, which is to say she begins her diary, with a cheery "Hi! My name is Nao, and I am a time being. Do you know what a time being is? Well, if you give me a moment, I will tell you. A time being is someone who lives in time, and that means you, and me, and everyone of us who is, or was, or ever will be."[26] The opening passage continues, "Right now, I am sitting in a French maid café in Akiba Electricity Town, listening to a sad chanson that is playing sometime in your past, which is also my present, writing this and wondering about you, somewhere in my future. And if you're reading this, then maybe by now you're wondering about me, too" (3). Delinquent from school, where she is viciously bullied by her classmates, Nao takes to hanging out at this café, which, we later learn, is a brothel of sorts. Born in Japan, Nao's family had moved to Sunnyvale, California, so that her computer engineer father could work in the dot.com industry. Bankrupted by the dot.com bubble bust in 2000, her family returns to Tokyo nearly destitute, and Nao finds herself socially abjected as an impoverished person bearing the taint of America. "This diary will tell the real life story of my great-grandmother Yasutani Jiko," Nao explains in the book's first chapter, in this way immediately establishing the book's interest in the compresence of lives and life stories (6). Indeed, Jiko's presence coheres the wide-ranging and disparate narratives comprising Ozeki's work and in doing so manifests its temporal aesthetic.

The book's structure and its generic ambiguity unsettle acceptance of Nao's introductory claims, however; they leave us uncertain whether the book is the result of the character Ruth's efforts at memoir, or whether Ruth, who lives in British Columbia with an artist husband named Oliver, as does the author, and who shares the first name with the author, ought to be read as a close approximation of Ozeki, which would in effect make this Ozeki's memoir. Or perhaps this book is best understood as an introduction to, or study of, Zen Buddhism or quantum physics. What *A Tale for the Time Being* suggests is that the answer to all these kinds of questions is "yes," and that this formal uncertainty and plurality is the architecture of the sensibility of not one, not two, not same, not different, that is its overarching aesthetic. The book in other words is not any of these, but not none of them either.

The alignments between Silko's and Ozeki's works do not, of course, erase their distinctiveness. They share a ground of disidentification from the modern liberal order; this is a coherence not based in identity nor requiring a single unifying political or intellectual horizon. Instead, as their works thematize, the entanglement of worlds, of being(s), is a condition of possibility even when it remains unacknowledged or is actively disavowed as such. In this way, they resonate, too, with Muñoz's theorization of brownness as naming ways of being, knowing, and living disidentified from the dictates, desires, and demands of dominant social formations. For Muñoz, brownness comes of the injuries constitutive of the modern world—of the reign of the liberal nation-state as the form of geopolitical organization and of capitalism as the political economy of the global order—but not only; brownness also refers to the production of bodies—through racialization and the naturalization of sex/gender difference—but not only; the Brown commons pulsates (his word)—with the joyful, full-bodied living of those who, despite every effort of the structures that persistently diminish, thrive in ordinary and nonordinary ways—but not only; it flows through and in kinship—with the fugitivity of blackness and the undercommons of Stefano Harney and Fred Moten's writings—but not only; and, as Alexandra Vazquez and José Quiroga have reminded us, Muñoz's brownness grew in and out of particular structures of feeling—that is, Cuban ethnicity—but not only.[27]

Muñoz unfurls a grammar wherein, in Ozeki's words, "Every instance of *either/or* is replaced by an *and*. And an *and*, and an *and*, and an *and*, and another *and* . . . adding up to an infinitely all-inclusive, and yet mutually unknowable, web of many worlds."[28] These worlds, these instances, are compresent. As a sensibility—a simultaneously conceptual and aesthetic orientation— brownness names the web of infinite worlds of otherwise living beings, a theory that resonates with, as Craig Womack has put it, "the weblike metaphysics of a novel like . . . *Ceremony*."[29] In time, Ozeki, Muñoz, and Silko are coincident despite their distinctive genealogies; the capaciousness of time affords this being with, this being that is always already relational. And in this state of being with, which is the state of being, we may come to understand and amplify reckoning as a form of rationalization important to the project of defunctioning liberal/colonial modernity.

Ozeki prompts us to ask, when is Nao? Homophonically enabling that question to refer to the character and to time itself, when is now/Nao, seemingly an invitation to sophistry, in Ozeki's book turns into/out to be a portal to an aesthetics and rationality emergent out of the materialities organized by global capitalism and corollary technologies of exposure and surveillance. This now, according to Ozeki, is precipitated by the deep history and reach of earlier emergent forms of commerce and circulation, the acknowledgment of which enables reckoning in the forms of disobedience and subterfuge. Ozeki and Silko together orient us to frame the challenge of the contemporary not in terms of the search for justice under capitalism (Spivak's memorable phrase) but rather the necessity of collective life despite it.

As in *Ceremony*, how to live the unbearable is a governing question for Ozeki. Where is the limit of survivability? Nao, burned by cigarettes and stabbed with scissors at school, and at one point nearly raped by classmates, suffers daily humiliation. A recording of the assault that takes place in the school bathroom is posted online, and Nao's underwear, stained with menstrual blood, is put up for sale. Nao's father, meanwhile, tries to kill himself in a series of tragically farcical and unsuccessful attempts. Unemployed and isolated, we come to learn late in the book that he resigned his job in California because it required him to create video games designed to train better soldiers—to "make killing fun." The comment on the partnership between capitalism and nationalism cannot be missed, and globalization is clearly shown to be a force that exacerbates the effects of their collaboration. Ozeki remembers the role of Enlightenment philosophies in the buttressing of these ideologies and political economies through Nao's father's preoccupation with the Great Minds of Western Philosophy, a series of books he rescues from someone's garbage pile. What, if anything, can be salvaged from that philosophy, Ozeki seems to ask. Whatever it is, it is not the source of salvation.

By the end of the book, Nao's father is making his living by helping others erase themselves from the virtual world; he and Nao both live outside of the field of representation. In this now, characterized by seemingly inexhaustible self-exposure through social media, virtual erasure is, according to Ozeki, tantamount to gaining the powers that accompany invisibility. In an era of the financialization and virtualization of everything, the novel observes, there is living that unfolds even, or perhaps especially, when it is not seen. In contrast to the enjoinder of modernity to be represented, Ozeki suggests that there is potency and survival and, simply, living, in being uncounted.

Nao's story is indeed at once hers and that of her "anarchist, feminist, novelist Zen Buddhist nun" great-grandmother (her father's grandmother), Jiko, and her great-uncle Haruki, a World War II kamikaze pilot who perished in the war and for whom her father was named. Haruki#1, as the pilot is referred to in the book, writes letters to his mother, Jiko, and those letters, along with his journal written in French, are found inside the Hello Kitty lunchbox along with Nao's diary.

Through the diary, translated by friends, Ruth discovers that Haruki#1 did not in fact kill himself by flying his plane into a U.S. battleship as he was ordered to do, and as Nao and her father believe him to have done. Instead, he flew his plane into the ocean rather than the ship, killing himself rather than doing harm to others. It is the thought of the broad impact his actions would have, not only on those killed but also on their family and friends, that underwrites his decision to end his own life. Beaten severely and daily by his training officer, Haruki#1's experience of military patriotism exemplifies the violence of exclusionary nationalism's reliance on turning persons into the machinery of war.

Ruth feels an urgency to deliver this information to Nao and Haruki and succeeds at doing so by time traveling to a time-place where/when she can leave the diary to be discovered by them. Encountering this time travel late in the book, the reader is prepared to accept this time travel not as fantasy and rather simply as a facet of the intimacy among subjects and stories and worlds that Ozeki has crafted thus far. This is both Ozeki's and Ruth's penultimate act of affording readerly agency; Ruth notices as she nears the end of Nao's diary that the remaining pages, which had been filled with writing, have gone blank, as if the words had fallen off the pages. Nao and her father had at this point decided separately to end their lives; the absence of narrative marks the possibility of their ends. Yet the pages become written again after Ruth visits Nao's world in her dreams—this time-travel trip during which she has the opportunity to speak with Haruki#2 and leave Haruki#1's diary for Nao and her father to discover. The present and the past, Ozeki suggests, are bilaterally connected; cause and effect are not unidirectional. But neither is this a suggestion that present actions can simply return us to past conditions. Rather, Ozeki shifts the framework of rationality to that organized by unity across time, space, place, and people.

Ozeki uses idioms and ideas drawn from quantum physics and Zen Buddhism in rendering this other rationality. Quantum physics is figured through the historical figures of Hugh Everett and Erwin Schrödinger. Schrödinger, an Austrian physicist working in the first half of the twentieth century, devised an experiment to explain quantum mechanics. Ozeki glosses this experiment in Appendix E:

> A cat is put into a sealed steel box. With him in the box is a diabolical mechanism: a glass flask of hydrocyanic acid, a small hammer aimed at the flask, and a trigger that will either cause the hammer to release, or not. The factor that controls the release is the behavior of a small bit of material being monitored by a Geiger counter. If . . . one of the atoms in the radioactive substance decays, the Geiger counter will detect it and trigger the hammer to shatter the flask, releasing the acid, and the cat will die. However, there is an equal probability that no atom will decay within that hour, in which case the trigger will hold and the cat will live.[30]

"The point of this thought experiment," the appendix continues, "is not to torture the cat. The point is not to kill it, or save it. . . . The point is to illustrate the perplexing paradox of the so-called measurement problem in quantum mechanics: what happens to entangled particles in a quantum system when they are observed and measured" (413). The cat and the atom represent the entangled particles, which indicates that they share certain characteristics or behaviors. In essence, the two behave as one; they are intimately entangled in one another—the decayed atom means the cat dies; the undecayed atom means the cat lives. Before the box is opened, the cat's state is unknown, so all positions are possible—it is in effect both alive and dead at the same time. This phenomenon, referred to as a *superposition*, describes all the possible positions of the entity under measurement (the entangled cat/atom). When an observer opens the box, the superposition collapses: the cat is either dead or alive, fixed in a single position. Schrödinger's point in positing this experiment was to argue that quantum theory ought not overweigh the importance of the subject (the observer) and objectivity (the cat is alive or dead/the atom is decayed or not).

Ozeki, however, rebuts Schrödinger's argument by introducing a physicist named Hugh Everett into her book. As she explains further by way of appendix, Everett was among the many physicists who attempted to resolve the paradox Schrödinger's experiment illustrated. Everett derived what came to be called the relative state theory, which held that instead of collapsing, every possibility according with a superposition branches off into distinctive worlds. Hence, there are infinite worlds: the cat is alive in some, dead in others. As Ozeki puts it, "Every instance of *either/or* is replaced by an *and*. And an *and*, and an *and*, and an *and*, and another *and* . . . adding up to an infinitely all-inclusive, and yet mutually unknowable, web of many worlds" (415). Having shown Ruth and Nao to be entangled particles as much as are the cat and atom, Ozeki prompts us to apprehend that so, too, are reader and text, Ozeki and her characters, history and fiction, and so on.

A Tale for the Time Being gives prominence to this relationality not only by the appearance of Schrödinger's cat and Everett in the appendixes, but as part of Ruth's and Nao's stories. They serve as ways of providing an understanding of being as constituted by moments upon moments, each of which represents a possibility, a decision, an orientation, and each of which is at once not-one and not-two, not-same and not-different, in that they exist infinitely, in every possible relation. In Jiko's words:

Up down, same thing. And also different, too . . .

When up looks up, up is down.

When down looks down, down is up.

Not one, not two. Not same, not different. (39–40)

The world in which this makes sense, the world that is one and the same and also multiple and different, is not that of modern rationality, but it isn't not that world either. Rather, bourgeois, capitalist modernity is a possibility of this not one, not two; it is a possibility among infinite others. Like Ruth, our task is to activate other possibilities, those that register and support living in relationality and in ways unfaithful to common sense.[31]

Reckoning with Entanglement

If, as Muñoz has suggested, brownness may be experienced in its performative dimensions more so than captured by direct explication or paradigmatic framing, brownness precedes but also extends beyond any singular form. That singularity is understood in Jean-Luc Nancy's terms as the singularity of "being singular plural"—an ontological condition of *being with* that neither negates the distinctiveness of and among beings, nor mistakes that distinctiveness for discrete and autonomous individuality. Thus it is that the experience of U.S. Latino/as and Chicano/as, according to Muñoz, may be understood as but one, albeit crucial, portal into this radical ontological condition. So, at the same time Muñoz's sense of brown emerges in and through the historical specificities that precipitate *latinidad*, including migration, linguistic coding, and the geographies of colonial modernity and Indigenous dispossession, it cannot—like the color brown itself—be isolated or reduced to those specificities. Brownness *is*—full stop; it is not a something, a particular thing, an adjectival appendage or cosmetic artifice; it is a name for minoritarian being and beingness. As a concept, brownness is the mode of knowing, the aesthetic rationality, that correlates with this ontological condition.[32]

I have been trying to suggest that Silko and Ozeki aestheticize an illiberal ontology akin to that of the brownness of being as theorized by Muñoz. Or, perhaps better stated, the works anchoring this chapter allow us, like Muñoz's thinking, to attune ourselves to this other, what I have been referring to as illiberal, way of being and knowing. My aim here is not to collapse distinctions among these works and the worlds and histories each emphasizes, but to ask the extent to which the elaboration of illiberal humanism has the capacity to facilitate encounters that illuminate coincidence and entanglement—that is, that such encounters are themselves a part of the logic and affordances of an illiberal onto-epistemology.

What I'm trying to elucidate is a way of being and knowing in the world that is shaped by the common experience of disidentification rather than solidarity through identity. Or, in other words, it is the world in which the misrecognitions naturalized by hegemonic sociality are apprehended as such; but the response to this phenomenon is not to strive for authenticity in an effort to correct misrepresentation. Rather, collectivity grows from the shared recognition of misrecognition. It is the relationality of the felt, often wordless connectivity that occurs among minoritarian subjects because of misrecognition, and precipitates the sociality of being with, of entanglement; it is that commonality necessary to persist, to thrive.

This is, I believe, an iteration of the Relation—the "interactive totality"—that Muñoz, Silko, and Ozeki bring to bear, to which Édouard Glissant gives vibrant enunciation. Specificity of grounds of emergence and enunciation of each iteration allows us to remember their nonequivalence, and their singular plurality refuses to allow the positivism of cultural relativism—the reigning episteme of liberal modernity—governing control over the meaning of "specificity." Rather than implying or positing propriety (specificity as possession), from this radically other view, specificity is an instantiation of the complexity of Relation. Can intellectual pathways come together as a critical mass without requiring dilution or the imposition of equivalence? What might come of dis- and rearranging our knowledge and pedagogical practices to those "that always sought linkages, blurrings, and chiaroscuros for the sake of progressive action"?[33] Perhaps this is what it means to "infer Relation, the overstepping that grounds [the] unity-diversity" of "evolving cultures"?[34]

Within all this, the role of the humanities must be, I believe, to amplify relationality in an effort to delegitimize and defunction the rationalism that so affirmatively justifies unlivability. This is both a simple and difficult project. It is simple insofar as we can deliberately unlearn received methods and epistemes, starting with recognition of the narrowness and parochialism of those generated through liberalism, and proliferating more worldly forms of knowing. It is difficult in that, for relationality to be meaningful as a response and corollary to entanglement, it is necessary to acknowledge and reside in irresolvable complicity and associated and historically induced antagonisms. Critiques of model minority discourse, largely emergent through Asian Americanist discourse, tell us much about the ways that minoritized subjects are structurally pitted against each other in the service of White supremacy. The point here is not to induce self-flagellation, but instead to insist on the study of how it is that the categorical differentiation of peoples through colonialism and racism precipitates the foreclosures of lives and of life through hierarchization and the management of proximity to humanness. It is crucial to avoid ascribing either tragedy or heroism to reckoning in this manner. Rather, circumstances moot the choice to act in accordance with entanglement: given the state of the world, we cannot not be with each other, not as a matter of choice, but because we are entangled. Perhaps in this way the humanities can enliven the dream of infinite parallel worlds encompassed by Schrödinger's thought experiment, in a refusal of the misery-inducing status quo as the only possible reality.

I have been suggesting in this book that part of our work must be to acknowledge how the humanities may enhance the efficacy of what Stuart Hall and Alan O'Shea have reminded us are the popularization and naturalization into common sense of the politics and policies that give rise to aggressive inequality. Drawing on Antonio Gramsci's theorizations, Hall and O'Shea cogently define common sense as

> a form of "everyday thinking" which offers us frameworks of meaning with which to make sense of the world. It is a form of popular, easily available knowledge which contains no complicated ideas, requires no sophisticated argument and does not depend on deep thought or wide reading. . . . It is pragmatic and empirical, giving the illusion of arising directly from experience, reflecting only the realities of daily life and answering the needs of "the common people" for practical guidance and advice."[35]

Hall and O'Shea call for the embrace of "the idea that common sense is a site of political struggle," and, like them, I am interested here both in illuminating how common sense operates within the world of the academy and in exploring the possibilities of proliferating "good sense"—what Gramsci (echoed by Hall and O'Shea) explains is the space of critique of common sense—through intellectual and pedagogical work.[36]

It is clear that diagnosis alone is insufficient to activate good sense in the dominant political economy; we are not lacking in evidence of colonialism, toxification, racism, and so on. It will, I think, and as I have tried to suggest here, be necessary to delegitimate common sense in part by concertedly emphasizing the frameworks and measures of life and living that follow from the relationality of being. The activation of relationality requires methods of critical inquiry unbound to the compartmentalized arrangements of knowledge organizing the liberal humanities, including especially its temporal and geographic distributions. Illiberal aesthetics provides rationalities that refute and refuse the logics of such ordering, which may be deployed toward the ends of making sense otherwise.

Chapter 4

Mis/Taken Universals

Time for me had always been measured in terms of the rising sun, its setting sister, and the dependable cycle of the moon. But at sea, I learned that time can also be measured in terms of water, in terms of the distance traveled while drifting on it. When measured in this way, nearer and farther are the path of time's movement, not continuously forward along a fast straight line. When measured in this way, time loops and curlicues, and at any given moment it can spiral me away and then bring me rushing home again. —MONIQUE TRUONG, *The Book of Salt*

Throughout this book, I have been making the case for the elaboration of an illiberal humanist aesthetic as a means of engaging the contemporary situation of the humanities without recourse to either defensiveness or resignation. Such an aesthetic reckons with the damages covered over and justified by the liberal rationality that organizes the received humanities and cognate humanism. Illiberal humanist reason takes issue with the structured assumptions driving and advanced by the individualizing and personalizing discourses of meritocracy and the moralization of failure characterizing the (neo)liberal hegemonic order. The human as illiberally constituted is inextricable from its conditions of possibility or, in other words, is radically indiscrete, irrevocably relational, and decidedly not autonomous. I have suggested that bringing into unconcealedness and amplifying this humanism is part of the twofold project of delegitimizing bourgeois liberalism and elaborating illiberal humanist onto-epistemologies. The logics of entanglement afforded by illiberal humanism remembers the intimate ties between the advantaged and disadvantaged, the wealthy and the poor, and the dominant and the subjugated, such that "between" names the irrevocable condition of socio-ontological relationality which is itself the object of study and analysis. Disidentified from the telos of Enlightenment liberalism and its neoliberal iteration, illiberal humanism in this way elicits attention to the grounds that subtend being and knowledge.

In contrast to Enlightenment philosophy's defining interest in transcendence of particularity or subjective experience toward universality, illiberal aesthetics (re)turn us again and again to the conditions of emergence and possibility underlying particularity and experience, including the particularity of the aspiration to universality disavowed by liberalism. Moreover, such aesthetics thematize how they are themselves at once products of and openings into apprehension of the long-lived, diverse, and contradictory effects of bourgeois liberalism in its constitutive interarticulation with settler colonialism, racial capitalism, and modern nationalism and imperialism; this is one of the ways they provide the aesthetics of entanglement and relationality that are key features of illiberal humanist ways of being and knowing. The seeming discreteness and solidity of a given work/text/object defrays in this view, a position from which the blurriness of its edges—its porousness, its openness, its relationality—may be sensed.

This chapter focuses on such textual indiscretion, a primary thematic interest of Monique Truong's 2004 novel, *The Book of Salt*, to suggest how it elicits a kind of critical promiscuity that refutes and refuses the compartmentalization of knowledge wrought by the geographies and temporalities of the received humanities/liberal humanism. By doing so, the novel gives rise to a sense of the universal as a category not of transcendence but of subtending grounds. Truong invites us to follow its lead in lingering at the edge of discretion, at the limits of knowledge, individuality, and objectivity, and in that way, to recognize the mistakenness of the universal-particular dyad constituting the modern/colonial epistemic order. *The Book of Salt*, in other words, turns the commonsensical deployment of the dyad inside out: what is effected is not a simple reversal whereby the particular (the colonized, the racially marked, the other) takes the place of the abstract universal (the ideal subject of modernity), but rather, a sensibility that understands that the desire for universality, trafficked forcibly beyond specific time and place of emergence by the processes that realize imperialism and colonialism, subtends the modern world. By giving universality affective and material life in this way, Truong identifies knowledge protocols as intimately linked to the production and legitimation of desires tethered to an array of institutional formations. *The Book of Salt*'s thematization of the intimacy of modernist and colonialist aesthetics thus helps us understand how the university organizes desire by its arrangements of knowledge, understanding necessary to making it work otherwise.

The novel also helps show that the kind of aesthetic inquiry I have been trying to elaborate operates in the vein of the "intended mistake," a formulation I borrow from Gayatri Spivak.[1] In her analysis of the prospects of aesthetic education in the era of globalization (or, for her, "globalizability"), Spivak identifies the intended mistake as a procedure of deliberately displacing "the Europe/non-Europe economy of correctness" or, in other words, the historical processes and corollary epistemologies that created and naturalized the bio- and geographic dichotomies characterizing the modern world, and to which we collectively refer as colonialism.[2] This procedure remembers the impossibility of simply (reductively) jettisoning Enlightenment philosophy altogether given that it is a thoroughgoing legacy that at once secures subjugation and facilitates the capacities for critique. Accordingly, the intended mistake focuses attention on this double bind itself—on the structured/authorized economies of meaning and value within which correctness is adjudicated—and mis-takes axiomatic concepts (like the universal) and understandings as a means of "mak[ing] room for justice."[3] In other words, the intended mistake enacts a pedagogy of disidentification oriented toward maintaining openings for worlds in which the idea of justice remains possible. For Spivak, it is those worlds, and hence the hope that aesthetic education might participate in creating the desire for them, that are increasingly disappeared by the processes to which globalization refers, namely, the abstraction and financialization of everything and everyone. Indeed, Spivak expresses this hope as itself an intended mistake—a "false hope" that "any reader will waste the time to learn to parse the desires (not the needs) of collective examples of subalternity."[4] Illiberal aesthetic inquiry, as a modality of the intended mistake, is in short a practice of identifying the mistaken assumptions and assertions of the world according to the received humanities, and to mis-take them toward the ends of learning to sense and make sense (out) of subjugated desires. This practice requires a suspension not of disbelief, but rather of belief in what is given/imposed as universally desirable, namely, freedom and happiness as defined by bourgeois liberalism.

The task at hand is to consider how the humanities might be organized to gather and amplify the desires that correlate with and materialize worlds capable of reckoning with and derailing the historic and ongoing diminishment of life under liberal/colonial modernity.

The shift in focus from needs to desires Spivak promotes does not result in a disavowal of the material conditions of existence of the dispossessed or subjugated. Desires are, we remember, historically constituted, contingent on environment and (de)legitimated through structured, disciplinary means. In this view, the contingency of desires on their conditions of possibility beyond individual control disrupts their commonsense appearance as universal and individually generated. To parse desires is at least partly an invitation to apprehend subjugated people as desiring subjects and thus to refuse the colonial epistemologies' need to produce such figurations as primitives and "little brown brothers." While it is not especially difficult to identify nonhegemonic desires, it is more challenging to defunction the economies of correctness by which desires are judged to be worthy, valuable, or not. Within governing economies, certain desires are minimized through particularization (e.g., "what women want," "queer desires") and/or through ascription as naive, idealistic, or utopian. The aesthetic judgment of bourgeois liberalism operates in this way, to narrow via common sense the parameters of acceptable and laudable desires. Rather than trying to expand such parameters, illiberal aesthetic inquiry takes the metrics of acceptability as object of knowledge, to remember and remind of their interested constructedness and to ask: What worlds correlate with the desires incommensurate to normative paradigms of judgment? To what and whose (dis)advantage is the regulation of permissible desires directed?

These are questions *The Book of Salt* provokes as it organizes sense and sensibility around undocumented figures and desires, specifically those exiled from the normative institutions of the modern nation and the colonial state. It is a novel that thematizes and aestheticizes displacement on multiple scales, a motif by which it renders the contingency wrought by colonial modernity. In this way, Truong rewrites the relationship between the aesthetic and the universal, from its Kantian iteration (in which the aesthetic capacitates transcendence of particularity in favor of the universality of the sensus communis) to an illiberal iteration wherein the aesthetic keys us into coloniality as the universal condition of modernity. The illiberal aesthetic mis-takes the universal and, from the grounds of history, remembers it as a category of violence and violation.

We know the universal is a category through which the geo- and bio-specificity of Enlightenment thought was covered over, and the establishment of contemporary globalization renews the imperative to suss out what is universalized and to whose (dis)advantage.[5] As Anna Tsing puts it as part of the project of studying "the global," "universals are indeed local knowledge in the sense that they cannot be understood without the benefit of historically specific cultural assumptions."[6] We may moreover acknowledge that universals index "knowing that moves—mobile and mobilizing—across localities and cultures" and, in the process of such movement, generate new interests, sometimes out of compromise and at other times, most devastatingly, as a consequence of domination.[7] Tsing submits that the universal is, across both dominant and liberatory practices and philosophies, that which we "cannot not want." "The universal," she explains, "offers us the chance to participate in the global stream of humanity. We can't turn it down. Yet we also can't replicate previous versions without inserting our own genealogy of commitments and claims."[8] Tsing allows us to understand how universals are remade into local varieties, specific to time, place, and people, and serve in this manner as a category of analysis that gives texture and meaning to such large-scale processes as globalization.

To this rendering of the analytic purchase of universals, I suggest a somewhat different proposition, one that comes not only of Truong's work but also of lingering with the syntagm of "cannot not want." This construct—drawn from Spivak's theorization of identity as that which we cannot not want—registers compromised desires and the contingency of will, a circumscription of the rational decision-making/"choice" assigned to autonomous subjects that remembers it, too, as an interested artifice of liberalism. We cannot not want precisely because historical conditions and geopolitical structures are beyond individual control; because liberal colonial modernity has made it impossible to opt wholly out of its governing political and cultural economies and social formations. But neither do desires line up tidily to the dictates of the dominant such that the doubled negation of the "cannot not" is always juxtaposed with wanting otherwise—with the wanting that finds dominant desires to be in themselves wanting, unsatisfactory, empty; with the wanting that is produced by the attempted universalization of liberalism's universal; with desires incommensurate to the economies of correctness. What do we make of—and with—the wanting that fails to as-pire to the universal? Which is to say, that remains disincorporated, outside the "stream of global humanity"? What sense(s) of justice, of life, reside in and correlate with, such mis-taken desires?

Alone and Unemployed

In *The Book of Salt*, Truong gives us a narrating subject far removed from the control of the regime of knowledge if not always physically distant from the seats of power. This narrator, Binh, is neither wholly reliable nor, it turns out, the author of the autobiography he seemingly narrates; he is an inau-thentic Native conjured through and as the desires of colonial modernity, the conceit of his nonauthorship figuring the colonial desire for authentic knowledge of the Native. Truong unsettles faith in the evidentiary force of writing as she links the desire for such authentic knowledge to modernist aesthetics, and she limns both the limits and potency of writing, of litera-ture, as well as the (body) politics of knowledge.

Through Binh, who is compelled to a precarious life in exile because of the intersecting forces of colonialism and cis-heteropatriarchy, Truong con-nects the regulation of desire with geopolitics. Set in the early twentieth century, this 2004 novel resonates with and provides a longer genealogy of the situation of the migrant worker in the context of contemporary global-ization.[9] The proliferation and movement of migrant workers keys us into the large-scale transformations wrought by the combination of the deliber-ate and heightened integration of local economies into a global capitalist net-work to ensure economic interdependence, initiated through earlier modes of capital cooperating with colonial conquest, and the political, cultural, and ideological processes that underwrite and are given shape not only by these economic shifts, but also by emergent technologies of transportation, transmission, and communication.[10] In Truong's novel, these broad-stroke characteristics of globalization are figured as the difficulty of making a life as labor made invisible by and to the institutions of modernity—specifically, the colonial state, social and literary establishments, and heteropatriarchal normativity, in their interrelations. *The Book of Salt* does not, however, un-fold in the tenor of a labor or class protest novel. Rather, it suggests the pos-sibilities for world making based on the queer desires—the nonnormative erotics and objectives incommensurate to common sense—of those made to be without the prospect of social mobility or economic advancement by dint of colonialism and capitalism. Neither are they desirous of such achievement, even as Truong's work remembers the difficulty of inhabiting that position; what romance there is to migrancy is sharply mitigated by the material vulnerability Binh faces. And it is also true, this novel submits, that queer desire crafts—or has the potential to craft—social formations necessary to navigating that vulnerability, formations that constitutively understand the irrevocable connection between dislocation and dispossession and the good life promised by modernity.

The Book of Salt is mostly set in 1930s Paris, though time and space flow indiscreetly throughout it. Binh, the first-person narrator and putative subject of the autobiography that is the novel's framing device, cannot hold at bay memories of his life in Vietnam previous to his contemporary status as an exile seeking refuge in Paris. Binh travels by sea to reach Europe and comes to work as a cook for "GertrudeStein," the fictionalization of Gertrude Stein, whose iconic status is marked by this compound name, and Miss Toklas (referred to together as "The Steins"). The younger son of a family dominated by a violent father who is deeply embedded in the life of the local Catholic church, Binh—the name he assumes as he crosses the ocean deep in the belly of a ship full of other would-be laborers set adrift—leaves Vietnam in disgrace after being discovered having sex with a male chef at the Consulate-General's residence where he'd been employed as a low-level kitchen worker. He is throughout the novel characterized by an intimate understanding of food—the power of its taste, the chemistry of its operations—and by his capacity to give sensory pleasure. Binh's understanding of food is a learned intuition, initiated by helping his mother cook to earn money for his family, and later, through repetition and mimicry in the Consulate-General's kitchen and during his employment at The Steins'.

The novel's opening establishes its thematic concern with knowledge: "Of that day I have two photographs, and, of course, my memories."[11] Documentation and ephemera, the visual record and the ephemeral trace, are the source material for his life story, which begins not with his birth or early life, but instead by recalling the end of his time with The Steins. "That day" is the day they leave Paris—and Binh—to return to the United States. The photographs capture GertrudeStein and Miss Toklas at the Gare du Nord, awaiting a train that will be the first part of their journey—by ship, then by air as they traverse the states, a tour of triumphant return. Binh features in the background of one of the photographs. "It shows my Mesdames sitting side by side and looking straight ahead," Binh explains. "I am over there on the bench, behind them, on the left-hand side. I am the one with my head lowered, my eyes closed. I am not asleep, just thinking, and that for me is sometimes aided by the dark" (9). He continues, "I am a man unused to choices, so the months leading up to that day at the Gare du Nord had subjected me to an agony, sharp and new, self-inflicted and self-prolonged. I had forgotten that discretion can feel this way" (9). Choice, the privileged value of bourgeois liberalism that individualizes life and defines freedom in terms of rationalist decision making abstracted from sociohistorical conditions, is rewritten here to acknowledge the precariousness of existence, the wearisomeness of striving for basic survival for those for whom mobility is compulsory.

What is his place in the world? What does it mean to be placed in the world? The novel's introductory chapter raises such questions as Binh's memory of "that day" unfolds to include receipt of a rare letter from his brother, Anh Minh, who lives in Vietnam. "'It is time for you to come home to Việt-Nam'" (8), writes Anh Minh, in response to Binh's earlier letter which had explained, "'My Mesdames may be going home.'" Binh had written to Anh Minh what will appear at this opening chapter's close in poetic form:

I do not want to start all over again.
Scanning the help-wanteds.
Knocking on doors.
Walking away alone.
And, yes, I am afraid. (10)

This refrain, a concise evocation of the irrelevance of the freedom to choose in the context of being unhomed in an inhospitable world, accidentally provides Binh truth. "I had meant to place a comma between 'alone' and 'I am afraid,'" he explains, "but on paper, a period instead of a comma had turned a dangling token of regret into a plainly worded confession. I could have fixed it with a quick flick of lead, but then I read the sentences over again and thought, *That* is true as well" (8). The errant pen renders insight; grammatical error expresses discomfort; an editing decision transforms the self from one who is apologetic to one who is disaggregated by fear.

Once again "Alone and Unemployed," a phrase that serves as a near-ontological description of Binh throughout the opening sections of the novel, it is the condition that bespeaks his desires: to touch and be touched, and to want to participate in the symbolic and material economies of modern life, but unable and unwilling to give what was necessary to do so, namely, himself as authentic Native.[12] Until he comes to work for The Steins, Binh fails repeatedly either to secure employment or to retain it. For some would-be employers, Binh is "nothing but a series of destinations with no meaningful expanses in between," his response to which is, "Thank you, but no thank you."[13] For others—"the collectors"—who hire him, he at first is grateful for the havens that their kitchens are for him: "Every kitchen is a homecoming, a respite, where I am the village elder, sage, and revered. . . . I allow myself to believe that it is the sheer speed of my hands, the flawless measurement of my eyes, the science of my tongue, that is rewarded. During these restorative intervals, I am no longer the mute who begs at this city's steps" (19). Inevitably, however, the "collectors are never satiated by my cooking. They are ravenous. The honey that they covet lies inside my scars. . . . They crave the fruits of exile, the bitter juices, and the heavy hearts" (19). Recognizing himself to be "but one within a long line of others" including the "Algerian orphaned by a famine, the Moroccan violated by his uncle, the Madagascan driven out of his village . . . these are the wounded trophies who have preceded me" (19), Binh cannot stay.

> After so many weeks of having that soft, steady light shined at me, I begin to forget the barbed wire rules of such engagements. I forget there will be days when it is I who will have the craving, the red, raw need to expose all my neglected, unkempt days. And I forget that I will wait, like a supplicant at the temple's gate, because all the rooms of the house are somber and silent. When I am abandoned by their sweet-voiced catechism, I forget how long to braise the ribs of beef, whether chicken is best steamed over wine or broth, where to buy the sweetest trout. I neglect the pinch of cumin, the sprinkling of lovage, the scent of lime. And in these ways, I compulsively write, page by page, the letters of my resignation. (20)

What is the nature of forgetting? Unintentional, it emerges to insulate against exposure, as a compulsive habit of refusing to be the proper wounded subject whose function is to secure the sympathetic superiority of the bourgeois liberal subject. That it is Paris, and the French, who are cast in that role surely comments on France's standing as a celebrated founding site of liberal democracy and its attendant promises of universal freedom, even as Binh's narration of his life at the Governor-General's kitchen prior to his migration to France remembers its colonialist history, the damage wrought by and for the sake of its much-heralded democratic vision. Binh forgets himself, which is to say, he fails to act obediently to perform the role assigned to him by colonial modernity. This was as true in the Governor-General's kitchen, where his desire to touch and be touched—his unkempt, raw need—writes his letters of exile. Unlike his brother, whose deliberately acquired fluency in the French of his employers signals his attachment to becoming *of* rather than simply *like* the French imperialists, Binh has no settled path to follow: "Me, what was I supposed to do? Twenty years old and still a *garde-manger*, sculpting potatoes into perfect little spheres, carving chunks of turnips into swans, the arc of their necks as delicate as Blériot's fingers, fingers that I wanted to taste. Equipped with skills and desires that no man would admit to having, what was I supposed to do?" (14–15).

Truong in this way tethers the aesthetic and the economic, elaborating as she does the conditions of labor required to enable the aestheticism and domesticity characterizing GertrudeStein and Miss Toklas's lives, characteristics rendered through both the former's seemingly insatiable appetite for things (art and ordinary objects alike) and the latter's near-obsessive preoccupation with food. As Y-Dang Troeung suggests, Binh's story may be seen as a "gift . . . to his imagined community of the underclass, the long line of servants, migrants, and queer exiles who have preceded him through the master's door."[14] Truong amplifies the practical knowledge and labor subtending intellectual and artistic endeavor, emphasizing through Binh that taste is quite literally crafted on the backs of laboring others. Differentially marking the impact of economic shifts—the market crash of the 1930s catalyzes The Steins' and other expatriate Americans' departure from France, as no longer were any funds coming to them, while Binh is left with precious few resources—*The Book of Salt* displaces the privileging of the impact of financial crisis on the middle class in favor of a much longer view of the "crisis ordinariness" of the underclass.[15] The difference between Binh and The Steins functions in this regard as an intimate difference/relation between undomesticated queer desire and the normativity of sustained coupledom; between the colonized in exile and the expatriate; between the craftsman (*garde-manger*) never elevated to the position of Artist (Chef) or the icon of such position (the writer). "How is it," David Eng suggests the novel asks, "that Stein and Toklas appear in history as the iconic lesbian couple of literary modernism and historical modernity while Binh can never appear?"[16] The occlusions and erasures effected by and operational in modern epistemology ensures that racialization, colonialism, and biopolitics (collectively, Walter Mignolo's body-politics) remain outside of history, disqualified from the "historical sensorium."[17]

That the novel is narrated in English underscores the fictionality of the autobiography: Binh's language is of food and feeling and not of text and words; words regularly fail him, he reports, and yet the often lyrical prose of his story suggests that it is readers who, like the collectors who employ him, fail to apprehend his offerings. Out of inauthenticity comes art: he is the failed subject of empire, the inappropriate son to his father, the un-French cook who makes French food better than the native born. In each way, he is incommensurate to the symbolic and material economies that organize the normative world. Indeed, when at the end of the novel Binh discovers hidden away a manuscript of his life story authored by GertrudeStein and titled "The Book of Salt," we recognize that his story can be present as fiction only if he is to remain unravaged, undisclosed. Truong reverses the usual course of irony, shifting the reader from holding the omniscient view of the story world to the ignorant subject of ironic discourse. We find that we, like Anh Minh, have been seduced by the language of power and turned toward a security in knowledge of the colonized and underclass laborer, a knowledge that turns out to rest on flawed but potent presumptions of the knowability of the other. Binh, of course, has no control over his narrative; he is a figure of Truong's imagination.

This is not to say that Binh is just fiction. Or, rather, perhaps it is to recast "just" from its diminishing deployment to its sense of ethical or political adequation: Binh does justice/is a just figure insofar as he defunctions a colonialist ethnographic reading of the novel. He is a figure that is an exercise of the "epistemic rights of the racially devalued," in Mignolo's terms; Truong has created a figure with which knowing is generated by listening to silence, to nondisclosure, to touch and taste and desire as speech. He cannot be reduced to a singular representation; he is unavailable to knowledge in that way, always in some way opaque.

Relations upon Relations

Truong's inspiration for Binh is the reference to Vietnamese cooks made in the *Alice B. Toklas Cookbook*, a 1954 volume authored by Toklas, and the disclosure of the manuscript's authorship at the end of Truong's novel formally links it to Gertrude Stein's *Autobiography of Alice B. Toklas* (1933). Stein's most commercially successful work, *Autobiography* is narrated in the first person by the putative subject of the narrative. It offers an account of their lives together from about 1907, when Alice first arrives in Paris, to the early 1930s. Alice, like Binh of Truong's novel, is necessary to Stein's artistic efforts; she presents herself as an exacting employer and social arranger who willingly lives in Stein's shadow. "About six weeks ago," the *Autobiography* closes, "Gertrude Stein said, it does not look to me as if you were ever going to write that autobiography. You know what I am going to do. I am going to write it for you. I am going to write it as simply as Defoe did the autobiography of Robinson Crusoe. And she has and this is it."[18] With these lines, what had already been marked by the juxtaposition of the title of the book with the author's name—namely, its fictionality—thus enters the novel in the moment of its closure, and writing itself is revealed to be the novel's penultimate subject. Having recorded and reported the intricate and unending labor required of Alice to sustain Stein, the author Stein makes the arguably triumphant move of accepting that labor as her due with this act of privileging writing itself.

Exemplary of modernist tendencies to pressure language to actualize itself—to remind us that writing is "about" nothing and is the thing itself— the *Autobiography*, despite its characterization as Stein's most accessible text by critics both contemporaneous and contemporary, offers a sense of the suppressed complexities through which subjects are linguistically crafted. Here, I mean to refer to the ways in which the literary subject (the subject of literature, the subject of a text) allegorizes subjectivity itself—that is, the conditions that make it possible to be known and to function as a subject. Self-subjectification is a process of alienation; the "I" on the page is never the selfsame as the singularity of being. The liberal philosophical mandate to know thyself is similarly an invitation to fiction, belying the sociogenic nature of identity formation. This fiction at once comes of and buttresses the colonial matrix of power/knowledge, which, as exemplified by Defoe's work, establishes itself as modern common sense in part through a literary pedagogy whereby the death of others for the sake of civilization is not merely acceptable but actively required to service Enlightenment.[19]

Initially published in 1719, Defoe's *The Life and Strange Surprising Adventures of Robinson Crusoe of York, Mariner: Who lived Eight and Twenty Years, all alone in an un-inhabited Island on the coast of America, near the Mouth of the Great River of Oroonoque; Having been cast on Shore by Shipwreck, wherein all the Men perished but himself. With An Account of how he was at least as strangely deliver'd by Pyrates. Written by Himself* is, according to Defoe, a historically based fictional autobiography. It tells the story of the eponymous Robinson Crusoe, a young Englishman of German, middle-class descent, who sets sail in September 1651 on what turns out to be the first of a series of adventuresome voyages he will take. Crusoe in turn becomes enslaved to a Moor; escapes; becomes a wealthy tobacco plantation owner in Brazil; and tries with uneven success to participate in the African slave trade before he ends up on the Island of Despair, the part of the story that is most familiar to contemporary audiences, having been popularized through retellings by everyone from Beatrix Potter to J. M. Coetzee. On this island, Crusoe creates, by dint of hard work and the residual material of English society that he harvests from his shipwrecked vessel, a relatively comfortable life herding the wild goats he has domesticated. He finds God while on the island, which allows him to resist despair, and frees one of the captives of the Native cannibals living on this ("uninhabited") island, later naming him Friday after the day of the week on which he appeared.

It is difficult to overstate the impact that Defoe's work has had on securing the pervasiveness of liberal philosophy both in its time and to contemporary hegemonic understandings of humanity.[20] A personification of the spirit of individual fortitude and economic rationalism, Robinson Crusoe stands as an idealization of the modern subject by achieving not only self-understanding, but also self-driven economic success. He is the figure of the merchant-philosopher, a personage that speaks to the inextricable weaving of the economic through enlightenment ontogeny. We see in Robinson Crusoe the justification for the enslavement and conquest of people and places: the development of civilization and the realization of the potentiality of humanity depend upon it. As Laura Doyle puts it, "what Defoe's narrative makes quietly clear is that . . . the African is the laborer through whom the Anglo-Saxon Protestant on the Atlantic turns loss into profit and captivity into redemption."[21] As one of the progenitors of the Anglophone bildungsroman, a form that is arguably the exemplary narrative form of modernity, Defoe's work continues to have material effectivity both in and beyond literary critical circles.

Defoe's prominence in Anglophone literary history, which is to say in the history of modernity, is at least in part attributable to the common understanding that he inaugurated a specifically nationalist writing. As Samar Attar reports, a particularly "extravagant" version of this argument is found in James Joyce's 1912 insistence that "the first English author to write without imitating or adapting foreign works, to create without literary models and to infuse into the creatures of his pen a truly national spirit . . . is Daniel Defoe."[22] That Defoe and his writings have been instrumental to cohering an English national identity is tautologically made by such claims. A substantial amount of scholarship from such other sources exists that makes a strong case for recognizing that foreign models may well have informed Defoe's *Robinson Crusoe*.

More specifically, as Attar and others have argued, the translation into Latin and then English, during Defoe's lifetime, of a work by a prominent twelfth-century Muslim-Andalusian philosopher, Ibn Ṭufayl (Abu Bakr Muḥammad Ibn ʿAbd al-Malik Ibn Muḥammad Ibn Muḥammad Ibn Ṭufayl al-Qaysī), and the resemblance between this earlier work and key tropes in *Robinson Crusoe* interrupt the asserted novelty and sovereign standing of the later work. Ibn Ṭufayl's tale, *Ḥayy Ibn Yaqẓan*, or "the living son of wakeful or aware," entered the English reading public sphere by the efforts of a well-established Oxford University orientalist, Edward Pococke, who offered a Latin translation in 1671. The university press published the translation, together with an Arabic version, under the title *Philosophus Autodidactus*. In 1674, Pococke's Latin version was translated into English (by a Quaker named George Keith), and in 1708, a translation by Simon Ockley directly from the Arabic to English was published under the rather lengthier title, *The Improvement of Human Reason, exhibited in the Life of Hai Ebn Yokdhan: Written in Arabick above 500 years ago; by Abu Jaafer Eban Tophail, In which is demonstrated, by what Methods one may, by the meer Light of Nature, attain the Knowledge of things Natural and Supernatural; more particularly the Knowledge of God, and the Affairs of another life.* Ockley's translation was reprinted in 1711 in London. Historical evidence suggests that Ṭufayl was fairly well known in Western Europe and in England specifically, just at the time Defoe was writing (Defoe lived between about 1660 and 1731).[23]

Ṭufayl's tale is structured as a letter to "Noble brother," who has, he says, "asked me to unfold for you, as well as I am able, the secrets of the oriental philosophy."[24] The opening section of the work reviews major philosophers and tenets of "oriental philosophy," and, indeed, the work functions as an introduction, the accuracy of which remains a source of debate, to the philosophy of Ibn Sina (or Avicenna).[25] The narrator explains that the addressee's request "set off a stream of ideas . . . which lifted [him] to a state of sublimity . . . a state so wonderful 'the tongue cannot describe' or explain it, for it belongs to another order of being, a different world."[26] The contours and thematic interests of Ṭufayl's work make its appeal to the eighteenth-century Enlightenment project clear: the opening discussion establishes as the task of the work the illumination of the "gradual progress" toward Truth that an individual makes, not through education or other facets of society, "but solely by intuition," and the truth of this journey cannot be written but instead must be experienced individually.[27] While the narrator turns to telling Ḥayy's story, the text also reads as an autobiographical account of his own journey to the ecstatic experience of Truth. Truth itself is unavailable through narrative; only the journey toward it may be laid out as an invitation and guide for others to follow. The narrator's experience thus remains distinctly his own, a strategy that accords with a philosophical belief that each person must work to connect the soul with the universal by means of inner contemplation. Knowledge of and openness to God is necessary to achieve Truth: religion and philosophy together produce the conditions whereby Truth can be approached.

Ḥayy's life begins without parents. He is either spontaneously generated on an equatorial island in the Indian Ocean by dint of its perfect environment, or is washed ashore in a small vessel into which he has been placed by a princess mother in fear of the wrath of her brother, the king, for the life of her child. Ḥayy grows up on an island wholly without human company, a scenario that allows the examination of the question, What is man outside of society?[28] Ḥayy is nurtured and nursed by a doe that serves as his foster mother and develops a strong emotional bond with her. As he grows up and develops practical knowledge—how to find food and to make himself physically comfortable on the island, how to deter the other animals from taking his food, how to use fire—he is in essence learning also how different he is from the other species on the island. Ḥayy comes to a gradual awareness of how he is uniquely equipped in some advantageous ways (with hands, for example) and vulnerable in others (without horns, for example). Upon the doe's death, that awareness of his species difference progresses apace as the narrative moves from telling of his grief to his efforts "to discern what could be wrong with his one-time provider" by means of what is in effect a vivisection, and finally to his detached insight that whatever it was that animated his foster mother, it was not to be found in the bodily matter of the doe's carcass. This initial intuition of the existence of a soul unfolds into ever-greater insight as to the ways in which the arrangements of nature point toward some kind of universal force that he thinks of as the Necessary Existent. By means of an intuitive knowledge formed by keen and contemplative observation of the natural world, Ḥayy determines that putting his soul into communion with that universal force is what is most important.

Another character, Asal, who is himself in search of divine enlightenment, arrives on the island in the latter half of the tale and is Ḥayy's first contact with another of the human species. Asal teaches Ḥayy human language and is astonished both by Ḥayy's tale of isolated life and by the spiritual illumination that has come of it. Asal convinces Ḥayy to journey back to civilization with him, to his friend Salaman's palace, in order to share with others dedicated to the path of enlightenment his own journey. Ḥayy readily agrees, but soon becomes distraught at the inability or unwillingness of those he finds to let go of the dogmatic principles of religion, an inability that makes spiritual communion with the Necessary Existent impossible. And thus Ḥayy, accompanied by Asal, retreats to the island as the tale closes.[29]

The similarities between Ṭufayl's and Defoe's work are plainly evident and buttress the argument that *Robinson Crusoe* is substantially informed by this earlier work. The occlusion of this plausible link between Ṭufayl's work and Defoe's is of course of a piece with the ways in which orientalism creates distance between—creates as distance—East from West, thus allowing for the originary claim of Enlightenment to rest squarely in Western Europe. It is this geo-graphic politics of knowledge that underwrites the bio-graphic politics of the self-authorizing subject of liberal philosophy.[30]

What I am suggesting is that *The Book of Salt* affords an intertextual geography that makes chronology irrelevant and finds intimate contact instead of distance. Reflective of the emphases of Julia Kristeva's 1968 theorization of intertextuality (rendered through her reworking of Mikhail Bakhtin's theory of dialogism according to which language and literature are conceived to be in constant states of flux as terms and texts gain meaning through their inevitable and not always intentional interactions with others), there is something radically democratizing in such an approach to language and cultural production: all texts are in effect intertexts given that texts and interpretation can neither be apprehended nor proceed independently of other texts and readings, a condition that undermines the possibility of hierarchical ordering. Nor can they be understood as fixed objects: they are better understood to be fields of articulation, of relations brought into relation.

As such, they bring to bear the grounds of laboring bodies—the body-politics of knowledge—that subtend in every instance the production of Knowledge: Binh, Alice, Friday, and the disavowed work of the oriental(ism) central to Enlightenment, each and collectively necessary to the positive image of colonial modernity figured by GertrudeStein, Gertrude Stein, and Crusoe.[31] Nonequivalently but interrelatedly, these texts in their interarticulation submit that the universal of global history is coloniality.

The theoretical register of this chapter in this regard engages the implications of illiberal humanism on the construct of the universal, in part as a way of considering whether, like aesthetics and reason, there is radical potential to the universal that might generatively be brought to bear in our efforts to address the current conjuncture. Is entanglement another name for, or kind of, universality? What happens to the epistemic function of the universal-particular dyad given the radical relationality of humanity in an illiberal key? How can particularity, specificity, continue to be acknowledged and valued—surely an important political task in the face of the homogenizing forces that globalization names and the long-lived efforts to eradicate difference to which colonialism refers—without recourse to cultural relativism and the tacit essentialism and positivism that give it purchase? Such questions turn us to consideration of comparison's history and analytic function. For, one of the effects of attuning to illiberal rationality—to making sense through relationality as the condition of being—is acknowledgment of the potency and politics of comparison and comparativity, as modes of knowing and knowledge production.

This is to remember that comparison is at the heart of liberal-colonial epistemologies, that affords the dichotomous logic by which people are sorted into different groups and kinds—as more and less capable, emotional, ideal, human—in correlation with the demands of racial capitalism and cis-heteropatriarchal ideologies. And it is comparison that gives primacy of place to the one who compares, to the subjective perspective of the agent of comparison. The authority of that agent is contingent on legitimacy secured through the credentializing mechanisms of normative institutions: the law, the academy, the culture industry, that is, those that structure and make commonsensical the dominant political economy. The agent of comparison functions in this dominant paradigm as the Knowing Subject, whose authority is reiterated by affirming the legitimacy of these institutions, and whose principal activity is one of judgment: of determining equivalence and putting entities into relation. This is the disinterested critic of disciplinary knowledge, whose own historicity and unavoidable interestedness are covered over: the "hard-eyed" professor who nominates and fixes into objects of knowledge in accordance with the representational schema constituting the university, the unreconstructed anthropologist reporting on the Native, the formalist literary critic, the "drive-by" sociologist, and so on.[32] Comparison, in brief, is deeply implicated in buttressing the authority of the liberal-colonial order, which is also to remember that the stakes in articulating the onto-epistemology of relationality are at once local, academic, and broadly political, always worldly.

Underlying any claim to or mobilization of the universal as a category of knowledge and thought is the comparative exercise and the unavoidable historicity of the agent of comparison. As R. Radhakrishnan points out, even in ordinary life, "comparisons are never disinterested. That in itself is not a major problem."[33] Rather, while acknowledging that "all epistemologies are perspectival with reference to their respective subjects . . . when it comes to comparison," we must recognize that the "epistemology of comparison is willed into existence by a certain will to power/knowledge. Such a will is never innocent of history and its burden" (16). Comparison is the mechanism by which a world and a subject are made identical: the agent of comparison, from his or her location, contrasts the units of analysis for the purposes of producing new knowledge that is somehow better: "more sophisticated, progressive, worldly, and cosmopolitan than a form of knowledge that is secure in its own identity and provenance" (18). For comparison to do something other, to act on behalf of the "other," it is thus necessary to "deconstruct[ ] the apparatus of recognition," that is, to dismantle the assumption that there is a self-contained positive identity in the first place that is put into relation (20). Radhakrishnan avers that comparison in this regard "opens up a mobile space of the 'between' that is nonsovereign—space that cannot be owned and administered as property" (21).

The space to which Radhakrishnan refers is that in which the affirmation of the sovereign subject and the world in which that subject is authorized has no place. Instead, its work is to refunction relationality itself. Resounding Édouard Glissant's theorization of the worldliness of literature and poetics, Shu-mei Shih reminds us that "as a being in the world, the text is not only organic to the world but also enters into relation."[34] Comparison may accordingly be understood to be a practice of "setting into motion historical relationalities between entities brought together for comparison, and bringing into relation terms that have traditionally been pushed apart from each other."[35] It is, Shih submits, in the "excavation of these relationalities" that the "ethical practice of comparison, where the workings of power are not concealed but necessarily revealed" reside.[36]

This is the story of how the world was made global in ways that underpin its contemporary modality; we might provisionally posit that this is the universality belied by universalism: "Imperialism (the thought as well as the reality of empire) does not conceive of anything universal but in every instance is a substitute for it."[37] The particular gives rise to the universal, not as an instance or derivative, but as a poetics of Relation, in Glissant's words. It is thus that the agent of comparison must be doubly, multiply conscious, simultaneously of the ways in which they have been cast as the object of study and their position as a knowing subject. What Mignolo describes as "the body-politics of knowledge," in other words, affords the onto-epistemic shift necessary to short-circuit the production of knowledge in its same old imperial guise. As Mignolo explains, "body-politics is the darker side and the missing half of bio-politics: body-politics describes decolonial technologies enacted by bodies who realized that they were considered less human at the moment they realized that the very act of describing them as less human was a radical un-human consideration. Thus, the lack of humanity is placed in imperial actors, institutions and knowledges that had the arrogance of deciding that certain people they did not like were less human."[38] From this more human/illiberal humanist position, knowledge and modes of knowing are recruited toward the aims of "the *regeneration* of life," rather than, by contrast, the ideal of civilization or the salvation of the economy. This knowing subject is radically different from the universal subject, not as universalism's particular, but instead as that standpoint formed by the compulsory imposition of a particular universalism and the radical relation to its governing epistemology. Comparison for this subject is a hermeneutic of relationality: it is the very act of investigating the conditions under and effects with which certain entities have been classified as fundamentally discrete and different and bringing into unconcealedness the irreducibly fluctuating entanglements that dis/organize humanity.

"What Keeps You Here?"

Dismissed from the Governor-General's house, betrayed by Bleriot, the *chef de cuisine*, "who insisted that I call him 'Chef' or, worse, 'Monsieur,' even when our clothes were on the floor," and banished from his family home by his father, the vituperous Old Man who continues to berate Binh long after he is dead, Binh takes to the sea on an uncertain journey, with little expectation, hope, or option.[39] "The world was enormous before I left my corner of it. But once I did, it grew even more immense. As for that corner, it continued to shrink until it was a speck of dust on a globe. Believe me," Binh explains, "I never had a desire to see what was on the other side of the earth. I needed a ship that would go out to sea because there the water is deep, deeper than the hemmed-in rivers that I could easily reach by foot. I wanted the deepest water because I wanted to slip into it and allow the moon's reflection to swallow me whole" (250). Self-dissolution would extinguish both desire and need and allow him to survive. That he reaches land aboard ship surprises him; without his shipmate, Bāo, and their intimate relationship, it is clear Binh would not have survived. That Bāo steals from Binh—this man, who "if he had only asked, I would have given this man of my own free will my mother's gold, my father's skin, my brother's hands, and all the bones that float loose in this body of mine now that he has gone" (242)—is an "unsatisfying and unbearable ending, I know. That is why the saga of the red pouch [holding my mother's gold], for me, never ends there on the docks of Marseilles: Bāo the sailor whose name means 'storm,' traveled the seven seas in seven months, returning eventually to the familiar embrace of the Mekong" (242). There is no moral judgment issuing from Binh, no indictment of Bāo. Binh's desire never ends, and in that perdurance resides hope for a world in which the fictionality of self-coherence can give way to the radical relationality he longs for.

His "Sweet Sunday Man," Lattimore, an African American sometime-expatriate lover, too, betrays Binh, by inducing him to steal one of Gertrude-Stein's manuscripts and abandoning Binh in the aftermath. "Choose something from the middle, you tell me. No one ever remembers what happens there. 'No.' 'Bee, they'll never even notice.' 'No'" (208–9). A long internal monologue, a plea to be asked for something else follows, formed as an explanation of the ways that The Steins sustain him not only by providing housing and wages, but because they recognize as well as appreciate the food that he prepares ("Do you understand, Sweet Sunday Man?"). Binh recognizes the request as an inducement to betrayal: "The infidelity, the betrayal, the savagery of it, even I am not capable of it, Sweet Sunday Man" (212). Immediately following that proclamation, Sweet Sunday Man moves the matter from affect to the economy of exchange, which, in the end, for Binh, turn out to be one and the same:

> "Bee, what about a photograph?"
> "Yes," I nod, acknowledging my childlike wish for an image of you and me.
> "We'll do it. We'll go to Lené Studio and have our photograph taken, once you . . ."
> An even exchange. A fair trade. A give for a take. I have played this game before, I think. (212, ellipsis original)

Once incorporated into this exchange economy, Binh finds he is capable of theft and infidelity, the promise of enduring connection—of love, perhaps—overwriting his need for security. A willful naivete ("childlike wish") comes into play, as Binh declaims "an even exchange" and a "fair trade," actively ignoring the differential material circumstances and impact of the act. Truong registers, too, the disruptive effects of commodity fetishism (Lattimore's obsession with the manuscript) to the possibilities of solidarity and community among racialized and colonized subjects.

The photograph for which Binh commits theft in the end remains uncollected. The image records Binh and Sweet Sunday Man, but is only half paid for, Lattimore having absconded with the manuscript despite his promise to the contrary, and Binh finds himself distracted by and drawn to another image, one of a stranger once encountered on a bridge, a fellow countryman (257). The man in the photograph, identified as Nguyen Ai Quoc, one of Ho Chi Minh's pseudonyms, draws Binh to him.

I would rather save my money, the sweat of my labor, for the man on the bridge . . . I thought. . . . Clever, I again thought. "Nguyen Ai Quoc" was obviously not the name with which the man on the bridge was brought into this world . . . The giveaway . . . was the combination "Ai Quoc." By itself, the words mean "love" and "country" in that order, but when conjoined they mean "patriot." Certainly a fine name for a traveler to adopt, I thought, a traveler whose heart has wisely never left home. (247)

The photograph of Binh and Lattimore, uncollected, remains an image rather than a document; its evidentiary weight remains unclaimed, and the desire for such formal documentation—proof of existence in the form of visual record—dissipates. The other, of Nguyen Ai Quoc, bespeaks the world made through colonialism and struggle for independence, a world of networks and unexpected arrivals and encounters, overlaid by economic exchange but never reducible to it. Indeed, Binh stays in Paris because, after sharing a day, a meal with the man on the bridge, Binh believes that "it was a city where something akin to love had happened, and it was a city where it could happen again" (258).

Nguyen Ai Quoc, who would become the prime minister and president of the Democratic Republic of Vietnam and whose government will lead to independence from France in 1954, anticipates liberation and figures a renewed possibility of home. Binh cannot in the time setting of the novel know the role that Ho Chi Minh will play in the years to come, but the reader cannot but flash into the magnitude of history that the man on the bridge prefigures. It is by staging this encounter between Binh and Nguyen, and by leaving us at the novel's close with the potentiality, both affective and world changing, that the merging of underclass, queer desires together with liberation from empire implies, that Truong leaves us, finally, with hope, but a kind of hope that is not uplifting so much as tethered to an unchosen state of aloneness: "'What keeps you here?' I hear a voice asking. Your question, just your desire to know my answer, keeps me, is my response. In the dark, I see you smile. I look up instinctually, as if someone has called out my name" (261). Desire sustains; desir*ing*, that self-dissolving sense of consubstantiality, affords the occupation of the position of both the desiring subject and the object of desire.

While Truong's novel tells the tale of colonialism's globalizing impact in terms of queer desire and turbulent unhomed mobility, it also identifies, through Má, Binh's mother, gendered domesticity itself as a site of the global. It is Má from whom Binh learns that kitchens can be sanctuaries from violence; it is the one place that the Old Man, her husband, will never enter. It is Má who teaches Binh the basic skills of cooking as she teaches him also the ability of storytelling to speak of errant desires—the stories of the "scholar-prince," he says, who will "rescue me from my life of drudgery and labor and embrace me. . . . I am filled with these stories. My mother fed them to me as we worked side by side" (80). It is the "steady rhythm to our movements that I still carry with me, a dream to lull me to sleep" (80), and it is Má who gives over her carefully saved escape pouch of money and of dreams when Binh is cast out of his home. Binh imagines—or reports; like so much in the novel, fiction and factuality blur—that Má's illicit affair with a temporary schoolteacher is the grounds of his birth; that he is the child of love rather than the distinctly patriarchal marriage between Má and the Old Man. Binh is Má's inexact double; she stays because she must, because she had been born into obedience, and because of her own mother's impoverishment, she is transferred to the Old Man in an act of pure economic rationalism. The labor of women, affective and economic, grounds potentiality. And not only mobility, but also confinement, remembers Truong, bespeaks the production of the modern world.

We can, by following Truong, give aesthetic texture to colonial modernity and see in it the ways that it fails to eradicate queerness, to discipline desire successfully, exhaustively, or, relatedly, to capture the underclass, the disidentified, the queer, the exiled. She makes these histories and movements sensible through her doubled aesthetics: Truong not only thematizes taste in *The Book of Salt* but aestheticizes aesthetics themselves in her rendering of Binh and The Steins. We may take from her work this practice of creating sense and sensibility out of aesthetics, of understanding aesthetics as operating in, and issuing out of, other sensibilities, always relational, infinitely present. This is, finally, an illiberal humanist practice, one that is outward facing and open to difference, relation, the in-finite.

An Illiberal University?

The insight Truong provides as to how we may go about disarranging compartmentalized knowledge protocols—namely, by pursuing archaeological methods unbound by the geographies and temporalities of modernity/

coloniality—does not, of course, lead directly to dis- and rearranging configurations of knowledge capable of bringing to bear the range of knowledge and ways of knowing and being I've referred to as afforded by illiberal humanisms. Indeed, given the stultifying inclinations of institutionality, I'm uncertain that the university can be remade to proliferate knowledge of the coloniality that underpins modernity, that illiberal humanisms can give rise to institutionalized forms of knowledge that remain undisciplined, disidentified, queer, and nonaligned with the seductions of capital and power. But such uncertainty, and the foreclosures on life and living that are associated with its production, do not strike me as reasons for resignation. Instead, I understand them to be conditions precipitating not only the need but the desire to inhabit the university in ways that hold open the possibility for justice, that create space for relationality to emerge, for entanglement to be revealed, for the refutation and displacement of the contracted, impoverished humanism of liberalism, for engendering encounters and un/learning toward these ends. These are simply the conditions that require work.

In these ways, illiberal humanisms suggest that we mis-take the university and use it as a means of unsettling the very grounds upon which it stands; that we mis-take the enjoinders to expertise and compartmentalized knowledge crystallized in seemingly discrete fields distributed across the naturalized geographies and temporalities of modernity, and work archaeologically to uncover the relationality and desires they obscure; that, finally, we take care not to mistake the university itself as the horizon for our work, our efforts, but rather insistently remember the project of remaking the world writ large. In this regard, an illiberal university must remain a question, a marker of a striving for the realization of a radically different world, one not dominated or secured by the aesthetics of racial capitalist modernity, but instead organized by the principles of uncontingent care and radical relationality brought forward by illiberal humanisms.

Conclusion

On the Humanities "After Man"

I have tried to show here that illiberal humanisms elucidate pedagogies and practices oriented toward the proliferation of onto-epistemologies and sensibilities disidentified from liberalism. In this way, they generate a materially grounded vision of the humanities that eschews the liberal values of civic virtue and progressive Enlightenment at the core of the liberal humanities and emphasizes instead study of the conditions and structures that give meaning to the human beyond the narrow, constrained confines of its bourgeois liberal definition. In this regard, this project responds to the manifold calls for the defense of the humanities characterizing contemporary popular and academic discourses. This book observes the difficulty of standing in defense of the humanities from the position of those for whom the humanities have long been a site of contestation in the struggle to make the academy, and through it, the world, not merely hospitable to but in fact organized around heretofore subjugated ways of knowing and being. I've suggested that if we consider critically just what it is we are being enjoined to defend, the history of the humanities' participation in the establishment and maintenance of the social hierarchies that distribute life chances differentially along the intersecting axes of race, gender, class, sexuality, and so on come to the fore. In the face of the impossibility of defending such a humanities, I've proposed to call attention to its histories and organizing politics in order to foster the emergence of different, defensible practices and arrangements of knowledge.

The stakes in posing and addressing such questions are in part located to the current condition of the U.S. academy. The rhetoric of the need to defend the humanities unfolds in concert with the pervasive rhetoric that posits the crisis of the university, both streams of thought pressing us to recognize that the university serves as a flashpoint for debate regarding broad social conditions. Intensive defunding of public higher education and related privatization is accompanied by high student debt and uncertain job prospects confronting graduates. The democratizing vision and function of education characterizing the post–World War II era has all but collapsed. What is the future of the university? And do the humanities have a place in it?

A related set of questions emerges from recognition of the ways that the combined and related forces of institutionalization and corporatization have mitigated the inaugural transformative energies and aims of politically engaged intellectual formations like ethnic studies and women's studies in the U.S. academy. The translation of radical difference into diversity accompanying the rise of the neoliberal corporate university has been well established. Can the university be mobilized toward redressing social inequality given contemporary conditions and, if so, how? What are the horizons of critical discourse organized around the redress of material inequality given the clear limitations of inclusion through incorporation as a means of effecting institutional and social transformation?

The Difference Aesthetics Makes has tried to address these interrelated issues—the rhetoric of defense and crisis, the contemporary condition of the university, the problem of the future and the place of the humanities, the role and transformative potential of politically engaged discourse—by mounting a critique of bourgeois liberal humanism as it pervades and organizes both the humanities and the relationship of minoritized difference to the U.S. university. This book has unfolded as a proposition to recognize both the injurious difference accompanying and advanced by aesthetics of liberal humanism, and the difference the aesthetics of illiberal humanisms makes to the work of social transformation.

By pointing to matters of sense and sensibility inhering in knowledge production, I have been trying in this book to elaborate a mode of engaging the contemporary situation of the humanities without recourse to either defensiveness or resignation. At the core of that mode is aesthetic inquiry, a form of address defined by a deliberate openness to disidentification and defamiliarization. While impossible intentionally to produce the experience of aesthetic encounter in the strict sense of staging an unexpected meeting with difference so as to provoke the experience of the extraordinary, it is,

I have suggested, both possible and necessary to inhabit and mobilize deliberately the edge of critical praxis—the meeting point of what is given as knowledge and that which challenges knowledge by persistently bringing to bear its inexhaustiveness and interestedness. Aesthetic inquiry stresses the partiality of knowledge and pays heed to the production of both common and disidentified sensibilities and their corollary rationalities. Coupled with the historicization of the humanities to acknowledge their long-lived contribution to the advancement of the variegated violence attending the establishment and sustenance of liberal/colonial modernity as the dominant (dominating) world historical model, this book intends to show how aesthetic inquiry elucidates suppressed ways of knowing and being and elicits illumination of the conditions and processes of subordination.

Illiberal humanisms teach us not to dwell in crisis or to accept commonsense explanations of their causes. Instead, they provide ways of being and knowing that remember the histories of violent subjugation subtending the modern world and its governing sensibilities. They ask us to take note of how such histories are aestheticized, made beautiful, reasonable, and acceptable, and at whose expense, and to work against the ways the received humanities and arrangements of knowledge support and legitimize such sensibilities, such aesthetics. They speak of desire, want, and wanting, and bring to bear a sense of the in-finite that comes of recognizing humanity beyond the constraints of liberalism.

I began this book by defining a "we" as those committed to the minoritarian project of mobilizing knowledge to transform the social field by, in part, attending to the arrangements and practices of knowledge production. Let me restate that now to ask: Who are we after Man? A "we" constituted by the writers/artists/theorists/critics grounding this book's discussions rewrites distance and difference in ways that, in Monique Truong's words expressed by Binh, "spirals me away and then brings me rushing home again." We are simultaneously of and not of; not one, not two, not same, not different; we are Relation, in-finite; we are being singular plural; we are of blackness and brownness, of queerness and radical alterity. We "agree not merely to the right to difference but, carrying this further, agree also to the right to opacity that is not enclosure within an impenetrable autarchy but subsistence within an irreducible singularity."[1] We are illiberal, decolonial, literary, incommensurate, and incommensurable. We acknowledge the great friction that comes of being "we" in a world still dominated by the demand to be understood and to understand each other as autonomous, discrete, individual(ist); we undertake the difficult work that comes of confronting openly and impolitically the complicity and compromise that situates us differentially in relation within the hierarchies of knowledge, of power, of the social. We undertake to make freedom meaningful and delinked from subjugation; to write self-determination from a stance in which the self is already radically illiberal, indigenous, decolonial; to write truth in ways that defunction the aestheticization of anti-Black violence and the inducement to capital that operates through the production and regulation of sex-gender in its interarticulation with racialization. We understand the nation and citizenship and bourgeois liberal democracy as categories and philosophies through which death is civilized, through which we are asked to kill as well as die on its behalf. We are entangled particles; we are matter; we matter.

A vast mandate arises from this "we," a mandate to face outward and confront the totality of the world, not as omniscient subjects but as entangled beings, and to remake the university, the humanities, from that view. This "we" is not a category of identity; it is a prompt to tune into and elucidate a grammar—rules of enunciation and organization and legitimacy—unbound to the received legacies of liberal modernity. We are the difference aesthetics makes, the difference aesthetics has made; we are the human, the humanities, after Man.

Postscript

The points of departure and inspiration constellating in the thoughts offered in this book are many and various. One that I have yet to note is how this project follows from *Imagine Otherwise: On Asian Americanist Critique*, published well over a decade ago. In it, I argued that Asian Americanist critique might conceive itself as subjectless in an act of strategic antiessentialism, in order that it might be defined not by the identity of its subject but instead as an epistemological and political project. Soon after its publication, I was asked two questions that, along with the encounters with the writing and artwork with which I've been concerned in the foregoing pages, provoked what became this project. The first of these was, if we take away the subject of Asian American studies, what are we left with? I understood this question to be both literal (why Asian American studies without the Asian American subject? To which my response was and continues to be, because tracing Asian racialization—the production of "Asian American" as a political and social and racial identity—illuminates the social, cultural, and political economic field in ways that cannot be done without doing so) and a comment on the ways that my argument had focused on dismantling without providing a sufficient alternative in the affirmative. It was, in short, a question about negation. The interest of *The Difference Aesthetics Makes* in providing such an alternative—hence the nomination of illiberal humanism and humanities—is in a way an albeit belated response.

The second question was, how might I visualize Asian American studies as subjectless? Sarah Sze's work, which graces the cover of that first book, immediately came to mind. Let me explain by way of briefly discussing another of her installations, one that has shaped the imaginary within which the present book was written. *Triple Point of Water*, an art installation by Sze, used to inhabit part of a courtyard of the Whitney Museum of American Art when it was located at Seventy-Fifth Street and Madison Avenue in New York City, and has for me long modeled the construction of a critical imaginary attuned to globalization.[1]

POSTSCRIPT.1 Sarah Sze, *Triple Point of Water*, 2003. Mixed media, dimensions variable. Courtesy of Tanya Bonakdar Gallery and Victoria Miro Gallery. © Sarah Sze.

By looking over the wall of the courtyard, one could see plants and orderly bottles of water, arranged irregularly on discontinuous landings of multiple heights, which were supported by PVC piping and interspersed with fish tanks and both live and fabricated foliage. This work could also be experienced by going into the museum and becoming a part of it for a while: one could step under, and into, and back from, each portion, each tableau. Perspective changed from the narrow unit (the single bottle, the specific tank) to a wider view depending on the position of the viewer; the piece enacted the impossibility of totality from a static position. The materials Sze used repetitively are mass produced and generic—PVC pipes, water bottles, even the fish tanks—yet the foliage, found emerging in unexpected angles, implied change, unpredictability, and tenacity—much like the water of the piece's title. The "triple point of water" refers to a state of equilibrium from which water can take liquid, solid, or gaseous form; it in this sense is a reference to both history and possibility—of all that allowed for its installation and location, and of that which may come from its encounter. The laboriousness of construction evident in the installation echoes the labor of industrial mass production, while its location in the courtyard, below street level, invokes underlying histories. What lies beneath the surface? What human activity produces this site, this art, as such? On whose labor does the Whitney, do the materials of art, rely?

I find *Triple Point of Water*, like Sze's work generally, helpful in reflecting on whether and how our work can elicit subjects not only equipped with the historical knowledge of people and labor, of colonialism and capital, subtending any given object—and perhaps especially those that appear, like her installation, politically neutral—but also, and perhaps more importantly, oriented toward the desire to garner such knowledge, in part because it is regularly installed in institutions like the Whitney, ones that bear more than a passing resemblance to universities in their social status and imprimatur as purveyors of culture. The Whitney Museum of American Art moved to its Upper East Side location in 1966. It was founded in lower Manhattan at the beginning of the twentieth century, largely through the efforts of Gertrude Vanderbilt Whitney, whose marriage to Harry Payne Whitney joined the fortunes of the Vanderbilts, amassed through profits from commercial transportation in the nineteenth century, and the Whitneys, whose wealth accumulated following Eli Whitney's invention of the cotton gin in 1839. Manhattan, the island on which people of the Lenape nation lived through the 1600s, became New York when the British took over control of the land from the Dutch, who claimed it as property from the Lenape. The Dutch East Indies Company's global network of trade established the context for the encounters between Europeans and the Lenape, and later, fear of Indians motivated the construction of Wall Street by the labor of enslaved Africans in the early 1600s. In very brief form, this interarticulation of conquest and dispossession, enslaved labor and global capital, underlies and is evoked by Sze's installation in the Whitney Museum. For, in making art out of mass-produced objects, by thematizing linkages among unlike objects, and by highlighting the recruitment of nature toward the ends of human endeavor, Sze points to the ways that what is given as art contains and is enabled by a foundational worldliness of violence and violation. In a sense, it is this sensibility, this aesthetic, that I have tried to convey in this book.

This project of elucidating entanglements toward the ends of ameliorating violence and suffering advanced by racial capitalism and colonialism is, I believe, a project of distinctive importance for Asian Americanists in the current conjuncture. We know that the form Asiatic racialization in the U.S. context has taken has been over and against the production of both White and other racial and Indigenous categories of identity. Critiques of model minority discourse, largely mounted by Asian Americanists, have resoundingly demonstrated this process and its effects. Certainly, the ascription of model qualities to Asian Americans obscures the wide-ranging heterogeneity indicated by, for example, the histories and experiences of refugees from the U.S. wars in Southeast Asia, or undocumented migrants—largely women—working in factories and in the informal care industries, in contrast to the largely highly educated, middle-class immigrants of the post-1965 Immigration and Naturalization Act.[2] At the same time, it also describes those who aspire to assimilate to the bourgeois ideals of hegemonic U.S. culture and politics. The model minority construct, in other words, not only tells us how Asian Americans are made to service racial capitalism by assigning differential capacities to minoritized groups, but also compels us to attend to how those racialized as Asians have cathected to bourgeois ideals such that many of us are now regularly a part of the machinery of hegemonic social reproduction: it is the case that significant numbers of those of us racialized as Asian American have increasingly organized and defined our lives and communities in terms of socioeconomic success, which is regularly defined in terms of credentials from the most prominent colleges and universities.[3] Especially in the era of the Knowledge Economy, which, as I've discussed in this book, features the commodification of innovation and amplifies the role of the university in the global economic scene, that Asian Americanist critique must redouble its efforts to interrogate the university's role in social stratification is readily apparent.

I hope *The Difference Aesthetics Makes* contributes to such an effort. In this regard, it is (not) an Asian Americanist work—that is, it is deeply informed by the study of Asian racialization in the United States but tries, at least, not to be led or bound by the administrative rubric of Asian American studies. Critical promiscuity is a leverage, I believe, against the seductions of institutionalization—a final proposition with which I close this book.

Notes

Introduction

1. Briefly, we may recall that the Renaissance-era renovation of education from the practical scholasticism of the medieval era to the cultivation of intellectual capacity marks a sea change in the constitution and orientation of higher education, especially with regard to the place and position of the human as object of study and politics. Across this shift, *studia humanitatis* became established as a (perhaps *the*) measure of cultivation and the erudition necessary to fulfill the promise of humanity. This held true in and through the eighteenth- and nineteenth-century Western European bourgeois revolutions that ushered in the constellation of the structures and social formations of Modernity, as humanities education was tasked with refining the liberal subject established and naturalized through the Enlightenment and post-Enlightenment eras. Rehearsals of this history are found in Wynter, "On Disenchanting Discourse"; Graff, *Professing Literature*; Harpham, *The Humanities and the Dream of America*; Marcus, "Humanities from Classics to Culture Studies"; Menand, *The Marketplace of Ideas*; Oakley, *Community of Learning*; Mignolo, "Geopolitics of Knowledge"; Mignolo, "Epistemic Disobedience." On the medieval university, see Kibre, *Scholarly Privileges*.

2. Wynter, "On Disenchanting Discourse," 434.

3. Wynter, "On Disenchanting Discourse," 433.

4. Wynter, "On Disenchanting Discourse," 433 (emphasis original).

5. This project in this regard aligns with Gayatri Spivak's effort in *Death of a Discipline* to articulate a form of collectivity that embraces difference—what she calls "planetarity"—through "*telepoiesis*," Jacques Derrida's term for the bringing into being of what remains at a distance (tele-). It may also be seen in Armstrong's terms as taking the deconstructive critique of aesthetic inquiry as a point of departure rather than as conclusion (*The Radical Aesthetic*, 2).

6. Ferguson and Hong, *Strange Affinities*.

7. Hall, "Cultural Studies," 60.

8. Hall, "Cultural Studies," 60. As Williams describes in *Marxism and Literature*, his position at that time "can be briefly described as *cultural materialism*: a theory of the specificities of material cultural and literary production within historical materialism" (5).

9. Strathern, "'Improving Ratings,'" quoted in de Bary, "Introduction," 7.

10. Quoted in de Bary, "Introduction," 7.

11. See Harney and Moten, *Undercommons*; Goh, "A Presentiment of the Death of Intellectuals"; and Ko, "How an 'Intellectual Commune' Organizes Movement."

12. The special issue of *Traces: A Multilingual Series of Cultural Theory and Translation*, "Universities in Translation: The Mental Labor of Globalization," edited by Brett de Bary, provides clarifying analyses of the relationship of the Knowledge Economy to both the contemporary situation of the university on a global scale and the particular forms of mental labor elicited within it. In that volume, see especially de Bary, "Introduction"; Lii, "Articulation, Not Translation"; Morris, "On English as a Chinese Language"; and Boutang, "Cognitive Capitalism." See also the essays collected in Douglass, King, and Feller, *Globalization's Muse*; and Altbach and Umakoshi, *Asian Universities*. Sheila Slaughter and Larry L. Leslie provide a book-length study of the impact of global economic policies on higher education in the United States, the United Kingdom, Australia, and Canada (*Academic Capitalism*).

13. See Altbach and Umakoshi, *Asian Universities*, on "massification."

14. More than forty schools now have branches outside of the United States. See Institute for International Education, *Open Doors*.

15. For example, Baruch College, one of the institutions in the City University of New York system in which I work, in its *Global Strategic Plan 2015–2019* explains, "As the world becomes increasingly globalized, we want to build on our intrinsic diversity . . . so our graduates may be more international and inclusive, and better prepared for the world that awaits them" (https://www.baruch.cuny.edu/globalinitiatives/).

16. See Bourdieu, *Distinction*, for an elaboration of these dynamics.

17. Some forty-eight land grant colleges and universities were established by the 1862 Act, and seventeen HBCUs by the 1890 iteration. Staley, "Democratizing American Higher Education."

18. Dunbar-Ortiz, *An Indigenous Peoples' History*, 142. Dunbar-Ortiz explains that the Homestead Act, the Morrill Act, and the Pacific Railroad Act were not only illegal in breaking treaties with Indigenous nations, but also vital to the consolidation of national territory: "Most of the western territories, including Colorado, North and South Dakota, Montana, Washington, Idaho, Wyoming, Utah, New Mexico, and Arizona, were delayed in achieving statehood, because Indigenous nations resisted appropriation of their lands and outnumbered settlers. So the colonization plan for the West established during the Civil War was carried out over the following decades of war and land grabs" (141).

19. Berlant, "Affect and the Politics of Austerity."

20. Berlant, "Affect and the Politics of Austerity."

21. These include Great Britain's 1988 Education Reform Act, Japan's University Incorporation Bill of 2003, and Korea's 2005 "Basic Plan for Developing National Universities." As Brett de Bary summarizes, "the adoption of New Management Reforms in higher education by governments around the world must be seen as continuous with the epochal reorganization of social and economic life inaugurated by the emergence of neoliberalism in 1979–80" ("Introduction," 5).

22. According to the National Center for Educational Statistics, in 2015, there were some 4,627 "Title IV–eligible" (federal financial aid eligible) colleges and universities in the United States, a decline of some one hundred such institutions since 2010. Of this total, 3,011 are four-year schools and 1,616 are two-year schools (Digest of Education Statistics, Table 317.10, https://nces.ed.gov/programs/digest/d15/tables/dt15_317.10.asp). In 2010, about 5.7 percent of the total U.S. population, or 21 million students, were enrolled in tertiary education. The U.S. Census Bureau reports that in 2016, 59 percent of adults in the U.S. had completed some college or more, while only a third held a bachelor's degree. Some 12 percent, according to its figures, had earned post-baccalaureate degrees (see Ryan and Bauman, *Educational Attainment in the United States*). There are some 1.6 million professors in degree-granting postsecondary institutions, with slightly more than half (52 percent) full-time and the rest part-time faculty members (National Center for Educational Statistics, "Fast Facts," 2017, https://nces.ed.gov/fastfacts/display.asp?id=61).

23. See Newfield, *Ivy and Industry*; and Newfield, *Unmaking the Public University*, for extensive analyses of these processes.

24. See Ferguson, *The Reorder of Things*; and Ferguson, *We Demand*.

25. See Berlant, "Affect and the Politics of Austerity."

26. Wilder, *Ebony and Ivy*, 11.

27. See Solomon, *In the Company of Educated Women*; Jacobs, "Gender Inequality and Higher Education"; Thelin, *A History of American Higher Education*.

28. Lowe, *Immigrant Acts*, 41.

29. Lowe, *Immigrant Acts*, 41.

30. Ferguson, *The Reorder of Things*.

31. See Chow, "Theory, Area Studies, Cultural Studies"; and Lee, *Life and Times of Cultural Studies* for helpful critical histories of the emergence of cultural studies. Womack, "A Single Decade," rehearses the relationship between Native literary studies and cultural studies in ways that punctuate the affordances and challenges of the latter in relation to the establishment of the former. See also Carby, *Cultures in Babylon*, for multifaceted discussions of the particular form cultural studies takes in the U.S.

context, namely, largely without strong engagement with class relations and social structures.

32. As Sue-Im Lee concisely captures, "As with scholarship in many other minority literatures, the emergence and growth of Asian American literary criticism in the larger sphere of American literary studies has depended upon its ability to represent the material realities of its marginalized constituents" ("Introduction," 1). Lee is one of the editors of *Literary Gestures*, the first collection of essays to engage aesthetics per se in Asian American literary studies. Dorothy Wang's *Thinking Its Presence* insightfully examines such matters contemporarily in relation specifically to poetry; see also Palumbo-Liu, "The Occupation of Form"; and Chiang, "Capitalizing Form," for more on the question of literature and literary history's meaningfulness in the contemporary era. For a sampling of other critical works since the 1990s that are similarly engaged with such issues, see, e.g., Elliott, Caton, and Rhyne, *Aesthetics in a Multicultural Age*; Levine, *Aesthetics and Ideology*; Eagleton, *The Ideology of the Aesthetic*; Hein and Korsmeyer, *Aesthetics in Feminist Perspective*; and the 2004 special issue of *American Literature*, Castiglia and Castronovo, "Aesthetics and the End(s) of Cultural Studies."

33. On this point, see the essays collected in and especially the introduction to Palumbo-Liu, *The Ethnic Canon*; Wall, "On Freedom and the Will to Adorn"; as well as Armstrong, *The Radical Aesthetic*; and Redfield, *The Politics of Aesthetics*.

34. See Berlant, *Cruel Optimism*, on the link between aesthetics and our ability to live within as well as to apprehend the present and its material and affective demands and conditions.

35. As Terry Eagleton puts it, "Anyone who inspects the history of European philosophy since the Enlightenment must be struck by the curiously high priority assigned by it to aesthetic questions" (*The Ideology of the Aesthetic*, 1). The centrality of the aesthetic to such intellectual traditions makes it difficult to summarize its position in the disparate kinds of work in which it finds expression. But a representative sampling is suggestive of its range and historical potency. One could start with Kant, for example, who is arguably at the center of the eighteenth-century European—and more specifically, German—efforts to address the problem of human subjectivity; *Critique of Judgment* (1790) is commonly held to be the text foundational to modern philosophical aesthetics. The pleasure associated with aesthetic encounter, and conceptualized as thoroughly subjective and thus inapposite as a principle upon which philosophical inquiry could be based, could be neither ignored nor subsumed into metaphysics or ethics, the branches of philosophy respectively announced in Kant's earlier treatises, *Critique of Pure Reason* (1781) and *Critique of Practical Reason* (1788). If these prior critiques had posited the principles—the a priori conditions—for making what for Kant were universally valid, objective, and moral judgments, the third *Critique* investigated what a priori conditions exist that make possible judgments of taste, specified as the ability to recognize beauty. (*Critique of Judgment* begins with a section titled "The Analytic of the Beautiful.") Eagleton provides an overview of, especially, the significance

of the aesthetic to the German idealist tradition in *The Ideology of the Aesthetic*. See also Levine's introduction to *Aesthetics and Ideology* for a discussion of the English and specifically literary genealogy of aesthetics; and Badiou, *Handbook of Inaesthetics*, for consideration of major schema from the classical period to the contemporary, by which art has been philosophically defined.

36. See Eze, "The Color of Reason"; and Brown, *The Primitive, the Aesthetic, and the Savage*, for overview of this history; see Lloyd, "Race under Representation," for discussion of the irremediably racial quality of modern aesthetic subjectivity. Jon M. Mikkelsen has collected and translated into English Kant's writings that more explicitly produce racial difference in *Kant and the Concept of Race*. See also Asad, "On Torture"; Asad, "What Do Human Rights Do?"; Weheliye, *Habeas Viscus*; and the various works of Mignolo and Wynter, for expansive critical engagement with humanism and its relationship to racial colonial modernity. The essays collected in Nuttall, *Beautiful Ugly*, illuminate the stakes of aesthetic philosophy from a specifically African-centered ground.

37. Andrew Bowie notes that Descartes's seventeenth-century "ego cogito ergo sum" prepares the way for this new philosophy to take hold in the eighteenth century; the distinction between Descartes and Kant, as exemplary eighteenth-century philosopher, lies in the latter's turn away from the former's reliance "upon God to guarantee the connection of ourselves to the order of the universe" (*Aesthetics and Subjectivity*, 1–2). Perhaps most immediately, see Spivak's *Critique of Postcolonial Reason* for an extended and extensive consideration of the role of reason in the production of the colonial world order; and Wynter, various.

38. See Schmidt, *What Is Enlightenment?*, for discussion of eighteenth-century debates and current responses to them. See also Baker and Reill, *What's Left of Enlightenment?*

39. For Friedrich Schiller, the "aesthetic education of man" was necessary for the elevation of mankind. Writing in 1794, in the aftermath of the French Revolution, Schiller, who was dismayed by the violence and the forms of governance that followed the revolution, submitted that it was only through the arts (through engagement with beauty) that man could encounter true knowledge. In *Eros and Civilization*, Herbert Marcuse takes up Schiller's concept of the *Spieltrieb*, or "play-drive," that is a utopic space of freedom.

40. Foucault, *The Order of Things*.

41. Marc Redfield provides an incisive summary:

> Without question, a utopian sublimation of historical contingency into form constitutes the telos of aesthetic discourse, but much of the political force of aesthetics resides in its historicism, in its projection of a temporal line running from the primitive to the modern, and then onward to a futurity, an ever-deferred end of history, that aesthetic experience prefigures. Acculturated subjects, actualizing

their human potential in aesthetic judgment, become capable of representing the less acculturated both in an aesthetic and political sense precisely because the difference between representative and represented has a temporal dimension. Someday, humanity will achieve itself as a national, and in the end, global subject; in the meantime, an acculturated minority speaks for the collective. (*The Politics of Aesthetics*, 12)

42. See, as prime example, Kant's 1775 "On the Different Races of Man." For extensive contemporary commentary on racism in Kantian thought, see Eze, "The Color of Reason."

43. "Biocentricity" is a term Wynter uses across her work. For an exemplary discussion, see David Scott, "The Re-Enchantment of Humanism."

44. As Srinivas Aravamudan's *Enlightenment Orientalism* shows, for example, a study of the figure of the Orient in the expressive cultural media of the era suggests both the pervasive presence of Asian figurations and a corollary uncertainty as to the geographic and cultural boundaries of Western subjectivity. See also Muthu, *Enlightenment against Empire*.

45. Lloyd, "Race under Representation."

46. This obviously condenses large swaths of history. I refer interested readers to work from a variety of intellectual traditions, including that by Giovanni Arrighi, Wendy Brown, Susan Buck-Morss, Judith Butler, Lisa Duggan, Michel Foucault, Simon Gikandi, David Harvey, Lisa Lowe, Uday Singh Mehta, Walter Mignolo, Cedric Robinson, Gayatri Spivak, and Sylvia Wynter.

47. As George Lipsitz observes in *The Possessive Investment in Whiteness*, Kant, for instance, believed in "fundamental differences in the rational capacities of blacks and whites" (177), a belief that animates the constative properties of aesthetic philosophy in instituting racial difference as part of the modern project. For more of this history, see the works cited in note 36 above.

48. Claire Colebrook points out that Nietzsche's privileging of youth bespeaks his emphasis on becoming ("Queer Aesthetics"). Becoming in this tradition is closely linked to becoming-beautiful, that is, the connotative meaning of what it means to be becoming. There is little room or concern for the possibility of becoming unbeautiful, or distasteful. I take up these issues more fully in chapter 1.

49. The literature on globalization and neoliberalism is vast. For broad-scoping analyses of globalization and neoliberalism as capitalist modalities, see, e.g., Duggan, *The Twilight of Equality?*; Melamed, *Represent and Destroy*; Brown, *Undoing the Demos*; Stiglitz, *Globalization and Its Discontents*; Sen, *Development as Freedom*; Harvey, *A Brief History*; and Harvey, *The Enigma of Capital*. Anna Tsing's *Friction* generatively questions how we might study something called "the global."

50. Serres, *Conversations on Science, Culture, and Time*, 60, 61. Muñoz's *Cruising Utopia*; and Berlant, *Cruel Optimism*, offer rich theorizations and studies of temporality along these lines.

51. Byrd, *The Transit of Empire*.

52. Lowe, *Intimacies of Four Continents*.

53. Sharpe, *In the Wake*.

54. Muñoz, *Cruising Utopia*.

55. Indeed, works like Chandan Reddy's *Freedom with Violence* and Jodi Byrd's *The Transit of Empire* powerfully demonstrate precisely the reverse effects of modernity—that is, the devastating effects it has had and continues to have. See also the essays collected in Goldstein, *Formations of United States Colonialism*, which collectively analyze the "colonial present" (Goldstein's phrase)—that is, how "the current moment is shaped by the fraught historical accumulation and shifting disposition of colonial processes, relations, and practices" (7).

56. See Hage, *Against Paranoid Nationalism*.

57. See Hong, *The Ruptures of American Capital*, for concise discussion of U.S. exceptionalism.

58. Latour, *We Have Never Been Modern*.

59. Rancière, *The Politics of Aesthetics*, 10.

60. For Kant, judgment results from the ordering of experience under or through concepts; judgment is the thought that results from the interaction of Sensibility and Understanding, respectively, the passive capacity to be affected sensorily by things, and the active work of producing thoughts by submitting sensation to the general concepts available to the mind. Sensibility is an individual, subjective phenomenon, while Understanding involves concepts that are generally present. Thus, judgment refers to the generalization of the individual phenomenon of sensation, and takes place regularly and in quotidian settings: I see the screen in front of me and I am aware it is a computer; this is a computer. Aesthetic judgment—or what he calls the judgment of taste, which means for him the thought that something is beautiful—is a distinctive form of judgment. In the *Critique of Judgment*, in his characteristic fashion, Kant systematizes his analysis of "what is required in order to call an object beautiful" (section 1n). Aesthetic judgments differ from cognitive judgments insofar as the latter routes individual experience through a general concept (my seeing the computer screen results in my judgment that this thing is a computer), while the former redirects the experience "back to the subject and to its feeling of life, under the name of the feeling of pleasure or displeasure" (section 1). It is in this sense that aesthetic judgments are subjective rather than objective.

61. Rancière, *The Politics of Aesthetics*, 2. Thus in what he calls the "ethical regime," art is evaluated for its utilitarian effects on communal and individual ethos and is seen, in a platonic sense, as mere craft; in the "representative regime," the arts operate in a semiautonomous sphere derived through the affiliation of certain practices with artistic endeavor—the arts and artists become professionalized in the representational regime. And what Rancière calls the "aesthetic regime" is coextensive with the rise of modernity according to this schema; modernity is conceived as fundamentally aesthetic in its coordination of who and what may be seen and heard in ways that make it possible, ideally, for any individual to create work that has the potential for recognition as art (24). Rancière makes the important point that while these regimes are historically emergent, they do not wholly displace one another and function instead palimpsestically.

I don't wish to claim the validity of Rancière's periodization of these regimes. What I do find useful is that he demarcates these distinguishable ways that aesthetics, understood as structuring the condition of sense experience (of what can be apprehended as art) and thus as a condition of community (of who has the capacity to experience that experience) has continued to be fundamental to the socialities and institutions that we have commonly referred to in political or ideological terms. What I emphasize for present purposes are the ways that, in effect, the culture wars of the latter decades of the twentieth century to varying degrees of explicitness were motivated by the aesthetics of politics.

62. Aristotle, *De Anima*, book 3, sections 1–2.

63. Kant, *Critique of Judgment*, section 20. Kant explains further,

> Cognitions and judgments must, along with the conviction that accompanies them, admit of universal communicability; for otherwise there would be no harmony between them and the Object, and they would be collectively a mere subjective play of the representative powers, exactly as skepticism would have it. But if cognitions are to admit of communicability, so must also the state of mind,—*i.e.* the accordance of the cognitive powers with a cognition generally, and that proportion of them which is suitable for a representation (by which an object is given to us) in order that a cognition may be made out of it—admit of universal communicability. For without this as the subjective condition of cognition, knowledge as an effect could not arise. This actually always takes place when a given object by means of Sense excites the Imagination to collect the manifold, and the Imagination in its turn excites the Understanding to bring about a unity of this collective process in concepts. But this accordance of the cognitive powers has a different proportion according to the variety of the Objects which are given. However, it must be such that this internal relation, by which one mental faculty is excited by another, shall be generally the most beneficial for both faculties in respect of cognition (of given objects); and this accordance can only be determined by feeling (not according to concepts). Since now this accordance itself must admit of universal communicability, and consequently also our feeling of it (in a given representation), and since

the universal communicability of a feeling presupposes a common sense, we have grounds for assuming this latter. And this common sense is assumed without relying on psychological observations, but simply as the necessary condition of the universal communicability of our knowledge, which is presupposed in every Logic and in every principle of knowledge that is not sceptical. (section 21)

64. Kant's elaboration on common sense:

In all judgements by which we describe anything as beautiful, we allow no one to be of another opinion; without however grounding our judgement on concepts but only on our feeling, which we therefore place at its basis not as a private, but as a communal feeling. Now this common sense cannot be grounded on experience; for it aims at justifying judgements which contain an *ought*. It does not say that every one *will* agree with my judgement, but that he *ought*. And so common sense, as an example of whose judgement I here put forward my judgement of taste and on account of which I attribute to the latter an *exemplary* validity, is a mere ideal norm, under the supposition of which I have a right to make into a rule for every one a judgement that accords therewith, as well as the satisfaction in an Object expressed in such judgement. For the principle, which concerns the agreement of different judging persons, although only subjective, is yet assumed as subjectively universal (an Idea necessary for every one); and thus can claim universal assent (as if it were objective) provided we are sure that we have correctly subsumed [the particulars] under it. (*Critique of Judgment*, section 22)

65. Rancière, *Dis-agreement*, 29.

66. See Hinderliter et al., *Communities of Sense*, for an array of essays engaging various facets of the implications of Rancière's theorization.

1. Knowledge under Cover

1. I mean to invoke José Muñoz's theorization of disidentification. For Muñoz, disidentification eschews the options of both identification with and counteridentification against the identities imposed by normative structures. Disidentification, instead, acknowledges the inadequacy of any identity category to capture complexity, and thus marks a position and practice of at once playing with and inhabiting that which exceeds and thus reworks an individual's relationship to identity. Likewise, I use disidentification as a means of signaling the need and possibility of playing with so as to transform the received legacies of the humanities, which are at once ours and yet inexhaustibly so.

2. Melamed, *Represent and Destroy*.

3. These contemporary conditions echo the formation of higher education in its early days in the United States. Then, private colleges for privileged classes were the accepted norm. Not until the Morrill Act of 1862 did the U.S. nation associate higher education

with a public good necessary to the future well-being of its citizens, and broader access to college is largely a twentieth-century phenomenon. The data on defunding of public universities and colleges is widely available; sources include Mortensen, "State Funding"; and the Center on Budget and Policy Priorities, "State-by-State Fact Sheets."

4. See Wilder, *Ebony and Ivy*.

5. Andrew Jewett reminds us of this history: "The freedoms enjoyed by American scholars today are a direct result of the political quiescence of their Cold War–era predecessors, who tempered public fears about the radicalism of academic 'eggheads' by vigorously constructing new weapons technologies and new ideological defenses of 'the West'" ("Academic Freedom and Political Change," 265). See also Oparah, "Challenging Complicity," for analysis of the intimate link between the contemporary university and the prison-industrial complex.

6. This division is inherited as part of the Humboldtian legacy, the philosophy of which—with its emphases on public duty and nationalist interest in the development of individuals into Enlightened subjects—continues to organize the ideal if not always the practical life of universities in the United States.

7. American Council of Learned Societies, *Report of the Commission on the Humanities*, 4, 5.

8. American Council of Learned Societies, *Report of the Commission on the Humanities*, 4, 5.

9. American Council of Learned Societies, *Report of the Commission on the Humanities*, 4, 5. The report explains further of the national interest in the humanities: "Upon the humanities depend the national ethic and morality, the national aesthetic and beauty or the lack of it, the national use of our environment and our material accomplishments—each of these areas directly affects each of us as individuals. On our knowledge of men, their past and their present, depends our ability to make judgments—not least those involving our control of nature, of ourselves, and of our destiny. Is it not in the national interest that these judgments be strong and good?" (7).

10. The report takes this quotation from John Adams as its epigraph: "I must study politics and war that my son may have liberty to study mathematics and philosophy. My sons ought to study mathematics and philosophy, geography, natural history and naval architecture, navigation, commerce, and agriculture, in order to give their children a right to study painting, poetry, music, architecture."

11. See Chatterjee and Maira's coedited *The Imperial University* for discussion of the production of the "liberal class" necessary to U.S. imperial conduct in and through the university.

12. See Lowe, *Intimacies of Four Continents*, which establishes long-lived and irrevocable links among settler colonialism, liberalism, and racial capitalism.

13. See, e.g., Canaday, *Straight State*; Reddy, *Freedom with Violence*; Gilmore, *Golden Gulag*.

14. See, especially, Harpham, *The Humanities and the Dream of America*; and Wilder, *Ebony and Ivy*. See also Readings, *University in Ruins*.

15. Readers will perhaps recognize Eve Sedgwick's theorization of ignorance (*Epistemology of the Closet*) and Lauren Berlant's theorization of cruel optimism (*Cruel Optimism*) in the language and critical sensibility of this chapter. I've offered a somewhat more extended discussion of Sedgwick's theory in Chuh, "It's Not about Anything."

16. Chang, *Hunger*, 11.

17. Chang, *Hunger*, 11–12.

18. Chang, *Hunger*, 12.

19. In "Transgressions of a Model Minority," Freedman argues suggestively that Chang's narrative choices link her work genealogically to the work of such Jewish writers as Bernard Malamud.

20. Chang, *Hunger*, 106.

21. Chang, *Hunger*, 114.

22. Officially the Republic of China, founded in mainland China in 1912 and by a government that relocated to the island of Taiwan in 1949, Taiwan is a country that has witnessed serial occupation over centuries—by the Dutch, the Portuguese, the Japanese—and its relationship to the People's Republic of China remains fraught. In 1971, Taiwan ceased to be the recognized representative of China to the United Nations, replaced at that time by the People's Republic of China. Part of what Chang's story imagines is the flight of people from the mainland to the island as well as the violence of the military rule that characterized Taiwan in the post–World War II era. See Ching, *Becoming Japanese*; Chen, *Asia as Method*; see also Hillenbrand, "The National Allegory Revisited."

23. Lisa Lowe's incisive critique of the ways that generational differences between mothers and daughters in Asian American cultural work are read as matters of culture rather than an effect of narrow definitions of what constitutes authentic American culture is usefully remembered here. See Lowe, *Immigrant Acts*; Lowe, "Heterogeneity, Hybridity, Multiplicity."

24. Berlant, *Cruel Optimism*.

25. Wynter, "On Disenchanting Discourse"; Ferguson, *The Reorder of Things*.

26. Gutiérrez y Muhs et al., *Presumed Incompetent*.

27. Lloyd, "Race under Representation," 61

28. Chakrabarty, *Provincializing Europe*.

29. As Lloyd explains, "although it is possible to conceive formally of an equable process of assimilation in which the original elements are entirely equivalent, the product of assimilation will always necessarily be in an hierarchical relation to the residual, whether this be defined as, variously, the primitive, the local, or the merely contingent" ("Race under Representation," 73).

30. Melamed, *Represent and Destroy*. There is an obvious resemblance between the organization of knowledge within English and the general reliance on the field-coverage model characterizing the arrangement of knowledge in the university. Disciplinary differences realized in the administrative units of departments attest to the university as an institution organized by liberal representational politics. Indeed, even a passing familiarity with the establishment and histories of interdisciplinary fields like Asian American studies enables recognition of the mobilizing force of representational politics in the student and scholar-activist movements of the 1960s and '70s. Like the globally distributed student protests erupting currently, those earlier movements argued for access and curricular equality as part of a broad-reaching agenda for social justice. The institutionalization of the interdisciplines, to borrow Roderick Ferguson's usage, was one way in which such goals were pursued. Over the decades since, women's and gender and ethnic studies programs have emerged, albeit erratically and unevenly across the academic landscape. Increasingly and at the same time, interdisciplinarity has gained a too-facile traction within departments as well as universities such that now an institutional commitment to interdisciplinarity sometimes is nearly as hollow as the ever-popular commitment to excellence. See Ferguson, *The Reorder of Things*. See also Readings, *University in Ruins*.

31. Castiglia and Castronovo, "Aesthetics and the End(s)," 424.

32. Castiglia and Castronovo, "Aesthetics and the End(s)," 424.

33. Castiglia and Castronovo, "Aesthetics and the End(s)," 425.

34. Castiglia and Castronovo, "Aesthetics and the End(s)," 426.

35. Castiglia and Castronovo, "Aesthetics and the End(s)," 426.

36. Pease, "Doing Justice," 159. Specifically, Pease identifies *Moby-Dick* as having "provided the field itself with a frame narrative that included the norms and assumptions out of which the field was organized" (159).

37. Melville's rise to canonical status, according to David Shumway, dates to the 1930s, a period during which the positivism of literary history dominated the still institutionalizing field of American Literature (*Creating American Civilization*).

38. Gordon, *Ghostly Matters*, 187, 188.

39. Gordon, *Ghostly Matters*, 187.

40. Gordon, *Ghostly Matters*, 188.

41. Gordon, *Ghostly Matters*, 188. In the course of her rich reading of Toni Morrison's *Beloved*, which is also a call to identify the ways that the "sociological imagination" can reproduce racist epistemologies, Gordon explains in a way worth quoting at length:

> Few teachers, especially sociology teachers, reading *Beloved* today would identify with schoolteacher, the educated master. . . . The repudiation of schoolteacher registers a desire to be included in one of the very crucial political questions *Beloved* poses: How can we be accountable to people who seemingly have not counted in the historical and public record? *"'But how will you know me? How will you know me?'"* After all, the question—how can we be accountable to people who have seemingly not counted?—has been a major impetus for a range of collectively organized efforts in critical scholarship. The rejection of the master and the concomitant identification with the slaves and their descendants produce a sense of inclusivity that such a question invites. *"'Mark me, too,' I said. 'Mark the mark on me too.'"* But this desire for inclusion, which is the essential quality of sympathetic identification, is a treacherous mistake. (187; emphasis original)

Gordon continues,

> In a text as evocative and successful in creating a sociological and mythical reality as *Beloved*, it is perhaps too easy to distance ourselves from the ones who count, to disclaim this onerous inheritance by sympathetically identifying with the others or by denying any identification whatsoever. (This book is not about me.) Yet Morrison's call for accountability suggests that it is our responsibility to recognize just where we are in this story, even if we do not want to be there. She also suggests that we cannot decline to identify as if such an (albeit worthy) act can erase or transcend the sedimented power relations in which we lived then and live now. Thus we will have to contend not only with those who do not count but are counted; we will also have to contend with those who have the right to count and account for things. (188; emphasis added)

My thanks to Jack Halberstam for his timely reminder of Gordon's work on this point.

42. I have commented on such debates in Chuh, *Imagine Otherwise*.

43. Kang, "Late (Global) Capital."

44. Kang, "Late (Global) Capital," 307.

45. Kang, "Late (Global) Capital," 312. See also Lye, "Unmarked Character."

46. Incommensurability is far from a new construct. We may remember, for example, Homi Bhabha's theorization of a "third space," Dipesh Chakrabarty's emphasis on singularity, and José Muñoz's articulation of queerness and/as a critical utopia: what I have been referring to as the linked concepts of the aesthetic state, radical difference, and incommensurate subjectivity find kinship in these works. See Bhabha, *The Location of Culture*; Chakrabarty, *Provincializing Europe*; Wiegman, "Introduction"; Muñoz, *Cruising Utopia*.

47. Melas, "Versions of Incommensurability."

48. Lowe, "The Intimacies of Four Continents," 208.

49. The "aesthetic state" is a term often associated with Schiller, and specifically with Schiller's take on Kant. My own definition of the aesthetic state rejects the autonomy of the aesthetic sphere that is foundational to Schiller's view. The debates regarding the putative autonomy of the aesthetic sphere in fact function as part of an aesthetic regime insofar as they regulate the determination of art and artists.

50. Gayatri Gopinath's acute insights into Allan deSouza's work inform my considerations ("Archive, Affect"). See also Shimakawa, *National Abjection*, for theorization of abjection and racialization, to think through the implications of deSouza's use of bodily detritus.

51. Eve Oishi has described this series of deSouza's work as "depicting physical space as empty of people yet entirely sculpted by human desire" ("Painting with an Eraser," 4).

52. Cohen summarizes further:

> Responses to this question are traditionally articulated in two different registers: the physical and the spiritual. The skin is the integument that encloses the visceral interior of the body, yet it is also the membrane within which, mysteriously and ethereally, the human essence is supposed to reside. The outside surface of the body and its first line of defense against the external world, the skin is also the psychically projected shield that contains the self within. Both tactile membrane and enclosure, the skin is a permeable boundary that permits congress between inside and outside, whether that interior is conceived in material or metaphysical terms. The skin thus forms the border not only between bodily interior and exterior but also between psychical and physical conceptions of the self. As a social signifier, moreover, the color, texture, and appearance of the skin have often been presumed to testify to what resides within or beneath it. (*Embodied*, 65)

53. "Vestibularity" here evokes Hortense Spillers's disarticulation of "flesh" and "body" in the context of thinking through Blackness and chattel slavery in "Mama's Baby, Papa's Maybe."

54. Bowie, *Aesthetics and Subjectivity*, 34.

55. Bowie, *Aesthetics and Subjectivity*, 34.

56. Kant, *Critique of Judgment*, section 1.

57. Pleasure in the beautiful is distinctive because it is "a disinterested and free satisfaction; for no interest, either of sense or of reason, here forces our assent" (Kant, *Critique of Judgment*, section 2).

58. Kant, *Critique of Judgment*, section 6.

59. Kant, *Critique of Judgment*, section 8.

60. See Butler, *Gender Trouble*; Butler, *Bodies That Matter*; Spillers, "Mama's Baby, Papa's Maybe"; and Salamon, *Assuming a Body*. See also Weheliye, *Habeas Viscus*, for an extended discussion of Spillers's theorization.

61. Performance studies scholars working with gender and sex and racial difference are perhaps foremost among those who have put the body in the foreground. Scholarship under the rubric of disability studies provides salient attention to normative ideas of corporeality and embodiment subtending and reproduced by critical discourse.

62. Images of this piece are widely available. See, for example, Carrie Mae Weems, *Ain't Jokin'*, *1987–1988*, http://carriemaeweems.net/galleries/aint-jokin.html; and Artnet, http://www.artnet.com/artists/carrie-mae-weems/mirror-mirror-from-the-aint-jokin -series-v5mNygRTHypuqoIPGPqkxg2.

63. I think here also of Glenn Ligon's paintings, especially his *Ain't I a Man*. See Ligon, *Yourself in the World*. These works resonate with Fanon's primal scene of mis/recognition; Darby English's *How to See a Work of Art in Total Darkness* takes up such matters in specific relation to art; see also Jorge Cortiñas's short play, *Look, a Latino!* for his dramatic treatment of visual mis/recognition with respect to Latino racialization; and Tina Campt's work with archival photography in *Image Matters* ("The materiality of the photo secures neither its indexical accuracy nor transparency; it leads us to question it instead. It exposes our own investments in the visual as evidence and indication of such attributions [as race and affiliation]," 127). Campt suggestively also proposes that we extend the "affective sensorium [of the materiality of the photographic image] . . . to include the sonic and musical registers" (128). Xu Bing's graphic crafting of the English alphabet into Chinese character form also comes to mind as work that challenges the truth function of the visual (see Tsao and Ames, *Xu Bing and Contemporary Chinese Art*). Miriam Thaggert provides contextualization in the Harlem Renaissance (*Images of Black Modernism*). See also Judith Butler on the racist episteme ("Endangered/ Endangering"); and Susan Buck-Morss on the long reach of visuality in the execution of empire ("Visual Empire"). In brief, across a wide terrain of work and focuses, artists and scholars have continued to interrogate the epistemic reliance on the visual, especially with regard to its relationship to the production of racial knowledge.

64. I understand difference not as the opposite of identity but instead as the radical condition upon which the dialectic of identity and difference assumes form:

$$\frac{\text{dialectic of identity/difference (political)}}{\text{difference (proto-political)}}$$

65. The literature on the coemergence of literary forms and national politics is immense. See, for example, Aravamudan, *Tropicopolitans*; Lukács, *Theory of the Novel*; Bhabha, *Nation and Narration*; Doyle, *Freedom's Empire*; Gilbert and Gubar, *Madwoman in the Attic*; Lowe, *Intimacies*; and Slaughter, *Human Rights, Inc.* Recall, also, the connection between the rise in print culture and the formation of the imagined community that is the nation, posited by Benedict Anderson in *Imagined Communities*.

2. Pedagogies of Liberal Humanism

1. See Wynter, "1492: A New World View"; Wynter, "On Disenchanting Discourse"; Wynter, "Unsettling the Coloniality"; Wynter, "The Ceremony Must Be Found"; Scott, "The Re-enchantment of Humanism"; and Wynter and McKittrick, "Unparalleled Catastrophe."

2. Wynter, "On Disenchanting Discourse," 208.

3. I am reminded of Alexandra T. Vazquez's consideration of the work of anthologies, especially as to their preoccupation with documentation. Referring to their deployment and uses in Cuba and the United States, Vazquez explains that "the anthology has been an enormously effective tool in the formal and informal education of a nation's population. The form was and is a way for an editor or small consensus to make nation a cohesive entity with an agreed-upon past, a fixed present, and an imposed future. National anthologies continue to traffic in the possibilities and dangers of this is who you are and who you will become" (*Listening in Detail*, 58–59, citations omitted). Importantly, Vazquez also notes: "it would be a mistake . . . to assume that its compilers were always driven by some version of: to exist means to be read. This would reduce too many labors of love into the failed fodder of representation. Rather, some corners of the anthological enterprise were raising difficult questions about black futurity: how can reading publics be nurtured? How can little sisters be taught? How can a book offer company? What happens when survival strategies are put together in print?" (59).

4. Gilmore, *Golden Gulag*, 28.

5. Cedric Robinson's theorization of Black Studies as a critique of modernity translates to the understanding of Black Literature as a critique of liberal humanism. See Sharpe, *In the Wake*, on the depth of anti-Blackness to the constitution of U.S. modern life.

6. See Spillers, "Mama's Baby, Papa's Maybe"; see also Weheliye's enrichment of her work in *Habeas Viscus*.

7. See, e.g., Hughes, "The Negro Artist and the Racial Mountain."

8. Jacqueline Goldsby's *A Spectacular Secret* establishes the centrality of both the practice and the aesthetic of lynching to the production of U.S. national culture and politics.

9. Hartman, *Scenes of Subjection*.

10. See Reddy, *Freedom with Violence*; and Nguyen, *The Gift of Freedom*, for analyses of the constitutive centrality of violence to modern concepts and practices of freedom.

11. Moten, *In the Break*, 5.

12. As David Lloyd puts it,

> the domain of aesthetic culture provides a site of reconciliation which transcends continuing political differences and accordingly furnishes the domain of human

freedom promised in theory by bourgeois states but belied in all but form by their practices. The aesthetic domain performs this function by virtue of the fact that, while bourgeois political theory postulates the essential identity of man, aesthetic works are held to furnish the representative instances of reconciliation which at once prefigure and produce an ethical subjectivity restored to identity with this universal human essence. ("Race under Representation," 379–80)

13. See Lloyd, "Race under Representation," for an extended consideration of the relationship between canon formation and this version of humanism.

14. Moten, *In the Break*, 5.

15. Hartman, *Scenes of Subjection*.

16. Hughes, *Ways of White Folks*, 3. Subsequent citations appear as page numbers in the text.

17. Attali, *Noise*, 6.

18. The scholarship that addresses sound, both as a sensory experience and as the experience of music, similarly recognizes the distinctive potency of the sonic. See Stadler, "Never Heard Such a Thing," for analysis of the relationships among sound, racial violence, and mediation. Other astute work attending to the sonic or aural include Redmond, *Anthem*; Nancy, *Listening*; Mendieta, "The Sound of Race"; Tongson, *Relocations*; Voegelin, *Listening to Noise and Silence*; and, again, Vazquez, *Listening in Detail*; and Moten, *In the Break*.

19. Attali, *Noise*, 6.

20. See Kadosh, Henik, and Walsh, "Synaesthesia"; and Spector and Maurer, "Synesthesia."

21. See Derrida, Porter, and Morris, "The Principle of Reason," for discussion of the centrality of the eye/vision to modern epistemology.

22. Nancy summarizes helpfully: "What truly betrays music and diverts or perverts the movement of its modern history is the extent to which it is indexed to a mode of signification and not to a mode of sensibility. Or else the extent to which a signification overlays and captures a sensibility" (*Listening*, 57). See also Bowie, *Aesthetics and Subjectivity*.

23. Rancière, "Politics of Literature," 12.

24. Schematically and chronologically, this includes Plato's interest in the relationship of music to emotion (*Republic*, book 3 in particular) and Aristotle's suggestion that music is an expression of human emotion (*Politics*, book 8); Arthur Schopenhauer's assertion that music is rightly conceived of as a copy of human "will" (*The World as Will and Idea*); Eduard Hanslick's effort to isolate the purpose of music against the fashion of ascribing to it the evocation of emotion (*On the Musically Beautiful*); Adorno's

dialectical treatment of music (*Essays on Music*); and Susan K. Langer's insistence that music is "isomorphic" with emotion (*Philosophy in a New Key*).

25. Hughes, *Ways of White Folks*, 46.

26. As Jean-Luc Nancy writes, the sonorous "enlarges [form]; it gives it an amplitude, a density, and a vibration or an undulation whose outline never does anything but approach. The visual persists until its disappearance; the sonorous appears and fades away into its permanence" (*Listening*, 2).

27. If Foucault reminds us that Man is a fabricated subject of knowledge, crafted within the changing schema of academic professionalization, contemporary interest in objects and things collectively restages philosophy's pervasive concern with their specificity and foundation.

28. Moten, *In the Break*, 180.

29. Rancière, "The Politics of Literature," 12, 13.

30. Rancière, *The Politics of Aesthetics*, 24.

31. Rancière, *The Politics of Aesthetics*, 25.

32. Wynter, "On Disenchanting Discourse," 467.

33. Morrison, "Recitatif," 243.

34. Quiroga, *Tropics of Desire*, 2. Derived in part from his participatory observation of a 1993 gay pride march in Buenos Aires, for Quiroga, open masking afforded the possibility of "manifesting solidarity with the cause of civil rights for a disenfranchised minority" regardless of the particular situation of the participant (1).

35. Quiroga, *Tropics of Desire*, 80.

36. Glissant, *Poetics of Relation*, 189.

37. Morrison, "Recitatif," 249, 250.

38. Redfield concisely encapsulates: "Acculturated subjects, actualizing their human potential in aesthetic judgment, become capable of representing the less acculturated both in an aesthetic and political sense precisely because the difference between representative and represented has a temporal dimension. Someday, humanity will achieve itself as a national, and in the end, global subject; in the meantime, an acculturated minority speaks for the collective" (*The Politics of Aesthetics*, 12).

39. Goldsby, *A Spectacular Secret*, 24.

40. In *A Spectacular Secret*, Goldsby compellingly documents and analyzes the ways that newspapers and postcards, as well as the affordability and availability of photographic technologies circulated and consolidated lynching in the U.S. imagination.

3. Making Sense Otherwise

1. Lowe and Lloyd, *The Politics of Culture*; Prakash, *Another Reason*; Spivak, *An Aesthetic Education.*

2. See Berlant, *Cruel Optimism*, especially chapter 3, "Slow Death (Obesity, Sovereignty, Lateral Agency)."

3. We may recognize in this constellation of issues the effects of the will to knowledge, the assumption of mastery and privileged place of expertise as subtending the continuing hold of the logic of compartmentalized knowledge. As Judith Halberstam submits, "terms like *serious* and *rigorous* tend to be code words, in academia as well as other contexts, for disciplinary correctness; they signal a form of training and learning that confirms what is already known according to approved methods of knowing" (*The Queer Art of Failure*, 6). Arguing the embrace of failure as a mode of operating in radical distinction from these disciplinary norms and demands, Halberstam reminds us that compartmentalized knowledge is a form of policing whereby compliant subjects are compulsorily interpellated. Radically disidentified from normative demands and desires, scholarship may proceed as a "project of learning and thinking altogether" (7). I want here to turn to (to take seriously!) the "altogether" that Halberstam identifies as the plural subjectivity afforded by letting go of our attachments to the received Order of Knowledge. For it identifies and reiterates what I think of and have been describing as illiberal humanist onto-epistemologies. Or in other words, it keys us into the potentiality of bringing to bear on and in the academy a different rationality. See also Harney and Moten, *The Undercommons.*

4. See introduction.

5. We may remember in the context of the liberal mandate Kant's seminal influence on the idea of the modern university as one in which individual subjectivity could be transcended to the plane of pure Reason ungrounded by or in history. The truths of the university were to be ahistorical, and autonomy is a condition necessary for such transcendence. Kant transformed the primacy of classical Reason (the supreme faculty, following Plato and Aristotle, that would guarantee the rightness of thought and behavior) into that of rationality (*Verstand*), the terrain of Logos upon which the structures of meaning and categories of condition through which self and society could be understood and measured. Lured by the promise of emancipation through self-consciousness, this individual is utterly constrained by and within this rationality, which becomes rationalism—a doctrinaire rationality—to think himself free.

6. See Berlant, *Cruel Optimism*, on lateral sovereignty.

7. On sovereignty, see Barker, *Native Acts*; the essays collected in Barker, *Sovereignty Matters*; and Coulthard, *Red Skins, White Masks*; on colonialism's relationship to gender and sexuality, see Lugones, "Toward a Decolonial Feminism"; and Lugones, "Heterosexualism and the Colonial/Modern Gender System"; as well as Rifkin, *The Erotics of Sovereignty.*

8. Byrd, *The Transit of Empire*.

9. See, e.g., Byrd, *The Transit of Empire*; Coulthard, *Red Skins, White Masks*. The essays collected in *Theorizing Native Studies*, edited by Audra Simpson and Andrea Smith, address the relationship of Native studies to theory and collectively argue the transformation of subjects and object(ive)s of knowledge effected by Native studies scholarship—that is, the constitution of the domain of theory is itself transformed. Alyosha Goldstein's edited volume, *Formations of United States Colonialism*, offers a range of analyses of the ongoingness of coloniality; in that volume, see especially Barker, "The Specters of Recognition."

10. Criticized for publicizing through this novel rituals and stories sacred to the Laguna peoples represented in it, *Ceremony* and the critical discourse around it reminds us of how the production of knowledge vis-à-vis dominant onto-epistemologies is inextricably coupled with the violence necessary to the establishment and maintenance of modernity. See especially Gunn, "Special Problems." A substantial number of essays analyzing *Ceremony* are oriented toward showing the extent to which it accurately reflects Laguna Pueblo lifeways. It is part of the grounds and argument of this book that it is necessary to delink from such positivist modes of producing knowledge and to interrogate the will to knowledge that subtends that modality. The instrumental objectification of subjugated peoples is a problem expressed through a variety of practices, from tokenization to the spectacular exoticization and dehumanization of people exhibited for anthropological or entertainment purposes. While this ethical problem is perhaps most obvious across identity formations, it is also a general problem of research. For the production of institutionalized knowledge always already takes place within structures organized to reproduce rather than unravel social hierarchies; it takes place in the very sites that buttress the bio- and necropolitics and material inequalities that give meaning to race, gender, and indigeneity. The academic as such is never selfsame with the subject-object of inquiry, even while that subject-object cannot be understood as having an autonomous existence as a subject-object of study, that is, in nonrelation to the researcher. See Smith, *Decolonizing Methodologies*; Trinh, *Woman, Native, Other*; and Spivak, *Outside in the Teaching Machine*, for analyses of the problem of research in relation to racial and colonial otherness. This is not to suggest that there is a universal identity as an academic that enjoys an unsocial existence. It is all too apparent that differential capacities for intellectual work are assigned within the academy in ways that register the hierarchies of the social totality broadly. My point, instead, is to note that this is not a problem of identity politics, narrowly construed—a problem of who may speak for whom, or of the authenticity of representation. Rather, it is one that requires the analysis and theorization of the rationalization of knowledge.

11. See Matsunaga, "Leslie Marmon Silko and Nuclear Dissent in the American Southwest," for an extended discussion of this novel's rendering of "nuclear colonialism." On the history of nuclear toxification of Indigenous lands, see LaDuke, *All Our Relations*, ch. 5.

12. See Vizenor, *Survivance*; see also Vizenor, *Manifest Manners*; Byrd, *Transit of Empire*; Coulthard, *Red Skins, White Masks*; and Goeman, *Mark My Words*, for capacious discussions of that vibrancy in literature, politics, and theory. Goeman specifically attends to writings by Native women including Silko (focused particularly on *Almanac of the Dead*) and offers in her analysis of the "manifest acts" that decimated Native peoples an understanding of how Silko registers the ways that they are "never complete or final, rather they are ongoing, and even as they continue to affirm patterns of dominance, they also engender resistance and complicity, thus producing and productive of socialities" (*Mark My Words*, 158).

13. Silko, *Ceremony*, 7–8.

14. Silko, *Ceremony*, 8.

15. I mean "mutuality" in the sense Sandy Grande theorizes it in *Red Pedagogy* in her call to remake critical education in ways attentive to settler colonialism and indigeneity.

16. On debates regarding blood genealogy in Indigenous politics, see Kauanui, *Hawaiian Blood*; and Barker, *Native Acts*.

17. Silko, *Ceremony*, 126.

18. Wynter, "The Ceremony Must Be Found," 29.

19. In the thick history she provides of the coming to dominance of the ethnoclass-specific humanism of bourgeois liberalism, Wynter remembers how *studia humanitatis* shifted from its Christian medieval worldview, with its center of gravity located in God, to the "de-godded" activities of the human. In the process, the ceremonies that yoked the human to the divine had to be rewritten such that the ordering of chaos that had been the purview of the divine but now fell to mere humans could "constitute itself as a new *ordo* or *studium*" ("The Ceremony Must Be Found," 28). The human thus rebirthed appears thoroughly natural (biological) and autochthonous: "the common thrust was directed toward the valorization of the new emerging sense of self, of that which defined itself no longer as Spirit but as Natural Reason carefully cultivated" (29). Wynter explains further, "Even more, a new higher sanction system, one based on the self-correcting processes of human knowledge was here being proposed and put in place, in the context of a normative knowledge whose axiom . . . had been that God had ordered the world according to certain principles, and the role of fallen man was merely to decipher these principles and abide by them, but not seek to question and have knowledge of things celestial which, unaided, his corrupted human knowledge could not encompass" (28). In contrast, the humanists drew upon the "non-Christian legacy of the Graeco-Roman tradition of thought and literature to project an alternative mode of life and being" (29).

20. Silko, *Ceremony*, 124.

21. See Chen, *Animacies*, for consideration of the ways in which toxicity keys us into the racialized and imperial flows of capital, bodies, and objects in the contemporary world. See also Byrd, *The Transit of Empire*, regarding the ways in which Japanese Americans were recruited into service of the U.S. nation's settler colonialism as a facet of internment.

22. Silko's *Almanac of the Dead* brings to bear similar aesthetic-theoretical insights; I am reminded also of LeAnne Howe's writings and their emphases on connections across given boundaries, spatial and otherwise. See also Robert Warrior's discussions in *Tribal Secrets*.

23. The stakes in and urgency of fostering the onto-epistemologies of relationality announce themselves in the ongoing struggles to forestall the toxification of land, water, and people, driven by the primacy of the rationalism that accompanies the petroleum economy. Native Americans and First Nations peoples have led in standing against the machinery of capitalism on this continent—the explosives, heavy land-shifting machines, fracking tools, and pipelines, but also the unsustainable logics and corollary economies that justify the continuing and renewed abrogation of tribal sovereignty. Despite clear evidence of the unsustainability of its effects, capitalist rationalism (itself justified by the liberal ideology of freedom) retains state support and, in turn, affirms the necessity of state police authority to protect the marketplace. A recent, highly publicized example of such resistance efforts is the Standing Rock Sioux nation's protest of the North Dakota Access Pipeline. Honor the Earth is an organization, cofounded by Winona LaDuke and led by Native peoples, that advances understanding of sustainability and tracks and supports struggles to forestall damage to planet and people, understood in their mutuality. See www.honorearth.org.

24. Here echo the insights of another Native writer and critic, Gerald Vizenor, who has elucidated a link between Zen Buddhism and Anishinaabe (Chippewa or Ojibwe) dream songs, a link he experienced as an "introduction to haiku, by chance of the military" (*Native Liberty*, 265). "Haiku," Vizenor explains, "in a sense, caught me out on the road as a soldier in another culture and gently turned me back to the seasons, back to the tease and native memories. The turns and imagistic scenes of haiku were neither exotic nor obscure, because nature is a sense of presence, not a tenure of experience, or pretense of discovery" (258). He need not identify as or even with, so much as find resonant in this other culture the inseparability of philosophy, religion, and literature that reorients him toward nature and delinked from the expectations of the categorical, the identity as a soldier. "Haiku created a sense of presence, and, at the same time, reminded me of a nature that was already wounded, desecrated, removed, and an absence in many places on the earth. Nature is a presence not a permanence, and a *haiku moment* is an aesthetic survivance," Vizenor explains (261). For him, this moment induces the literary: "My very first literary creations were haiku scenes, and since then, that imagistic sense of nature has always been present in my writing" (260). This, too, is being with; not an erasure of difference but rather being sensate to

it; allowing difference to resonate through and in the relationality of self to place and other. Vizenor, like Ozeki, like Silko, iterates a geography in which Japan and Native America remain distinctive but are not held apart. Deployed to do harm by and as part of the U.S. Army, aesthetic encounter provokes a turn toward Relation.

25. I mean to invoke Édouard Glissant's theorization of Relation, a state of "interactive totality," a condition that poetics is uniquely capable of and necessary to bringing forth (*Poetics of Relation*); see also Fred Moten's poetic-theoretical offering of the "blur" that names the ineradicable connectedness of people and histories (*Black and Blur*, 2017).

26. Ozeki, *A Tale for the Time Being*, 3.

27. See, all by Muñoz, "The Brown Commons"; "Wildness and the Brown Commons"; "Feeling Brown"; "Feeling Brown, Feeling Down"; and "'Gimme Gimme This.'" Muñoz's book project on this topic was as yet incomplete when he died in December 2013. I draw from published related pieces, including lectures given, in crafting this discussion. Vazquez and Quiroga identified Hialeah, Florida, as a ground of Muñoz's theorization of Brownness in the remarks they delivered at the 2014 American Studies Association Annual Meeting.

28. Ozeki, *A Tale for the Time Being*, 415.

29. Womack, "A Single Decade," 5.

30. Ozeki, *A Tale for the Time Being*, 413.

31. Ozeki weaves this sensibility in other ways, too, which I summarize briefly here and/but for purposes of space will leave to other occasions for further discussion: through the novel's insights into gender performativity as a fixing of position and the erotics and pleasures to be found in disidentifying from normative gender scripts; its invocation of scale and the entanglement of all beings across the human, natural, animal, object, and even literary worlds; its attention to geopolitics and historical events like the dispossession of First Nations, 9/11, and the tsunami and aftereffects on the Fukushima nuclear power plant and decimation of surrounding areas; its attention to social media and the virtuality of the internet as characterizing the historical present; the violence of Japanese imperialism as well as its prominent engagement with Marcel Proust's magnum opus *In Search of Lost Time* (or *Remembrance of Things Past*), the seven-volume work characterized by a multiplicity of perspectives and the thematization of life as accumulated time. In this wide-ranging way, Ozeki produces an aesthetic of attunement, of deep engagement with the entanglement of all beings and beingness.

32. As a small detour through the history of color, remember that, in the tradition of Western civilization aesthetics and especially art history, color has been held to be far subordinate to form. From the classical age until, really, the twentieth century, color was understood to be superficial rather than substantive, unruly and even defiant: it could not be classified easily and thus troubled the scientific rationalist–driven efforts to taxonomize everything taking hold in the eighteenth and nineteenth centuries, and

remaining strongly influential today, of course. Color needed to be disciplined—it had to be carefully framed—an understanding that, of course, lent itself to defiance by figures who refused to frame, to use color not to refer to something or anything, but as meaningful in and of itself. What would it mean to experience color not as metaphoric but in and for itself? I think that's also what Muñoz is asking through and with his sense of brown—that is, that brownness is not metaphoric, referential, or propositional but, again, *is*.

33. Quiroga, *Tropics of Desire*, 3.

34. Glissant, *Poetics of Relation*.

35. Hall and O'Shea, "Common-Sense Neoliberalism," 1.

36. Hall and O'Shea, "Common-Sense Neoliberalism," 3. See Gramsci, *Selections from the Prison Notebooks*, 323–26 and 348–51, for focused consideration of "good" and "common sense."

4. Mis/Taken Universals

1. Spivak, *Aesthetic Education*; see especially the introduction.

2. Spivak distinguishes between globalization and globalizability to emphasize the point that "the globe" is given to us only in "capital and data"—that is, to emphasize its virtual, abstract nature. See "Introduction," 21.

3. Spivak, "Introduction," 21.

4. Spivak, "Introduction," 34.

5. See Mignolo, "Epistemic Disobedience," on "eurocentered epistemology's conceal [ment of] its own geo-historical and bio-graphical locations," a procedure necessary to "succeed in creating the idea of universal knowledge as if the knowing subjects were also universal" (160). A matter at the heart of the decolonial thinking Mignolo has elaborated across his oeuvre, he points in this essay quite precisely to the onto-epistemology of the colonial matrix of power—"a racial system of social classification that invented Occidentalism . . . , that created the conditions for Orientalism; distinguished the South of Europe from its center . . . and, on that long history, remapped the world as first, second and third during the Cold War" (161). This is and was the fantasy that continues to pervade knowledge production in the academy: "Once upon a time," Mignolo narrates, "scholars assumed that the knowing subject in the disciplines is transparent, disincorporated from the known and untouched by the geo-political configuration of the world in which people are racially ranked and regions are racially configured" (160). Condensing the vast history whereby modernity's darker side is occluded in favor of the idealization of Enlightenment, Mignolo re-sounds the need to delink from the illusions of the universal knowing subject and universal knowledge.

6. Tsing, *Friction*, 7.

7. Tsing, *Friction*, 7. The approach Tsing takes in *Friction* is a practical one, which is to say that she investigates the life of universals in their practiced forms. Through her analyses of especially environmental politics in Indonesia, Tsing establishes globalization as naming and having heterogeneous effects through the encounters it provokes between or among universals.

8. Tsing, *Friction*, 2. As Tsing demonstrates, tracing the animating force of the universal is a method of apprehending the specificity of entanglement—the friction, in her terms—that is, the sticky encounters in and through which ideas are materialized and the materiality of ideas is made apparent (6). Tsing's project shows how paradigms and analyses of globalization tell an incomplete story when they neglect to attend to the ways that "congeries of local/global interaction" constitute "global forces" (3). Narrated as an unstoppable force of homogenization driven by the insatiable engine of capitalism, globalization appears undifferentiated such that "all cultural developments [are packaged] into a single program: the emergence of the global era" (3). Such theories have limited explanatory power, not least because they substitute naming for analysis. In their stead, in Tsing's view, we may take up globalization as a genuine object of knowledge by formulating it as a question rather than an answer: "how does one study the global?" (2). For Tsing, undertaking such a study means repeated encounters with universals which, in cultural anthropology, the field to which she in part addresses herself, has been met with "curmudgeonly suspicion" (7), steeped as it is in a belief in the cultural specificity of universals.

9. For example, Nana Oishi summarizes that the "forces of globalization are increasing the demand for cheap and docile migrant female labor in all regions. Between 1960 and 2000, the number of migrant women around the world increased more than twofold, from 35 million to 85 million; by 2000, women constituted 48.6 percent of the world's migrants" (*Women in Motion*, 2); Rachel Parreñas attends to migrant Filipina domestic workers and what she identifies as the "international division of reproductive labor" ("Migrant Filipina Domestic Workers"); Robyn M. Rodriguez attends to the ways that the Philippine state has made "national heroes" of Filipino migrants ("Migrant Heroes"); and Alejandro Portes studies the formation of transnational communities as a result of migration for work ("Globalization from Below"). While the story of capitalist expansion is familiar, the modality of global capital bears the potential of "turning globalization into the final apotheosis of capital against its adversaries, be they state managers or organized workers" ("Globalization from Below," 254). See also Douglass, "The Race for Human Capital," which is concerned with people employed in caregiving and other low-wage service industries, who for a variety of reasons are recruited as "human resources" and developed as "human capital" for and find jobs abroad, and who may have little interest in permanent relocation. Strikingly, Douglass uses the phrase "human capital" without comment on its transformation of humanity into the abstractions of capitalism.

10. As Alejandro Portes succinctly puts it, the "success of these [migratory] initiatives [that crisscross the earth in search of accumulation] is generally correlated inversely with the economic autonomy achieved by national states and the social and economic prerogatives earned by local labor. For the most part . . . the momentum acquired by global capitalist expansion is such as to sweep away everything in its path, confining past dreams of equality and autonomous national development to the dustbin of history" ("Globalization from Below," 253).

11. Truong, *The Book of Salt*, 1. Subsequent citations appear as page numbers in the text.

12. See Trinh, *Woman, Native, Other*; and Barker, "The Specters of Recognition," for consideration of the problem and appeal of recognition and authenticity in relation to colonial and Indigenous politics and aesthetics.

13. Truong, *The Book of Salt*, 18.

14. Troeung, "'A Gift or a Theft,'" 130.

15. See Berlant, *Cruel Optimism*, on crisis ordinariness.

16. Eng, "The End(s) of Race," 1483.

17. I draw the phrase from Berlant, *Cruel Optimism*. See also Freeman on "erotohistoriography" in *Time Binds*.

18. Stein, *The Autobiography of Alice B. Toklas*, 252.

19. On this point, see Maldonado-Torres, *Against War*; Reddy, *Freedom with Violence*; and Nguyen, *Gift of Freedom*.

20. See Slaughter, *Human Rights, Inc.*, for a rich consideration of the career of Robinson Crusoe in the establishment of human rights discourse and law, for example.

21. Doyle, *Freedom's Empire*, 188. In her reading, Doyle remembers that the relationship with Xury, also enslaved to the Moors along with Crusoe, prefigures the ways that Friday is necessary to Crusoe's freedom. These relationships, she incisively observes, "unveil[] the faithless and profiteering logic of the Anglo-Saxons' relation to Africans on the Atlantic" (188).

22. Attar, *Vital Roots*, 19.

23. See Attar, *Vital Roots*; Baeshen, "'Robinson Crusoe' and 'Ḥayy Bin Yaqzan'"; and Kugler, *Representations of Race and Romance*. For discussion and analysis of *Ḥayy Ibn Yaqẓan*, including its cultural and historic contexts, philosophical sources, and relationships to gender and nature, see the essays in Conrad, ed. *The World of Ibn Ṭufayl*.

24. Goodman (trans.), *Ḥayy Ibn Yazqan*, 95.

25. The medieval Islamic philosopher Abū Ali Al-Husayn Ibn Sinā lived 980–1037.

26. Goodman (trans.), *Ḥayy Ibn Yazqan*, 95.

27. Goodman (trans.), Ḥayy Ibn Yazqan, 97.

28. See "Introduction," in Goodman (trans.), Ḥayy Ibn Yazqan.

29. There is substantial critical literature on the merits and purposes of Ṭufayl's tale. See, e.g., Gutas, "Ibn Ṭufayl on Ibn Sina's Eastern Philosophy"; Hourani, "The Principal Subject of Ibn Ṭufayl's Ḥayy Ibn Yaqẓan". On Ibn Sinā's philosophy, see Butterworth, "Medieval Islamic Philosophy and the Virtue of Ethics."

30. See Garcia, *Islam and the English Enlightenment*, for more on the compresence of Islamic and Enlightenment thought.

31. That Crusoe "rescues" Friday from the cannibalistic Natives on the Island of Despair is notable for the ways that it pits the enslaved against the Indigenous and, by doing so, affirms Crusoe's heroism.

32. Derrida, *Eyes of the University*; Trinh, *Woman, Native, Other*; Ferguson, *Aberrations in Black*.

33. Radhakrishnan, "Why Compare?," 16.

34. Shih, "Comparison as Relation," 80.

35. Shih, "Comparison as Relation," 79.

36. Shih, "Comparison as Relation," 79.

37. Glissant, *Poetics*, 117.

38. Mignolo, "Epistemic Disobedience," 174.

39. Truong, *The Book of Salt*, 248.

Conclusion

1. Glissant, *Poetics of Relation*, 190.

Postscript

1. *Triple Point* is the title Sze used for her massive and multiaspect United States Pavilion installation at the 2013 Venice Biennale. See Sze, *Sarah Sze* for commentary and images.

2. Insightful analyses of the histories, processes, and impact of migration from Asia to the United States may be found in Lubhéïd and Cantú, *Queer Migrations*; Hing, *Making and Remaking Asian America*; and Palumbo-Liu, *Asian/American*.

3. This discussion echoes ideas in my essay, "Asians Are the New . . . What?" collected in *Flashpoints for Asian American Studies*, edited by Cathy Schlund-Vials. There, I am especially interested in analyzing the significance of Asian American efforts to contest affirmative action policies in higher education.

Bibliography

Adorno, Theodor W. *Aesthetic Theory*. Translated by Robert Hullot-Kentor. Minneapolis: University of Minnesota Press, 1997.

Adorno, Theodor W. *Essays on Music*. Edited by Richard Leppert. Translated by Susan H. Gillespie et al. Oakland: University of California Press, 2002.

Adorno, Theodor W. *Philosophy of New Music*. Translated by Robert Hullot-Kentor. Minneapolis: University of Minnesota Press, 2006.

Ahmed, Sarah. *The Promise of Happiness*. Durham, NC: Duke University Press, 2010.

Altbach, Philip G., and Toru Umakoshi, eds. *Asian Universities: Historical Perspectives and Contemporary Challenges*. Baltimore, MD: Johns Hopkins University Press, 2004.

American Council of Learned Societies. *Report of the Commission on the Humanities*. New York: American Council of Learned Societies, 1964.

Anderson, Benedict. *Imagined Communities: Reflections on the Origin and Spread of Nationalism*. New ed. New York: Verso, 2006.

Aravamudan, Srinivas. *Enlightenment Orientalism: Resisting the Rise of the Novel*. Chicago: University of Chicago Press, 2012.

Aravamudan, Srinivas. *Tropicopolitans: Colonialism and Agency, 1688–1804*. Durham, NC: Duke University Press, 1999.

Armstrong, Isobel. *The Radical Aesthetic*. Oxford: Wiley-Blackwell, 2000.

Asad, Talal. "On Torture, or Cruel, Inhuman, and Degrading Treatment." *Social Research* 63, no. 4 (winter 1996): 1081–1109.

Asad, Talal. "What Do Human Rights Do? An Anthropological Enquiry." *Theory and Event* 4, no. 4 (2000).

Attali, Jacques. *Noise: The Political Economy of Music*. Translated by Brian Massumi. Minneapolis: University of Minnesota Press, 1985.

Attar, Samar. *The Vital Roots of European Enlightenment: Ibn Tufayl's Influence on Modern Western Thought*. Minneapolis, MN: Lexington Books, 2007.

Badiou, Alain. *Handbook of Inaesthetics*. Translated by Alberto Toscano. Stanford, CA: Stanford University Press, 2005.

Baeshen, L. M. S. "Robinson Crusoe and 'Ḥayy Bin Yaqzan': A Comparative Study." Ph.D. dissertation, University of Arizona, 1986.

Baker, Keith, and Peter Reill, eds. *What's Left of Enlightenment? A Postmodern Question*. Stanford, CA. Stanford University Press, 2001.

Barker, Joanne. *Native Acts: Law, Recognition, and Cultural Authenticity*. Durham, NC: Duke University Press, 2011.

Barker, Joanne, ed. *Sovereignty Matters: Locations of Contestation and Possibility in Indigenous Struggles for Self-Determination*. Lincoln: University of Nebraska Press, 2006.

Barker, Joanne. "The Specters of Recognition." In *Formations of United States Colonialism*, edited by Alyosha Goldstein, 33–56. Durham, NC: Duke University Press, 2014.

Berlant, Lauren. "Affect and the Politics of Austerity: An Interview Exchange with Lauren Berlant." By Gesa Helms and Marina Vishmidt. *Variant*, no. 39/40. http://www.variant.org.uk/39_40texts/berlant39_40.html.

Berlant, Lauren. *Cruel Optimism*. Durham, NC: Duke University Press, 2011.

Berlant, Lauren. "Slow Death (Sovereignty, Obesity, Lateral Agency)." *Critical Inquiry* 33, no. 4 (summer 2007): 754–80.

Bhabha, Homi K. *The Location of Culture*. New York: Routledge, 1994.

Bogues, Anthony, ed. *After Man, Towards the Human: Critical Essays on Sylvia Wynter*. Kingston: Ian Randle, 2006.

Bourdieu, Pierre. *Distinction: A Social Critique of the Judgement of Taste*. Translated by Richard Nice. Cambridge, MA: Harvard University Press, 1984.

Boutang, Yann Moulier. "Cognitive Capitalism and Education: New Frontiers." In *Universities in Translation: The Mental Labor of Globalization*, edited by Brett de Bary, 317–30. Traces: A Multilingual Series of Cultural Theory and Translation, vol. 5. New York: Columbia University Press, 2010.

Bowie, Andrew. *Aesthetics and Subjectivity: From Kant to Nietzsche*. 2nd ed. New York: Manchester University Press, 2003.

Brown, Tony C. *The Primitive, the Aesthetic, and the Savage: An Enlightenment Problem*. Minneapolis: University of Minnesota Press, 2012.

Brown, Wendy. *Undoing the Demos: Neoliberalism's Stealth Revolution*. Cambridge, MA: Zone Books, 2015.

Buck-Morss, Susan. *Hegel, Haiti, and Universal History*. Pittsburgh: University of Pittsburgh Press, 2009.

Buck-Morss, Susan. "Visual Empire." *Diacritics* 37, no. 2/3 (summer–fall 2007): 171–98.

Butler, Judith. *Bodies That Matter: On the Discursive Limits of "Sex."* New York: Routledge, 1993.

Butler, Judith. "Critique, Dissent, Disciplinarity." *Critical Inquiry* 35, no. 4 (summer 2009): 773–95.

Butler, Judith. "Endangered/Endangering: Schematic Racism and White Paranoia." In *Reading Rodney King, Reading Urban Uprising*, edited by Robert Gooding-Williams, 15–22. New York: Routledge, 1993.

Butler, Judith. *Gender Trouble: Feminism and the Subversion of Identity*. New York: Routledge, 1990.

Butterworth, Charles E. "Medieval Islamic Philosophy and the Virtue of Ethics." *Arabica* 34, no. 2 (July 1987): 221–50.

Byrd, Jodi. *The Transit of Empire: Indigenous Critiques of Colonialism*. Minneapolis: University of Minnesota Press, 2011.

Campt, Tina M. *Image Matters: Archive, Photography, and the African Diaspora in Europe*. Durham, NC: Duke University Press, 2012.

Canaday, Margot. *The Straight State: Sexuality and Citizenship in Twentieth-Century America*. Princeton, NJ: Princeton University Press, 2010.

Carby, Hazel V. *Cultures in Babylon: Black Britain and African America*. London: Verso, 1999.

Castiglia, Christopher, and Russ Castronovo, eds. "Aesthetics and the End(s) of American Cultural Studies." Special issue, *American Literature* 76, no. 3 (September 2004).

Center on Budget and Policy Priorities. "State-by-State Fact Sheets: Higher Education Cuts Jeopardize Students' and States' Economic Future." CBPP, August 2016. http://www.cbpp.org/research/state-by-state-fact-sheets-higher-education-cuts-jeopardize-students-and-states-economic.

Chakrabarty, Dipesh. *Provincializing Europe: Postcolonial Thought and Historical Difference*. Princeton, NJ: Princeton University Press, 2000.

Chang, Lan Samantha. *Hunger: A Novella and Stories*. New York: Norton, 1998.

Chatterjee, Piya, and Sunaina Maira, eds. *The Imperial University: Academic Repression and Scholarly Dissent*. Minneapolis: University of Minnesota Press, 2014.

Chen, Kuan-Hsing. *Asia as Method: Toward Deimperialization*. Durham, NC: Duke University Press, 2010.

Chen, Mel. *Animacies: Biopolitics, Racial Mattering, and Queer Affect*. Durham, NC: Duke University Press, 2012.

Chiang, Mark. "Capitalizing Form: The Globalization of the Literary Field: A Response to David Palumbo-Liu." *American Literary History* 20, no. 4 (winter 2008): 836–44.

Ching, Leo. *Becoming Japanese: Colonial Taiwan and the Politics of Identity Formation*. Berkeley: University of California Press, 2001.

Chow, Rey. "Theory, Area Studies, Cultural Studies: Issues of Pedagogy in Multiculturalism." In *Learning Places: The Afterlives of Area Studies*, edited by Masao Miyoshi and H. D. Harootunian, 103–18. Durham, NC: Duke University Press, 2002.

Chuh, Kandice. "Asians Are the New . . . What?" In *Flashpoints for Asian American Studies*, edited by Cathy Schlund-Vials, 220–37. New York: Fordham University Press, 2017.

Chuh, Kandice. *Imagine Otherwise: On Asian Americanist Critique*. Durham, NC: Duke University Press, 2003.

Chuh, Kandice. "It's Not about Anything." *Social Text* 32, no. 4 (2014): 125–34.

Cohen, William A. *Embodied: Victorian Literature and the Senses*. Minneapolis: University of Minnesota Press, 2008.

Colebrook, Claire. "Queer Aesthetics." In *Queer Times, Queer Becomings*, edited by E. L. McCallum and Mikko Tuhkamen, 25–46. Albany: State University of New York Press, 2011.

Conrad, Lawrence, ed. *The World of Ibn Ṭufayl: Interdisciplinary Perspectives on Ḥayy Ibn Yaqẓān*. London: Brill, 1996.

Coulthard, Glen Sean. *Red Skins, White Masks: Rejecting the Colonial Politics of Recognition*. Minneapolis: University of Minnesota Press, 2014.

Davis, Rocío G., and Sue-Im Lee, eds. *Literary Gestures: The Aesthetic in Asian American Writing*. Philadelphia: Temple University Press, 2006.

de Bary, Brett. "Introduction." In *Universities in Translation: The Mental Labor of Globalization*, edited by Brett de Bary, 1–23. Traces: A Multilingual Series of Cultural Theory and Translation, vol. 5. New York: Columbia University Press, 2010.

Defoe, Daniel. *Robinson Crusoe*. Edited by Michael Shinagel. New York: Norton, 1975.

Derrida, Jacques. *Eyes of the University: Right to Philosophy 2*. Translated by Jan Plug et al. Stanford, CA: Stanford University Press, 2004.

Derrida, Jacques. *Rogues: Two Essays on Reason*. Translated by Pascale-Anne Brault and Michael Naas. Stanford, CA: Stanford University Press, 2005.

Derrida, Jacques, Catherine Porter, and Edward P. Morris. "The Principle of Reason: The University in the Eyes of Its Pupils." *Diacritics* 13, no. 3 (autumn 1983): 2–20.

Douglass, John Aubrey. "The Race for Human Capital." In *Globalization's Muse: Universities and Higher Education Systems in a Changing World*, edited by John Aubrey Douglass, C. Judson King, and Irwin Feller, 45–63. Berkeley, CA: Berkeley Public Policy Press, 2009.

Douglass, John Aubrey, C. Judson King, and Irwin Feller, eds. *Globalization's Muse: Universities and Higher Education Systems in a Changing World*. Berkeley, CA: Berkeley Public Policy Press, 2009.

Doyle, Laura. *Freedom's Empire: Race and the Rise of the Novel in Atlantic Modernity, 1640–1940*. Durham, NC: Duke University Press, 2008.

Duggan, Lisa. *The Twilight of Equality? Neoliberalism, Cultural Politics, and the Attack on Democracy*. Boston: Beacon, 2004.

Dunbar-Ortiz, Roxanne. *An Indigenous Peoples' History of the United States*. Boston: Beacon, 2014.

Eagleton, Terry. *The Ideology of the Aesthetic*. Malden: Blackwell, 1990.

Elliott, Emory, Louis Freitas Caton, and Jeffrey Rhyne, eds. *Aesthetics in a Multicultural Age*. New York: Oxford University Press, 2002.

Eng, David L. "The End(s) of Race." *PMLA* 123, no. 5 (October 2008): 1479–93.

English, Darby. *How to See a Work of Art in Total Darkness*. Cambridge, MA: MIT Press, 2007.

Eze, Emmanuel Chukwudi. "The Color of Reason: The Idea of 'Race' in Kant's Anthropology." In *Postcolonial African Philosophy: A Critical Reader*, edited by Emmanuel Chukwudi Eze, 103–40. Cambridge, MA: Blackwell, 1997.

Ferguson, Roderick A. *Aberrations in Black: Toward a Queer of Color Critique*. Minneapolis: University of Minnesota Press, 2003.

Ferguson, Roderick A. "Administering Sexuality; or, The Will to Institutionality." *Radical History Review* 100 (winter 2008): 158–69.

Ferguson, Roderick A. *The Reorder of Things: The University and Its Pedagogies of Minority Difference.* Minneapolis: University of Minnesota Press, 2012.

Ferguson, Roderick A. *We Demand: The University and Student Protests.* Oakland: University of California Press, 2017.

Ferguson, Roderick A., and Grace Kyungwon Hong, eds. *Strange Affinities: The Gender and Sexual Politics of Comparative Racialization.* Durham, NC: Duke University Press, 2011.

Foucault, Michel. "The Masked Philosopher." In *Ethics: Subjectivity and Truth*, edited by Paul Rabinow. Translated by Robert Hurley et al., 321–28. New York: New Press.

Foucault, Michel. *The Order of Things: An Archaeology of Human Sciences.* New York: Pantheon, 1971.

Freedman, Jonathan. "Transgressions of a Model Minority." *Shofar: An Interdisciplinary Journal of Jewish Studies* 23, no. 4 (summer 2005): 69–97.

Freeman, Elizabeth. *Time Binds: Queer Temporalities, Queer Histories.* Durham, NC: Duke University Press, 2010.

Garcia, Humberto. *Islam and the English Enlightenment, 1670–1840.* Baltimore, MD: Johns Hopkins University Press, 2012.

Gikandi, Simon. *Slavery and the Culture of Taste.* Princeton, NJ: Princeton University Press, 2011.

Gilbert, Sandra M., and Susan Gubar. *The Madwoman in the Attic: The Woman Writer and the Nineteenth-Century Literary Imagination.* New Haven, CT: Yale University Press, 1979.

Gilmore, Ruth Wilson. *Golden Gulag: Prisons, Surplus, Crisis, and Opposition in Globalizing California.* Berkeley: University of California Press, 2007.

Glissant, Édouard. *Poetics of Relation.* Translated by Betsy Wing. Ann Arbor: University of Michigan Press, 1997.

Goeman, Mishuana. *Mark My Words: Native Women Mapping Our Nations.* Minneapolis: University of Minnesota Press, 2013.

Goh, Byeong-Gwon. "A Presentiment of the Death of Intellectuals in Korean Society." Translated by Lee Seok-Won. In *Universities in Translation: The Mental Labor of Globalization*, edited by Brett de Bary, 27–49. Traces: A Multilingual Series of Cultural Theory and Translation, vol. 5. New York: Columbia University Press, 2010.

Goldsby, Jacqueline. *A Spectacular Secret: Lynching in American Life and Literature.* Chicago: University of Chicago Press, 2006.

Goldstein, Alyosha, ed. *Formations of United States Colonialism.* Durham, NC: Duke University Press, 2014.

Goodman, Lenn Evan, trans. *Ibn Tufayl's Ḥayy Ibn Yaqzān: A Philosophical Tale.* Chicago: University of Chicago Press, 2003.

Gopinath, Gayatri. "Archive, Affect, and the Everyday: Queer Diasporic Re-visions."

In *Political Emotions: New Agendas in Communication*, edited by Janet Staiger, Ann Cvetkovich, and Ann Reynolds, 165–92. New York: Routledge, 2010.

Gordon, Avery F. *Ghostly Matters: Haunting and the Sociological Imagination*. Minneapolis: University of Minnesota Press, 1997.

Graff, Gerald. *Professing Literature: An Institutional History*. Chicago: University of Chicago Press, 1987.

Gramsci, Antonio. *Selections from the Prison Notebooks*, edited and translated by Quintin Hoare and Geoffrey Nowell Smith. New York: International, 1971.

Grande, Sandy. *Red Pedagogy: Native American Social and Political Thought*, 2nd ed. Lanham, MD: Rowman and Littlefield, 2015.

Gunn, Paula Allen. "Special Problems in Teaching Leslie Marmon Silko's 'Ceremony.'" *American Indian Quarterly* 14, no. 4 (autumn 1990): 379–86.

Gutas, Dimitri. "Ibn Ṭufayl on Ibn Sina's Eastern Philosophy." *Oriens* 34 (1994): 222–41.

Gutiérrez y Muhs, Gabriella, Yolanda Flores Niemann, Carmen G. González, and Angela P. Harris, eds. *Presumed Incompetent: The Intersections of Race and Class for Women in Academia*. Logan: Utah State University Press, 2012.

Hage, Ghassan. *Against Paranoid Nationalism: Searching for Hope in a Shrinking Society*. North Melbourne: Pluto, 2003.

Halberstam, Judith. *The Queer Art of Failure*. Durham, NC: Duke University Press, 2011.

Hall, Stuart. "Cultural Studies: Two Paradigms." *Media, Culture and Society* 2 (1980): 57–72.

Hall, Stuart, and Alan O'Shea. "Common-Sense Neoliberalism." *Soundings* 55 (winter 2013): 8–24.

Hanslick, Eduard. *On the Musically Beautiful*. Indianapolis: Hackett, 1986.

Harney, Stefano, and Fred Moten. *The Undercommons: Fugitive Planning and Black Study*. New York: Minor Compositions, 2013.

Harpham, Geoffrey Galt. *The Humanities and the Dream of America*. Chicago: University of Chicago Press, 2011.

Hartman, Saidiya V. *Scenes of Subjection: Terror, Slavery, and Self-Making in Nineteenth-Century America*. New York: Oxford University Press, 1997.

Harvey, David. *A Brief History of Neoliberalism*. New York: Oxford University Press, 2007.

Harvey, David. *The Enigma of Capital and the Crises of Capitalism*. New York: Oxford University Press, 2010.

Hein, Hilde, and Carolyn Korsmeyer, eds. *Aesthetics in Feminist Perspective*. Bloomington: Indiana University Press, 1993.

Hillenbrand, Margaret. "The National Allegory Revisited: Writing Private and Public in Contemporary Taiwan." *Positions: East Asia Cultures Critique* 14, no. 3 (winter 2006): 633–62.

Hinderliter, Beth, William Kaizen, Vered Maimon, Jaleh Mansoor, and Seth McCormick, eds. *Communities of Sense: Rethinking Aesthetics and Politics*. Durham, NC: Duke University Press, 2009.

Hing, Bill Ong. *Making and Remaking Asian America through Immigration Policy, 1850–1990.* Stanford, CA: Stanford University Press, 1994.

Hong, Grace Kyungwon. *The Ruptures of American Capital: Women of Color Feminism and the Culture of Immigrant Labor.* Minneapolis: University of Minnesota Press, 2006.

Hong, Grace Kyungwon, and Roderick A. Ferguson, eds. *Strange Affinities: The Gender and Sexual Politics of Comparative Racialization.* Durham, NC: Duke University Press, 2011.

Hourani, George F. "The Principal Subject of Ibn Ṭufayl's Ḥayy Ibn Yaqẓan." *Journal of Near Eastern Studies* 15, no. 1 (January 1956): 40–46.

Hughes, Langston. "The Negro Artist and the Racial Mountain." *The Nation,* June 23, 1926.

Hughes, Langston. *The Ways of White Folks.* New York: Vintage, 1990.

Hutner, Gordon, and Feisal G. Mohamed. "The Real Humanities Crisis Is Happening at Public Universities." *New Republic,* September 6, 2013.

Institute for International Education. *Open Doors Report on International Educational Exchange.* New York: IIE, 2015.

Jacobs, Jerry A. "Gender Inequality and Higher Education." *Annual Review of Sociology* 22 (1996): 153–85.

JanMohamed, Abdul R., and David Lloyd. "Introduction: Toward a Theory of Minority Discourse." *Cultural Critique,* no. 6 (spring 1987): 5–12.

Jewett, Andrew. "Academic Freedom and Political Change: American Lessons." In *Universities in Translation: The Mental Labor of Globalization,* edited by Brett de Bary, 263–78. Traces: A Multilingual Series of Cultural Theory and Translation, vol. 5. New York: Columbia University Press, 2010.

Kadosh, Roi Cohen, Avishai Henik, and Vincent Walsh. "Synaesthesia: Learned or Lost?" *Developmental Science* 12, no. 3 (May 2009): 484–91.

Kang, Laura Hyun Yi. "Late (Global) Capital." In *The Routledge Companion to Asian American and Pacific Islander Literature,* edited by Rachel Lee, 301–14. New York: Routledge, 2014.

Kant, Immanuel. *Critique of Judgment.* Cambridge Edition. Cambridge: Cambridge University Press, 2001. Original work published 1790/1793.

Kant, Immanuel. *Critique of Pure Reason.* Translated by Norman Kempt Smith. New York: Palgrave Macmillan, 2007. Original work published 1787.

Kauanui, Kēhaulani J. *Hawaiian Blood: Colonialism and the Politics of Sovereignty and Indigeneity.* Durham, NC: Duke University Press, 2008.

Kibre, Pearl. *Scholarly Privileges in the Middle Ages.* Cambridge, MA: Medieval Academy of America, 2013.

Kim, Young M. "Minorities in Higher Education." Washington, DC: American Council on Education, 2011. http://diversity.ucsc.edu/resources/images/ace_report.pdf.

Ko, Mi-Sook. "How an 'Intellectual Commune' Organizes Movement: A Brief Report on the Experiment 'Research Space Suyu+Nomo.'" Translated by Lee

Seok-Won. In *Universities in Translation: The Mental Labor of Globalization*, edited by Brett de Bary, 371–84. Traces: A Multilingual Series of Cultural Theory and Translation, vol. 5. New York: Columbia University Press, 2010.

Komunyakaa, Yusef. *Dien Cai Dau*. Middletown, CT: Wesleyan University Press, 1988.

Kugler, Emily M. N. "Representations of Race and Romance in Eighteenth-Century English Novels." Ph.D. dissertation, University of California, San Diego, 2007.

LaDuke, Winona. *All Our Relations: Native Struggles for Land and Life*. Brooklyn, NY: South End Press, 1999.

Langer, Susan K. *Philosophy in a New Key: A Study in the Symbolism of Reason, Rite, and Art*. 3rd ed. Cambridge, MA: Harvard University Press, 1996.

Latour, Bruno. *We Have Never Been Modern*. Translated by Catherine Porter. Cambridge, MA: Harvard University Press, 1993.

Lee, Richard E. *Life and Times of Cultural Studies: The Politics and Transformation of the Structures of Knowledge*. Durham, NC: Duke University Press, 2004.

Lee, Sue-Im. "Introduction: The Aesthetic in Asian American Literary Discourse." In *Literary Gestures: The Aesthetic in Asian American Writing*, edited by Rocío G. Davis and Lee, 1–14. Philadelphia: Temple University Press, 2006.

Levine, George, ed. *Aesthetics and Ideology*. New Brunswick, NJ: Rutgers University Press, 1994.

Levine, George. "Introduction: Reclaiming the Aesthetic." In *Aesthetics and Ideology*, edited by George Levine. New Brunswick, NJ: Rutgers University Press, 1994.

Ligon, Glenn. *Yourself in the World: Selected Writings and Interviews*, edited by Scott Rothkopf. New Haven, CT: Yale University Press, 2011.

Lii, Ding-Tzann. "Articulation, Not Translation: Knowledge-Production in an Age of Globalization." In *Universities in Translation: The Mental Labor of Globalization*, edited by Brett de Bary, 165–76. Traces: A Multilingual Series of Cultural Theory and Translation, vol. 5. New York: Columbia University Press, 2010.

Lipsitz, George. *The Possessive Investment in Whiteness: How White People Profit from Identity Politics*. Philadelphia: Temple University Press, 1988.

Lloyd, David. "Genet's Genealogies: European Minorities and the Ends of the Canon." In *The Nature and Context of Minority Discourse*, edited by Abdul R. JanMohamed and David Lloyd, 369–93. New York: Oxford University Press, 1991.

Lloyd, David. "Race under Representation." *OLR* 13 (1991): 62–94.

Lott, Eric. *The Disappearing Liberal Intellectual*. New York: Basic Books, 2006.

Lowe, Lisa. "Heterogeneity, Hybridity, Multiplicity: Asian American Differences." In *Immigrant Acts: On Asian American Cultural Politics*, 60–83. Durham, NC: Duke University Press, 1999.

Lowe, Lisa. *Immigrant Acts: On Asian American Cultural Politics*. Durham, NC: Duke University Press, 1999.

Lowe, Lisa. "The Intimacies of Four Continents." In *Haunted by Empire: Geographies of Intimacy in North American History*, edited by Ann Laura Stoler, 191–212. Durham, NC: Duke University Press, 2006.

Lowe, Lisa, and David Lloyd, eds. *The Politics of Culture in the Shadow of Late Capital.* Durham, NC: Duke University Press, 1997.

Lugones, Maria. "Heterosexualism and the Colonial/Modern Gender System." *Hypatia* 22, no. 1 (winter, 2007): 186–209.

Lugones, Maria. "Toward a Decolonial Feminism." *Hypatia* 25, no. 4 (fall 2010): 742–59.

Luibhéid, Eithne, and Lionel Cantú, eds. *Queer Migrations: Sexuality, U.S. Citizenship, and Border Crossings.* Minneapolis: University of Minnesota Press, 2005.

Lye, Colleen. "Unmarked Character and the 'Rise of Asia': Ed Park's *Personal Days.*" *Verge: Studies in Global Asias* 1, no. 1 (spring 2015): 230–54.

Maldonado-Torres, Nelson. *Against War: Views from the Underside of Modernity.* Durham, NC: Duke University Press, 2008.

Marcus, Steven. "Humanities from Classics to Cultural Studies: Notes toward the History of an Idea." *Daedalus* 135, no. 2 (spring 2006): 15–21.

Marcuse, Herbert. *Eros and Civilization: A Philosophical Inquiry into Freud.* Boston: Beacon, 1955.

Matsunaga, Kyoko. "Leslie Marmon Silko and Nuclear Dissent in the American Southwest." *The Japanese Journal of American Studies* 25 (2014): 67–87.

McKeon, Michael, ed. *Theory of the Novel: A Historical Approach.* Baltimore, MD: Johns Hopkins University Press, 2000.

McKittrick, Katherine. *Demonic Grounds: Black Women and the Cartographies of Struggle.* Minneapolis: University of Minnesota Press, 2006.

McKittrick, Katherine, ed. *Sylvia Wynter: On Being Human as Praxis.* Durham, NC: Duke University Press, 2015.

Melamed, Jodi. *Represent and Destroy: Rationalizing Violence in the New Racial Capitalism.* Minneapolis: University of Minnesota Press, 2011.

Melas, Natalie. "Versions of Incommensurability." *World Literature Today* 69, no. 2 (spring 1995): 275–80.

Menand, Louis. *The Marketplace of Ideas: Reform and Resistance in the American University.* New York: Norton, 2010.

Mendieta, Eduardo. "The Sound of Race: The Prosody of Affect." *Radical Philosophy Review* 17, no. 1 (2014): 109–31.

Mignolo, Walter. *The Darker Side of Western Modernity.* Durham, NC: Duke University Press, 2011.

Mignolo, Walter. "Epistemic Disobedience, Independent Thought and Decolonial Freedom." *Theory, Culture and Society* 26, no. 7–8 (2009): 159–81.

Mignolo, Walter. "Geopolitics of Knowledge and the Colonial Difference." *South Atlantic Quarterly* 101, no. 1 (winter 2002): 57–96.

Mignolo, Walter. "On Comparison: Who Is Comparison What and Why?" In *Comparison: Theories, Approaches, Uses,* edited by Rita Felski and Susan Stanford Friedman, 99–119. Baltimore, MD: Johns Hopkins University Press, 2013.

Mikkelsen, Jon M., ed. and trans. *Kant and the Concept of Race: Late Eighteenth-Century Writings.* Albany: State University of New York Press, 2014.

Mitchell, W. J. T. *Picture Theory*. Chicago: University of Chicago Press, 1994.

Morris, Meaghan. "On English as a Chinese Language: Implementing Globalization." In *Universities in Translation: The Mental Labor of Globalization*, edited by Brett de Bary, 177–96. Traces: A Multilingual Series of Cultural Theory and Translation, vol. 5. New York: Columbia University Press, 2010.

Morrison, Toni. "Recitatif." In *Confirmation: An Anthology of African American Women*, edited by Amiri Baraka and Amina Baraka, 243–61. New York: William Morris, 1983.

Mortensen, Thomas G. "State Funding: A Race to the Bottom." Washington, DC: American Council on Education, winter 2012.

Moten, Fred. *Black and Blur*. Durham, NC: Duke University Press, 2017.

Moten, Fred. *In the Break: The Aesthetics of the Black Radical Tradition*. Minneapolis: University of Minnesota Press, 2003.

Muñoz, José Esteban. "The Brown Commons: The Sense of Wildness." Lecture at Eastern Michigan University, April 1, 2013. https://www.youtube.com/watch?v=F-YInUlXgO4.

Muñoz, José Esteban. *Cruising Utopia: The Then and There of Queer Futurity*. New York: New York University Press, 2009.

Muñoz, José Esteban. *Disidentifications: Queers of Color and the Performance of Politics*. Minneapolis: University of Minnesota Press, 1999.

Muñoz, José Esteban. "Feeling Brown: Ethnicity and Affect in Ricardo Bracho's *The Sweetest Hangover*." *Theatre Journal* 52, no. 1 (March 2000): 67–79.

Muñoz, José Esteban. "Feeling Brown, Feeling Down." *Signs* 31, no. 3 (spring 2006): 675–88.

Muñoz, José Esteban. "'Gimme Gimme This . . . Gimme Gimme That': Annihilation and Innovation in the Punk Rock Commons." *Social Text* 116, 31, no. 3 (fall 2013): 95–110.

Muñoz, José Esteban. "Wildness and the Brown Commons." Lecture at Feminist Theory Workshop, Duke University, Durham, NC, March 2013. https://www.youtube.com/watch?v=huGN866GnZE.

Muthu, Sankar. *Enlightenment against Empire*. Princeton, NJ: Princeton University Press, 2003.

Nancy, Jean-Luc. *Being Singular Plural*. Translated by Robert D. Richardson and Anne E. O'Byrne. Stanford, CA: Stanford University Press, 2000.

Nancy, Jean-Luc. *Listening*. Translated by Charlotte Mandell. New York: Fordham University Press, 2007.

Newfield, Christopher. *Ivy and Industry: Business and the Making of the American University, 1880–1980*. Durham, NC: Duke University Press, 2003.

Newfield, Christopher. *Unmaking the Public University: The Forty-Year Assault on the Middle Class*. Cambridge, MA: Harvard University Press, 2008.

Ngai, Sianne. *Our Aesthetic Categories: Zany, Cute, Interesting*. Cambridge, MA: Harvard University Press, 2012.

Nguyen, Mimi. *The Gift of Freedom: War, Debt, and Other Refugee Passages*. Durham, NC: Duke University Press, 2012.

Nuttall, Sarah, ed. *Beautiful Ugly: African and Diaspora Aesthetics*. Durham, NC: Duke University Press, 2006.

Oakley, Francis. *Community of Learning: The American College and the Liberal Arts Tradition*. New York: Oxford University Press, 1992.

Oishi, Eve. "Painting with an Eraser." In *Allan deSouza: The Lost Pictures*, edited by Deepak Talwar. New York: Talwar Gallery, 2004.

Oishi, Nana. *Women in Motion: Globalization, State Policies, and Labor Migration in Asia*. Cambridge, MA: Harvard University Press, 2001.

Oparah, Julia C. "Challenging Complicity: The Neoliberal University and the Prison-Industrial Complex." In *The Imperial University: Academic Repression and Scholarly Dissent*, 99–121. Minneapolis: University of Minnesota Press, 2014.

Ozeki, Ruth. *A Tale for the Time Being*. Text Publishing, 2013.

Palumbo-Liu, David. *Asian/American: Historical Crossings of a Racial Frontier*. Stanford, CA: Stanford University Press, 1999.

Palumbo-Liu, David, ed. *The Ethnic Canon: Histories, Institutions, and Interventions*. Minneapolis: University of Minnesota Press, 1995.

Palumbo-Liu, David. "The Occupation of Form: (Re)theorizing Literary History." *American Literary History* 20, no. 4 (2008): 814–35.

Parreñas, Rachel. "Migrant Filipina Domestic Workers and the International Division of Reproductive Labor." *Gender and Society* 14, no. 4 (August 2000): 560–80.

Pease, Donald. "Doing Justice to CLR James's *Mariners, Renegades, and Castaways*." *Boundary 2* 27, no. 2 (2000): 1–19.

Plato. *Republic*. New York: Penguin Classics, 2007.

Portes, Alejandro. "Globalization from Below: The Rise of Transnational Communities." In *The Ends of Globalization: Bringing Society Back In*, edited by Don Kalb, Marco van der Land, Richard Staring, Bart Van Steenbergen, and Nico Wilterdink, 253–70. Lanham, MD: Rowman and Littlefield, 2000.

Prakash, Gyan. *Another Reason: Science and the Imagination of Modern India*. Princeton, NJ: Princeton University Press, 1999.

Quiroga, José. *Tropics of Desire: Interventions from Queer Latino America*. New York: New York University Press, 2000.

Radhakrishnan, R. "Why Compare?" In *Comparison: Theories, Approaches, Uses*, edited by Rita Felski and Susan Stanford Friedman, 15–33. Baltimore, MD: Johns Hopkins University Press, 2013.

Rancière, Jacques. *Dis-agreement: Politics and Philosophy*. Translated by Julie Rose. Minneapolis: University of Minnesota Press, 1999.

Rancière, Jacques. *The Politics of Aesthetics: The Distribution of the Sensible*. Translated by Gabriel Rockhill. New York: Continuum International, 2004.

Rancière, Jacques. "The Politics of Literature." *SubStance* 33, no. 1 (2004): 10–24.

Readings, Bill. *The University in Ruins*. Cambridge, MA: Harvard University Press, 1997.

Reddy, Chandan. *Freedom with Violence: Race, Sexuality, and the US State*. Durham, NC: Duke University Press, 2011.

Redfield, Marc. *The Politics of Aesthetics: Nationalism, Gender, Romanticism*. Stanford, CA: Stanford University Press, 2003.

Redmond, Shana L. *Anthem: Social Movements and the Sound of Solidarity in the African Diaspora*. New York: New York University Press, 2014.

Rifkin, Mark. *The Erotics of Sovereignty: Queer Native Writing in the Era of Self-Determination*. Minneapolis: University of Minnesota Press, 2012.

Robinson, Cedric J. *Black Marxism: The Making of the Black Radical Tradition*. Chapel Hill: University of North Carolina Press, 2000.

Rodriguez, Robyn M. "Migrant Heroes: Nationalism, Citizenship and the Politics of Filipino Migrant Labor." *Citizenship Studies* 6, no. 3 (2002): 341–56.

Roitman, Janet. *Anti-crisis*. Durham, NC: Duke University Press, 2014.

Ryan, Camille L., and Kurt Bauman. *Educational Attainment in the United States: 2015*. Washington, DC: U.S. Census Bureau, 2016.

Salamon, Gayle. *Assuming a Body: Transgender and Rhetorics of Materiality*. New York: Columbia University Press, 2010.

Schmidt, James, ed. *What Is Enlightenment? Eighteenth-Century Answers and Twentieth-Century Questions*. Berkeley: University of California Press, 1996.

Schopenhauer, Arthur. *The World as Will and Idea*. London: Dobimick, 2014. Original work published 1906.

Scott, David. "The Re-enchantment of Humanism: An Interview with Sylvia Wynter." *Small Axe 8*, September 2000, 119–207.

Sedgwick, Eve Kosofsky. *Epistemology of the Closet*. Berkeley: University of California Press, 1990.

Sen, Amartya. *Development as Freedom*. Oxford: Oxford University Press, 1999.

Serres, Michel. *Conversations on Science, Culture, and Time: Michel Serres with Bruno Latour*. Translated by Roxanne Lapidus. Minneapolis: University of Minnesota Press, 1995.

Sharpe, Christina. *In the Wake: On Blackness and Being*. Durham, NC: Duke University Press, 2016.

Shih, Shu-mei. "Comparison as Relation." In *Comparison: Theories, Approaches, Uses*, edited by Rita Felski and Susan Stanford Friedman, 79–98. Baltimore, MD: Johns Hopkins University Press, 2013.

Shimakawa, Karen. *National Abjection: The Asian American Body Onstage*. Durham, NC: Duke University Press, 2002.

Shimakawa, Karen. "What Constitutes 'the Political'?" Roundtable remarks, American Studies Association 2011 Annual Meeting, Baltimore, MD, October 2011.

Shumway, David R. *Creating American Civilization: A Genealogy of American Literature as an Academic Discipline*. Minneapolis: University of Minnesota Press, 1994.

Silko, Leslie Marmon. *Ceremony*. New York: Penguin, 1977.

Simpson, Audra, and Andrea Smith, eds. *Theorizing Native Studies*. Durham, NC: Duke University Press, 2014.

Slaughter, Joseph. *Human Rights, Inc.: The World Novel, Narrative Form, and International Law*. New York: Fordham University Press, 2007.

Slaughter, Sheila, and Larry L. Leslie. *Academic Capitalism: Politics, Policies and the Entrepreneurial University*. Baltimore, MD: Johns Hopkins University Press, 1997.

Smith, Linda Tuhiwai. *Decolonizing Methodologies: Research and Indigenous Peoples*. 2nd ed. London: Zed, 2012.

Solomon, Barbara Miller. *In the Company of Educated Women: A History of Women and Higher Education in America*. New Haven, CT: Yale University Press, 1985.

Spector, Ferrinne, and Daphne Maurer. "Synesthesia: A New Approach to Understanding the Development of Perception." *Developmental Psychology* 45, no. 1 (January 2009): 175–89.

Spillers, Hortense. "Mama's Baby, Papa's Maybe: An American Grammar Book." *Diacritics* 17, no. 2 (1987): 64–81.

Spivak, Gayatri Chakravorty. *An Aesthetic Education in the Era of Globalization*. Cambridge, MA: Harvard University Press, 2012.

Spivak, Gayatri Chakravorty. *A Critique of Postcolonial Reason: Toward the Vanishing History of the Present*. Cambridge, MA: Harvard University Press, 1999.

Spivak, Gayatri Chakravorty. *Death of a Discipline*. New York: Columbia University Press, 2003.

Spivak, Gayatri Chakravorty. *Outside in the Teaching Machine*. New York: Routledge, 1993.

Stadler, Gustavus. "Never Heard Such a Thing: Lynching and Phonographic Modernity." *Social Text 102* 28, no. 1 (2010): 87–105.

Staley, David J. "Democratizing Higher Education: The Legacy of the Morrill Land Grant Act." *Origins: Current Events in Historical Perspective* 6, no. 4 (January 2013). http://origins.osu.edu/article/democratizing-american-higher-education-legacy-morrill-land-grant-act.

Stein, Gertrude. *The Autobiography of Alice B. Toklas*. New York: Vintage, 1990. Original work published 1933.

Steyerl, Hito. "Missing People: Entanglement, Superposition, and Exhumation as Sites of Indeterminacy." *E-flux* 38 (October 2012): 1–10.

Stiglitz, Joseph E. *Globalization and Its Discontents*. New York: Norton, 2002.

Strathern, Marilyn. "'Improving Ratings': Audit in the British University System." *European Review* 5 (1997): 305–21.

Sze, Sarah. *Sarah Sze: The Triple Point of Water*. Exhibit. New York: Whitney Museum of American Art, July 3–October 9, 2003.

Sze, Sarah. *Triple Point*. New York: Gregory R. Miller and Bronx Museum of the Arts, 2013

Thaggert, Miriam. *Images of Black Modernism: Verbal and Visual Strategies of the Harlem Renaissance*. Amherst: University of Massachusetts Press, 2010.

Thelin, John. *A History of American Higher Education*. 2nd ed. Baltimore, MD: Johns Hopkins University Press, 2011.

Tongson, Karen. *Relocations: Queer Suburban Imaginaries*. New York: New York University Press, 2011.

Trinh, T. Minh-ha. *Woman, Native, Other*. Bloomington: Indiana University Press, 1989.

Troeung, Y-Dang. "'A Gift or a Theft Depends on Who Is Holding the Pen': Postcolonial Collaborative Autobiography and Monique Truong's *The Book of Salt*." *Modern Fiction Studies* 56, no. 1 (spring 2010): 113–35.

Truong, Monique. *The Book of Salt*. Wilmington, DE: Mariner, 2004.

Tsao, Hsingyuan, and Roger T. Ames. *Xu Bing and Contemporary Chinese Art*. Albany: State University of New York Press, 2011.

Tsing, Anna. *Friction: An Ethnography of Global Connection*. Princeton, NJ: Princeton University Press, 2005.

Ty, Eleanor. *Unfastened: Globality and Asian North American Narratives*. Minneapolis: University of Minnesota Press, 2010.

Vazquez, Alexandra T. *Listening in Detail: Performances of Cuban Music*. Durham, NC: Duke University Press, 2013.

Vizenor, Gerald. *Manifest Manners: Narratives on Postindian Survivance*. Lincoln: University of Nebraska Press, 1994.

Vizenor, Gerald. *Native Liberty: Natural Reason and Cultural Survivance*. Lincoln: University of Nebraska Press, 2009.

Vizenor, Gerald, ed. *Survivance: Narratives of Native Presence*. Lincoln: University of Nebraska Press, 2008.

Voegelin, Salomé. *Listening to Noise and Silence: Towards a Philosophy of Sound Art*. New York: Continuum, 2010.

Wall, Cheryl A. "On Freedom and the Will to Adorn: Debating Aesthetics and/as Ideology in African American Literature." In *Aesthetics and Ideology*, edited by George Levine, 283–304. New Brunswick, NJ: Rutgers University Press, 1994.

Wang, Dorothy. *Thinking Its Presence: Form, Race, and Subjectivity in Contemporary Asian American Poetry*. Stanford, CA: Stanford University Press, 2014.

Warrior, Robert Allen. *Tribal Secrets: Recovering American Indian Intellectual Traditions*. Minneapolis: University of Minnesota Press, 1995.

Weheliye, Alexander G. *Habeas Viscus: Racializing Assemblages, Biopolitics, and Black Feminist Theories of the Human*. Durham, NC: Duke University Press, 2014.

Wiegman, Robin. "Introduction: On Location." In *Women's Studies on Its Own: A Next Wave Reader in Institutional Change*, edited by Robin Wiegman, 1–43. Durham, NC: Duke University Press, 2002.

Wilder, Craig Steven. *Ebony and Ivy: Race, Slavery, and the Troubled History of America's Universities*. New York: Bloomsbury, 2013.

Williams, Raymond. *Marxism and Literature*. Oxford: Oxford University Press, 1977.

Womack, Craig S. "A Single Decade: Book-Length Native Literary Criticism between 1986 and 1997." In *Reasoning Together*, edited by Native Critics Collective. Norman: University of Oklahoma Press, 2008.

Woods, Clyde Adrian. *Development Arrested: Race, Power, and the Blues in the Mississippi Delta*. New York: Verso, 1998.

Wynter, Sylvia. "Beyond Miranda's Meanings: Un/silencing the 'Demonic Ground' of Caliban's 'Woman.'" In *Out of the Kumbla: Caribbean Women and Literature*, edited by Carol Boyce Davies and Elaine Savory Fido, 355–72. Trenton, NJ: Africa World, 1994.

Wynter, Sylvia. "Beyond the Word of Man: Glissant and the New Discourse of the Antilles." *World Literature Today* 63, no. 4 (autumn 1989): 637–48.

Wynter, Sylvia. "1492: A New World View." In *Race, Discourse and the Americas: A New World View*, edited by Vera Lawrence and Rex Nettleford, 5–57. Washington, DC: Smithsonian Institution Press, 1995.

Wynter, Sylvia. "The Ceremony Must Be Found: After Humanism." *Boundary 2* 12, no. 3 (spring–autumn 1984): 19–70.

Wynter, Sylvia. "On Disenchanting Discourse: 'Minority' Literary Criticism and Beyond." *Cultural Critique*, no. 7 (autumn 1987): 207–44.

Wynter, Sylvia. "Unsettling the Coloniality of Being/Power/Truth/Freedom: Towards the Human, after Man, Its Overrepresentation—an Argument." *New Centennial Review* 3, no. 3 (fall 2003): 257–333.

Wynter, Sylvia, and Katherine McKittrick. "Unparalleled Catastrophe for Our Species? Or, to Give Humanness a Different Future: Conversations." In *Sylvia Wynter: On Being Human as Praxis*, edited by Katherine McKittrick, 9–89. Durham, NC: Duke University Press, 2015.

Index

Foucault, Michel, vii, 135n40, 136n46, 148n27

Glissant, Édouard, 14, 71, 74, 95, 116, 148n36, 153n25, 154n34, 157n37
globalization, 13–14, 20, 91, 100, 102–3, 114, 126, 136n49, 154n2, 155n7, 155n8, 155n9; and the Knowledge Economy, 7–8, 132n12; and neoliberalization, 28, 75–76
"good life," 9–14, 104
Gordon, Avery, 40, 143n41

Ḥayy Ibn Yaqẓan (Ibn Tufayl), 111–13
Hall, Stuart, 6–7; and Alan O'Shea, 96. *See also* cultural studies
Hartman, Saidiya, 56–57
Higher Education Facilities Act of 1964, 9
Homestead Act of 1862, 9, 132n18
Hughes, Langston, 5, 24, 146n7; and *The Ways of White Folks*, 54–68, 73
humanism: illiberal, xi–xii, 1–6, 11, 20–21, 54, 95, 98–99, 114, 121–24, 126; liberal, xi–xii, 1–6, 18, 24, 27, 36–37, 50–54, 57, 74–75, 97–99, 136n46; 116–17, 120–21, 122–23. *See also* aesthetics; humanities
humanities, xi, 1–5, 26–28, 124–26; "after Man," 25, 52, 54, 125; and crisis, 28–29, 31, 123–24; and desire, 101; defense of, 1, 10; history of, 17, 29–31, 131n1, 140n5, 140n9; and liberalism, 24; and U.S. nationalism, 27, 30–32, 37–38, 140n9. *See also* aesthetics; humanism; National Endowment for the Humanities

Ibn Tufayl, 111–13
identity: formal properties of, 49–50; politics of, 13
immigrant narrative, 34–35
incommensurability, xi–xii, 24, 143n46; and Black women's subjectivity, 47–50; and comparison, 42, 114–17; and disidentification, 43, 75, 149n3; and rationality, 26, 67, 75, 78, 82, 84, 87; and subjectivity, 42–50, 101–3, 108, 124–25, 143n46
Indian Education Act of 1972, 9
intended mistake, 100–101, 121. *See also* aesthetic inquiry; Spivak, Gayatri
intertextuality, 99, 113

Kang, Laura, 40–41
Kant: and the aesthetic idea, 45–46; on judgment, 46–47, 134n35, 137n60, 138n63; racism of, 19, 135n36, 136n47; on Reason, 149n5; on sensus communis, 22–23, 139n64; on universality, 101–2. *See also* aesthetics
Knowledge Economy, 7–8, 129, 132n12

liberal subject, 3, 14, 18, 22, 34, 56, 106, 131n1
literariness, 66, 72–73
literature: history of, 52–53, 67–68, 145n65; modification of, 54, 68, 72–73
Lloyd, David, 37, 135n36, 142n29, 146n12, 147n13
Lowe, Lisa: *Intimacies*, 31–32; on institutionalization of ethnic studies, 12–13; and "other humanities," vii, 43, 75

Massenet, Jules: *Thaïs*, 63–65
Melamed, Jodi, 38, 136n49, 142n30, 154n5
Melas, Natalie, 42
Mignolo, Walter, 108, 116, 135n36
minoritized discourses: and aesthetics, 16–17; challenges for, 13–14, 77–78; conditions of, 12–13; distinctiveness of, 21, 27
Morrill Act of 1862, 8–9, 139n3